60

CLASSIC
AUSTRALIAN
POEMS

GEOFF PAGE is the author of eighteen collections of poetry, four verse novels, *A Reader's Guide to Contemporary Australian Poetry* and *80 Great Poems from Chaucer to Now*. He has reviewed Australian poetry (for *The Canberra Times* and ABC radio, in particular) for more than 40 years. He was in charge of the English department at Narrabundah College, ACT, from 1974 to 2001, and has been writer-in-residence at a number of academic institutions. His most recent books are the verse novel, *Lawrie & Shirley: The Final Cadenza* and the poetry collection, *Seriatim*. He was winner of the Patrick White literary award in 2001.

60

CLASSIC AUSTRALIAN POEMS

WITH COMMENTARIES BY GEOFF PAGE

UNSW
PRESS

A UNSW Press book

Published by
University of New South Wales Press Ltd
University of New South Wales
Sydney NSW 2052
AUSTRALIA
www.unswpress.com.au

National Library of Australia
Cataloguing-in-Publication entry
Title: 60 classic Australian poems/[selected by] Geoff Page.
ISBN: 978 1 921410 79 6 (pbk.)
Notes: Includes index.
Subjects: Poetry – Collections.
Other Authors/Contributors: Page, Geoff, 1940–
Dewey Number: A821.008

Design Di Quick
Printer Ligare

 Supported by the ACT Government

CONTENTS

ACKNOWLEDGMENTS

This book, like its predecessor *80 Great Poems from Chaucer to Now*, owes much to my former students and colleagues at Narrabundah College, ACT. It was here, in the (now-threatened) freedom of the ACT education system, that I wrote and taught for many years units such as 'Poetry Now' and was able to observe which modern and contemporary Australian poems worked with senior students and which didn't. It also reflects the reviewing done since 1967 for *The Canberra Times* and, more recently, for the ABC's 'Book Show' radio program.

Like the earlier book, this one also derives in part from the articles on classic poems in English which I wrote every few weeks for *The Canberra Times* between 2003 and 2006, particularly with the support of literary editors Jennifer Moran and Gia Metherell. Having had a positive response to those early articles, particularly the ones on Australian poems, I was encouraged to include 23 Australian poems in *80 Great Poems from Chaucer to Now* and later to write 37 more essays for this book, *60 Classic Australian Poems*.

Many people contributed in different ways to this project, but I should acknowledge, above all, the indefatigable support of my partner Alison Hastie. A few articles and the introduction have also been run past my friend and colleague Alan Gould, but he can take no responsibility for my arguments and opinions. I would also like to thank Professor Peter Pierce for selecting and discussing my poem, 'The Publisher's Apprentice', an inclusion insisted upon by my publishers.

Likewise, I thank the living poets – and the heirs of recently deceased ones – who kindly gave permission for the reproduction of these poems in *The Canberra Times*, as well as in the earlier and present volumes.

Thanks are also due to the ACT Government, which kindly provided the money to pay appropriate permission fees to poets and copyright holders.

I also wish to thank the team at UNSW Press, particularly Heather Cam, Phillipa McGuinness and my editor, Marie-Louise Taylor. It's been a pleasure to work with such dedicated and enterprising people.

I have also been an honorary visiting fellow at ADFA, University of New South Wales, throughout the book's preparation and am grateful for the practical assistance rendered.

INTRODUCTION

I

This book, as with my *80 Great Poems from Chaucer to Now*, grew out of more than 40 years writing poetry – as well as reading it, teaching it and organising live readings. As with the earlier book, each poem is followed by a short essay discussing its merits and suggesting why it might be considered a 'classic', problematic though that term is.

Of course, there are rather more than 60 classic Australian poems. Some enthusiasts might argue for ten times that, but 60 is a manageable number. It enables a clear focus on the poems concerned. I have, however, listed in an appendix a number of other modern or contemporary Australian poems I would have been happy to write about had space allowed.

The choices made here reflect a range of intentions. One of them was to rejoice in Australian poetry as a 'broad church', to get away from narrow preconceptions of what it might or should be. I also wanted to celebrate the sheer quality of our best poetry and thereby imply how well it bears comparison with that of other countries in the Anglosphere – and more widely via translation. Another key intention was to focus on poems which seem, to me at least, to be unequivocally enjoyable, even if that enjoyment is sometimes hard-won. A lesser hope was that by arranging the poems by poet's birth date, I might offer some sense of Australian poetry's development – though, naturally, this is difficult with only one poem per poet. I'm aware, too, that the order of birth dates does not necessarily reflect when the poems were composed or published.

Another consideration was to focus on a group of poets who were prominent in the middle-to-last decades of the last century but whose work is now in danger of dropping, undeservedly, into obscurity. Unfortunately, this priority has meant that my selection from poets currently in mid-career has had to be limited. My appendix lists many of them. They, I hope, will feature in some later book.

The term 'classic' is, as I've admitted, a difficult one. It clearly means more than merely being popular, a poem which has been frequently anthologised. It must also refer to something more than durability – though that, in many ways, is admirable enough. While an 'instant' classic is found only in advertising, a contemporary 'classic' is imaginable – and arguable. Several of the poems I've discussed here are quite recent but will, I suggest, be around for many years after we have departed.

Of course, the term 'classic' must always be something of a marketing strategy – and there can never be any final agreement on exactly which poems are or are not to be accorded this status. Time has a way of making these decisions for us – but time is not always fair, especially in the short to medium term. The canon of great poems in English does reflect some convergence of taste over the centuries, but it's not much use, except as a crude yardstick, for evaluating the poems of one's contemporaries.

As this selection will make clear, my own preference for poems I want to take with me into the future (or assist getting there) involves two inescapable criteria. The poem must be: a. emotionally moving (often with moral implications); or b. memorably entertaining. A 'classic' poem should be, in one sense or another, a life-changing experience. You will never be able to contemplate its subject in the future without to some extent calling the poem back to mind. Many such poems may affect your moral compass as well.

Clearly, some comic poems (as opposed to satirical ones) cannot be expected to do all this but they will, like a well-told joke, satisfy and extend your sense of humour. A few, like Bruce Dawe's 'Drifters', do both at the same time. We smile at the 'brown kelpie pup … dashing about tripping everyone up' but we also flinch at the poignancy in its last line when the long-suffering wife says to her chronically itinerant husband 'Make a wish, Tom, make a wish'. As

Alan Gould has argued in his essay, 'The Yes-Wow Molecule', a great poem is one that simultaneously defamiliarises and refamiliarises, the end product of which is gratitude in the mind of the beholder.

As with any anthology, the choices made here will inevitably be controversial. Some readers will lament my starting with Adam Lindsay Gordon rather than Charles Harpur or Henry Kendall. Others may complain that their favourite contemporary poet has been left out. Many will say that, given my 'desert-island' restriction of 'one-poet/one-poem', they would have stuffed something very different in their kitbag. It cannot be otherwise. We all have our favourites and any book like this will necessarily be subjective.

II

To make more sense of my selections – and to provide newcomers to Australian poetry with some context – it may be useful to outline briefly the story of Australian poetry so far. We should begin, of course, with Aboriginal song cycles (many of them thousands of years old). I've not sampled or discussed them here, however, owing primarily to difficulties with translation – and 'whitefella' limitations in regard to their more arcane contents.

From song cycles we jump abruptly into the mixed bag – or curate's egg – of Australian poetry in the nineteenth century. Barron Field's inaugural effort, 'The Kangaroo', was not auspicious. ('Kangaroo, Kangaroo!/Thou Spirit of Australia!' and so on). Unfortunately, despite the popularity of political satire (and genteel poetasting) in metropolitan and country newspapers, most of the nineteenth century did not fare at all well for poetry in the Australian colonies. The anonymous lyrics of bush songs and the work of popular figures such as 'Frank the Poet' (Francis McNamara) do hold historical and scholarly interest, but they don't quite provide the 'classics' this book is concerned with (though McNamara's 'A Convict's Tour to Hell' comes close).

Nor, alas, do those well-known founding figures of Australian poetry, Charles Harpur and Henry Kendall, supply what we're looking for. Neither Harpur's 'A Midsummer Noon in the Australian

Forest' nor Kendall's famous 'Bellbirds' seems to merit an unequivocal essay of commendation, for all of the latter's sub-Tennysonian musicality. A similar misfortune occurs when re-reading Barcroft Boake's well-known 'Where the Dead Men Lie'.

Thus it is with the ballads of Adam Lindsay Gordon, A.B. 'Banjo' Paterson and Henry Lawson that my sample begins. Though Gordon was not Australian-born his early poem, 'The Sick Stockrider' (1870), is pretty clearly the beginning of the Australian ballad tradition, a tradition carried on (in rather different ways) by Paterson and Lawson – and even by 'bush' poets of today. Though these narratives of outback equestrianism and/or comic escapades are rarely lyrical in any Keatsian sense, they certainly helped to create the Australian city-dweller's concept of himself (though not perhaps so much of herself) as a handy egalitarian who knows quite a bit about horses. These ballads were widely published in colonial newspapers and magazines (such as *The Bulletin* – from 1880) and were recited around campfires by successive generations of Australians.

It was the dominance of this school that the gifted but ill-fated Christopher Brennan tried to escape with his symbolist poetry in the 1890s and early 1900s. His now-famous correspondence with the French symbolist poet, Stéphane Mallarmé, served merely to emphasise his isolation. A very different contemporary of Brennan's, John Shaw Neilsen, with a much more limited education, wrote delicate lyric poetry (with only a few poeticisms) – but he, too, failed, for different reasons, to find a viable audience in his lifetime. The work of their slightly younger and short-lived contemporary, Lesbia Harford, has become known only recently.

C.J. Dennis, by contrast, was much more in tune with his times. His collection *The Songs of a Sentimental Bloke* (1915) sold 60 000 copies in less than 18 months. Though radically different from the ballads of Lawson and Paterson (still being published at the time), Dennis' idiosyncratic take on Melbourne working-class slang and mores also succeeded in finding an important place in the Australian psyche.

It was not until the arrival of Kenneth Slessor, however, in the late 1920s and early '30s that Australia finally acquired a genuinely sophisticated modern poet. While Lawson, Paterson and, to a lesser extent, C.J. Dennis tended (with some exceptions) to look backwards with nostalgia, Slessor understood the changes that the modernism of T.S. Eliot and Ezra Pound had wrought in Britain and America around 1910. Born in 1901, Slessor was the forerunner of (and inspiration to) a still-unequalled generation of Australian poets who began to publish during and just after World War 2. These included R.D. FitzGerald (who had started in the '30s and was only a year younger than Slessor), A.D. Hope, Douglas Stewart, David Campbell, James McAuley, Judith Wright and Rosemary Dobson. Though these poets varied considerably one from another, they were all were marked by a sophistication of technique and thought which, before Slessor, had not (despite the best efforts of Brennan) been seen in our poetry.

As the '50s turned into the '60s other names of roughly the same vintage began to emerge. William Hart-Smith, the only free-verse writer of his generation, was one. Roland Robinson, with his lyrical landscapes and Aboriginal connections, was another. Both of these poets had early ties to the Jindyworobak movement, which aspired (rather simplistically) to incorporate elements of Aboriginal culture into the mainstream of Australian poetry. Others of the same generation, such as Gwen Harwood and Dorothy Hewett, were delayed by child bearing – as well as political activism, in Hewett's case. Some, such as Ronald McCuaig, did not write as much as they might have, but nevertheless produced some distinctly memorable work. John Blight, like Gwen Harwood, really only became well known in the 1960s, despite his having published two collections in the '40s and '50s. Also emerging in the 1960s (though more mutedly because of the distance involved) were the London expatriates, Peter Porter (b. 1929) and the multi-talented Clive James (b. 1939).

So dominant was this post-World War 2 generation that the next, born in the early to mid-1930s and emerging in the early '60s, had difficulties breaking through the orthodoxies of their predecessors. Bruce Dawe, who began to publish prolifically in the 1960s, showed how 'high' and 'low' linguistic registers might happily be combined in the one poem – to both comic and serious effect.

Thomas Shapcott, Judith Rodriguez and David Malouf (all, in one way or another, from Brisbane) found other ways of creating the slightly more discursive and flexible poetry they had in mind (though Shapcott was, in his own way, to re-energise the sonnet in Australian poetry). The Manly-based Bruce Beaver, two years older than Dawe, was another talent heading in the same direction.

To those younger poets who started publishing in the small magazines of the late 1960s, the Shapcott–Rodriguez–Malouf group was an 'in-between' cohort. Some of this so-called 'Generation of '68', often identified with Sydney poet John Tranter, explicitly rejected the 'iambic pentameter/rhyming quatrain' conventions of the post-World War 2 generation and looked to New York sophisticates like John Ashbery or Frank O'Hara for their inspiration. A second group, identified with the even then well-known Les Murray, was much better disposed to Slessor (and the poets he had influenced). They aspired to continue, in modified form, something of the same tradition. Although there were real issues of aesthetics at stake (and some interesting cross-factional respect), a good deal of the quarrelling was ultimately personal in nature – even internecine. Groups which to outsiders appeared to be phalanxes of agreement were, on closer inspection, seen to be rent by dissension. There was also, just to complicate matters, a considerable rivalry between Sydney and Melbourne, even among those of the same opinions.

There is little use, at this distance, in enumerating which poets were associated with each group since many reconciliations have occurred in the interim and most contestants have now quietly agreed to disagree over the key aesthetic principles involved. It may be that the whole age group has grown old together and that more recent divisions have now replaced the ones they felt compelled to fight over. There is at the moment, for instance, considerable rivalry between young (or youngish) poets who see all language as being deeply 'problematic' in the manner of the postmodernists and those, often slightly older, poets who want to use language 'transparently' to achieve the communication and/or effects they aspire to. There has also developed in the past 20 years or so a considerable rivalry between 'performance' poets and 'literary' poets – the 'stage' versus the 'page', as it were. One group sees poetry as essentially a public matter, while the other prefers to emphasise the private interaction between the poet and his or her individual reader – which doesn't, it seems, dissuade performance poets from publishing their books or literary poets from playing to the crowd at public readings.

III

With only 60 places available, it has not been possible to represent all these trends adequately. Bronwyn Lea (b. 1969), the final poet in the book, is but the first in a line of youthful female poets who have published impressive first collections in the past ten years or so.

To return, however, to the word 'classic', I have found poems which are arguably classics from every one of the periods outlined above (except, alas, for the years before 1870). I have not sought to be politically correct but I do notice in retrospect that women poets – along with poets from certain minority groups – are all represented here with poems which are, to my way of thinking, definitely classics. Poetic quality and demographics don't necessarily coincide, but in recent years it's become more obvious that a good poem may come from anywhere across the human spectrum – in addition, that is, to the already rich offerings from the proverbial 'dead white English males'.

'The Sick Stockrider'

Hold hard, Ned! Lift me down once more, and lay
  me in the shade.
    Old man, you've had your work cut out to guide
Both horses, and to hold me in the saddle when I
  sway'd
    All through the hot, slow, sleepy, silent ride.
The dawn at 'Moorabinda' was a mist rack dull and
  dense,
    The sunrise was a sullen, sluggish lamp;
I was dozing in the gateway at Arbuthnot's bound'ry
  fence,
    I was dreaming on the Limestone cattle camp.
We crossed the creek at Carricksford, and sharply
  through the haze,
    And suddenly the sun shot flaming forth;
To southward lay 'Katâwa', with the sandpeaks all
  ablaze
    And the flush'd fields of Glen Lomond lay to
  north.
Now westward winds the bridle path that leads to
  Lindisfarm,
    And yonder looms the double-headed Bluff;
From the far side of the first hill, when the skies are
  clear and calm,
    You can see Sylvester's woolshed fair enough.
Five miles we used to call it from our homestead to
  the place

Where the big tree spans the roadway like an
arch;
'Twas here we ran the dingo down that gave us such
a chase
Eight years ago — or was it nine? — last March.

'Twas merry in the glowing morn, among the
gleaming grass
To wander as we've wander'd many a mile,
And blow the cool tobacco cloud, and watch the
white wreaths pass,
Sitting loosely in the saddle all the while.
'Twas merry 'mid the blackwoods when we spied
the station roofs,
To wheel the wild scrub cattle at the yard,
With a running fire of stockwhips and a fiery run of
hoofs;
Oh! the hardest day was never then too hard!

Aye! we had a glorious gallop after 'Starlight' and his
gang,
When they bolted from Sylvester's on the flat;
How the sun-dried reed-beds crackled, how the
flint-strewn ranges rang
To the strokes of 'Mountaineer' and 'Acrobat'.
Hard behind them in the timber, harder still across
the heath,
Close beside them through the tea-tree scrub we
dash'd;
And the golden-tinted fern leaves, how they rustled
underneath!
And the honeysuckle osiers, how they crash'd!
We led the hunt throughout, Ned, on the chestnut

and the grey,
And the troopers were three hundred yards
behind,
While we emptied our six-shooters on the
bushrangers at bay,
In the creek with stunted box-tree for a blind!

There you grappled with the leader, man to man,
and horse to horse,
And you roll'd together when the chestnut
rear'd;
He blaz'd away and missed you in that shallow
watercourse —
A narrow shave — his powder singed your beard!

In these hours when life is ebbing, how those days
when life was young
Come back to us; how clearly I recall
Even the yarns Jack Hall invented, and the songs
Jem Roper sung;
And where are now Jem Roper and Jack Hall?

Ay! nearly all our comrades of the old colonial
school,
Our ancient boon companions, Ned, are gone;
Hard livers for the most part, somewhat reckless as a
rule,
It seems that you and I are left alone.

There was Hughes, who got in trouble through that
business with the cards,
It matters little what became of him;
But a steer ripp'd up MacPherson in the

Cooraminta yards,
   And Sullivan was drown'd at Sink-or-swim;
And Mostyn – poor Frank Mostyn – died at last a
   fearful wreck,
   In the 'horrors' at the Upper Wandinong,
And Carisbrooke the rider at the Horsefall broke his
   neck,
   Faith! the wonder was he saved his neck so
   long!

Ah! those days and nights we squandered at the
   Logans in the Glen –
   The Logans, man and wife, have long been dead.
Elsie's tallest girl seems taller than your little Elsie
   then;
   And Ethel is a woman grown and wed.

I've had my share of pastime, and I've done my share
   of toil,
   And life is short – the longest life a span;
I care not now to tarry for the corn or for the oil,
   Or for the wine that maketh glad the heart of
   man.
For good undone and gifts misspent and resolutions
   vain,
   'Tis somewhat late to trouble. This I know –
I should live the same life over, if I had to live again;
   And the chances are I go where most men go.

The deep blue skies wax dusky and the tall green
   trees grow dim,
   The sward beneath me seems to heave and fall;
And sickly, smoky shadows through the sleepy

sunlight swim,
    And on the very sun's face weave their pall.
Let me slumber in the hollow where the wattle
    blossoms wave,
    With never stone or rail to fence my bed;
Should the sturdy station children pull the bush
    flowers on my grave,
    I may chance to hear them romping overhead.

Though Adam Lindsay Gordon (1833–70) was born on a plantation in the Azores, this poem, first published in the year of his death, has a genuinely Australian flavour and was recited around campfires for decades afterwards. Certainly Gordon was a romantic figure with his horsemanship, his reputed aristocratic connections, his scandalous exile as a kind of 'remittance man' and his suicide at 37 on Brighton Beach, Melbourne.

Gordon has, perhaps deliberately, embodied something of his own mythology in 'The Sick Stockrider'. The speaker seems to have lived rather more than Gordon's 37 years, but he has clearly been, like Gordon and by his own admission, a great horseman and a lover of escapades. Unlike Gordon himself, who ended his own life in depression, he regrets nothing and would 'live the same life over, if (he) had to live again'.

Realistically, as might be expected when delivered by a dying man, the narrative wanders somewhat after its arresting beginning. Initially, the stockman is dazedly recalling the 'hot, slow, sleepy, silent ride' that has brought him to this location, but by the end of the first stanza he has recovered enough to boast about the dingo he and Ned chased down together some eight or nine years earlier.

More exploits follow (chasing the 'wild scrub cattle'; fighting it out with 'Starlight' and 'his gang'), but soon he is reduced to less energetic musings and speculations (the fate of sundry companions, destroyed by the hazards of being 'hard livers' (alcoholism, drownings, droving misadventures and so on). Eventually the mood becomes more valedictory – and somewhat philosophical. The stockrider feels no need for any 'last rites'; he thinks 'the chances are I go where most men go'. He wants no marker for his grave and will be content if, by chance, he happens to hear 'the sturdy station children … romping overhead'.

The persona generated by this monologue slips very readily into Australian outback mythology and, indeed, may have done something to create it. He's adventurous, skilled with horses, a good 'mate', has few if any domestic or property attachments – and is more than a little self-dramatising. As a member of the 'old colonial school', Gordon knew what he was talking about. He'd experienced at least a few of these adventures himself and was nursing his wounds (both physical and mental) at the time of his death.

On the other hand, the reader can sense that Gordon, for all his efforts, is not yet truly assimilated. The landscape, despite the scattering of place names, is still rather generalised, even English, in its descriptions. The trees are merely 'big', 'tall' or 'green'; the 'morn' is 'glowing'; the grass is 'gleaming'. In 1869, when 'The Sick Stockrider' was written, there is no sense yet of the washed-out, hyperheated, intensely Australian landscapes created by the impressionist painters Streeton and Roberts in the 1890s. Gordon has caught the mythology, and something of the diction, but not yet the landscape to put them in.

Clearly, however, Gordon started something with this poem. The personality type of the stockrider was going to be around for a century and more – either in reality or in shared nostalgia. Quite a few Australian males still measure themselves against 'The Sick Stockrider' and by no means all of them live in the country. Women, of course, are mentioned only briefly and sentimentally in the poem. Logan, with whom both the narrator and Ned squandered 'days and nights', did actually have a wife but she has 'long been dead'. Ned, the narrator's faithful friend, does seem to have a daughter but little is made of her.

It's as if 'The Sick Stockrider' created the template which later and perhaps more sophisticated balladists like 'Banjo' Paterson and Henry Lawson could utilise. It's interesting to note, too, that the structure Gordon uses here is essentially the same as that used by Paterson in his even more famous 'The Man from Snowy River', namely a kind of 'fourteener' followed by a line of iambic pentameter. Consider, for instance, 'Now *west*ward *winds* the *bridle-path* that *leads* to *Lindisfarm*/And *yonder looms* the *double-headed Bluff*' and compare it with the opening lines from Paterson's poem: 'There was *movement at* the *station for* the *word* had *passed around*/That the *colt* from *old* R*egret* had *got away*'. Apart from an extra unstressed syllable at the beginning of Paterson's lines, the metre is the same. One also sees the buried ballad stanza here, the four stresses followed by three stresses in the first line and then the five stresses of iambic pentameter in the second.

But it is more than these similarities with Paterson's classic that explain why 'The Sick Stockrider' been such a popular and durable poem despite infelicities such as its unspecific landscape and its occasional sentimentalities and poeticisms. Certainly, something of the author's own romantic aura surrounds the poem, even invades it, but this in itself could not be enough. There were plenty of wild versifiers ('Breaker' Morant among them) whose poems have not survived nearly as well.

Clearly, it has a little to do with the frequent and resonant use of Australian place names (a technique that was to be used ad nauseam by latter balladists and bush poets). It probably has more to do with the laconic philosophy and the self-mythologising of the narrator: the reckless rider, the good mate, the nostalgic anecdotalist, the man who is content enough to say that he will 'go where most men go' and will be content to lie in his (probably early) grave hearing someone else's children 'romping overhead'.

The sick stockrider is a likeable, if unrealistic, figure and it's not hard to see why he – and his author – have survived so well, despite our changing mores and increasingly urban and multicultural society. Adam Lindsay Gordon, in 'The Sick Stockrider', was on to something essential – whether we care to admit it or not.

A.B. 'BANJO' PATERSON (1864–1941)

'The Travelling Post Office'

The roving breezes come and go, the reed-beds
    sweep and sway,
The sleepy river murmurs low, and loiters on its
    way,
It is the land of lots o' time along the Castlereagh.

. . .

The old man's son had left the farm, he found it
    dull and slow,
He drifted to the great North-west where all the
    rovers go.
'He's gone so long,' the old man said, 'he's dropped
    right out of mind,
But if you'd write a line to him I'd take it very kind;
He's shearing here and fencing there, a kind of waif
    and stray,
He's droving now with Conroy's sheep along the
    Castlereagh.
The sheep are travelling for the grass, and travelling
    very slow;
They may be at Mundooran now, or past the
    Overflow,
Or tramping down the black-soil flats across by
    Waddiwong,
But all those little country towns would send the
    letter wrong,
The mailman, if he's extra tired, would pass them in

his sleep,
It's safest to address the note to 'Care of Conroy's
    sheep',
For five and twenty thousand head can scarcely go
    astray,
You write to 'Care of Conroy's sheep along the
    Castlereagh'.

By rock and ridge and riverside the western mail
    has gone,
Across the great Blue Mountain Range to take the
    letter on.
A moment on the topmost grade, while open fire
    doors glare,
She pauses like a living thing to breathe the
    mountain air,
Then launches down the other side across the plains
    away
To bear the note to 'Conroy's sheep along the
    Castlereagh'.

. . .

And now by coach and mailman's bag it goes from
    town to town,
And Conroy's Gap and Conroy's Creek have marked
    it 'Further down'.
Beneath a sky of deepest blue where never cloud
    abides,
A speck upon the waste of plains the lonely
    mailman rides.
Where fierce hot winds have set the pine and myall
    boughs asweep

He hails the shearers passing by for news of
    Conroy's sheep.
By big lagoons where wildfowl play and crested
    pigeons flock,
By camp fires where the drovers ride around their
    restless stock,
And past the teamster toiling down to fetch the
    wool away
My letter chases Conroy's sheep along the
    Castlereagh.

First published in 1895, 'The Travelling Post Office' is one of only two Australian ballads included in John Leonard's classic Oxford anthology, *Seven Centuries of Poetry in English*. It sits there, chronologically by poet's date of birth, with Housman and Hopkins, as if to remind us how different Australia was in those days from the 'mother country'.

Academics, understandably, have pretty much written the bush ballads out of our literary history and point to Kenneth Slessor (writing in the 1920s and 1930s) as the first 'real' Australian poet of quality (if we set aside Aboriginal song cycles). Australia, in the 114 years or so since 'The Travelling Post Office' was written, has become a much more complex society and yet it is remarkable how much a poem of this kind can still have an impact.

The impression, of course, would be less on the quarter of our population born overseas, but, even here, the poem is likely to set up some sort of resonance, if only as an echo of the country they thought they were coming to. There is a deep nostalgia in the poem – felt not only now but even when it was written. Unlike his rival, Henry Lawson, 'Banjo' Paterson tended to idealise the 'bush' and the heroic, if laconic, qualities of those who lived and worked there.

For Paterson, Australia (or western NSW) is a country of spacious plains and slow-flowing rivers; a land of few words and great distances. And it is unproblematic, apart from the occasional severities of the climate. Although none of this country was without its Aboriginal inhabitants, Paterson (and his contemporary audience) usually failed to see them, except in comic set pieces such as his 'Frying Pan's Theology'. Whether this was a deliberate suppression of what they did know, or whether it was simply blithe innocence, can only be speculated on. Certainly, not all of Paterson's contemporaries were unaware of the Aborigines and their plight – Mary Gilmore, for one.

It is significant, too, that Paterson's variety of 'bush poetry' survives quite vigorously today in various pub venues and folk festivals, even though the humorous and sentimental have tended to replace the heroic and nostalgic. It's also a fact that these poems rarely find their way into a mainstream anthology of Australian poetry. David Campbell, John Manifold and Les Murray have written what might be called 'literary ballads' of the first quality, but most 'bush poetry' one now encounters is notable for its simplicity of viewpoint and technique. So what is it that we can still collect, as it were, from 'The Travelling Post Office'?

The first thing is the idealised landscape. The winds are 'breezes', the river 'loiters', the sky is of the 'deepest blue where never cloud/abides', the wildfowl 'play' in the 'big lagoons' and so on. This is the sense of the pastoral, going right back to ancient Greece – an idyllic place where pleasant (and only pleasant) things happen; a place remote from Athens or from Sydney, let alone London.

Allied with this is Paterson's use of exotic and/or resonant place names – 'Mundooran', 'the Overflow' and particularly Aboriginal names like 'Waddiwong' that often seem a little humorous to those who don't live there. The Aborigines, Paterson seems to be implying, may have disappeared but they left us their place names. There's also the countervailing sense of ownership in names like 'Conroy's Gap' and 'Conroy's Creek'. The Castlereagh river also has an interesting resonance. Named after a not particularly attractive English politician (see Shelley's 'The Mask of Anarchy') it readily evokes a long, slow, western river with lots of billabongs and places to camp for the night. One might well spend a lifetime 'along the Castlereagh'. A lot of Paterson's Sydney readers would hardly have known where it flowed, but that's beside the point. They were still prey to its spell.

Then, of course, there's the narrative. In 'The Man from Snowy River' Paterson told an heroic story of an underdog's success. In 'The Man from Ironbark' we have a lively farce about a country bumpkin come to town. In 'The Travelling Post Office', the story is minimal but no less real. The narrator is talking to an old farmer, who in turn tells him about his son working in 'the great Northwest where all the/rovers go'. Then we get the story of the mailman's imagined travels along the Castlereagh, trying to deliver the old man's letter. It's a story without an ending – which, in turn, reflects the vastness of the landscape in which the story is located.

Another important reason for the poem's appeal is its use of the ballad stanza, albeit disguised as a 'fourteener'. Whichever way it's arranged there's no doubt that the ballad stanza is a very effective technique for telling a story (see Coleridge's 'The Rime of the Ancient Mariner', for instance). Many hymns also use the same format (which conveniently leaves a musical rest at the end of every second line).

Numerologists may have attributed too much to the number 7, but there certainly is something compelling about it as far as poetry goes. In 'The Travelling Post Office' Paterson sticks to his form closely, not even reversing the stress in the first foot, as most writers of iambic verse often do. Although he generally handles the form well, Paterson does occasionally slip in an extra or archaic word to get his rhyme – as with 'away' in 'across the plains away' and 'abides' in 'where never cloud abides'.

Many of us in these latterly sophisticated days are tempted to leave poems like 'The Travelling Post Office' well behind. The history and sociology of the poem are simplistic at best; the iambics are resolutely unvarying; the emotional manipulation of phrases like 'along the Castlereagh' is obvious. In some ways it's a very superficial poem, but, paradoxically perhaps, it also goes a long way down. The nostalgia for the pastoral seems to be universal no matter how many generations we are away from it. The virtues of the ballad stanza appear similarly timeless.

DAME MARY GILMORE (1865–1962)

'Nationality'

I have grown past hate and bitterness,
I see the world as one;
But though I can no longer hate,
My son is still my son.

All men at God's round table sit,
And all men must be fed;
But this loaf in my hand,
This loaf is my son's bread.

Mary Gilmore, a youthful utopian socialist in William Lane's Paraguayan experiment (1892–1902), lived through two world wars and the Great Depression. Though modern poetry in Australia is generally considered to have started with the work of Kenneth Slessor (b. 1901), the poetry of Mary Gilmore was an important precursor to it. She had very clear ideas about Australia's past, much of which she had seen at first hand, and in poems such as 'Botany Bay' and 'Fourteen Men' she wrote about its positive and more negative features.

Although first published in 1942, 'Nationality' seems to look back over the country's previous 150 years or so, even while it is obviously influenced by the fighting going on while it was being written. There have been serious arguments about just where Gilmore, the person, stood in relation to her poem. Is she expressing her own deep conviction, saying that 'This loaf is my son's bread'? Is she, perhaps, criticising this point of view in a world where the fate of humanity could no longer remain a matter of national borders? Or is she simply giving us a neat, dictionary definition of what the word means and leaving us to make up our own minds (or continue with our own prejudices)?

In some ways, 40 and more years after her death, it doesn't really matter what Gilmore's view (outside the poem) was. 'Nationality' is still very much one of those poems that make a clear philosophical and/or moral point. It is in no way a lyric celebrating the beauties of Australian 'nature'; nor is it a fragment of autobiography. It is a poem where the poet reduces the essence of an idea down to a mere eight lines – which can be readily memorised and left to do their work in the world. In many ways, despite its ambiguities, 'Nationality' is political poetry at its best. Some readers will see it as a sympathetic embodiment of their own attitudes to both their family and their nation. Other readers may see it as the embodiment of a viewpoint doomed to extinction in this globalised world of free-trade agreements and increasingly porous borders.

In such a context, it is important to look at the poem carefully, line by line, rather than making impulsive claims based on its impact as a whole. Gilmore (or Gilmore's narrator) starts by saying she has 'grown past hate and bitterness' and now 'see(s) the world as one'. She wants to move away from the extreme nationalism that led to the destruction of millions in World War 1 and the one during which she is writing. She is not going to be persuaded to 'hate' her country's 'enemies'. But there is one thing she cannot go past – or get away from: 'My son is still my son'. Some psychologists such as Kohlberg have seen this strong preference for family over those in the wider community as a 'less-developed' morality than that which can impersonally assess the situation and give appropriate support in terms of abstract principles. And, certainly, this preference for one's 'son' has led to extensive nepotism and corruption in many societies around the world.

Gilmore (or her narrator) would, nevertheless, be quite unfazed by this accusation. She has stated her 'bottom line' and, in the second stanza, she goes on to reinforce her point more practically and more forcefully. Instead of talking about general principles, about 'world government' and 'the international community' and so on, she gets straight down to basics. Bread, a major staple around most of the world, with its biblical resonance ('man shall not live by bread alone' and so on), is ideal for her purposes.

Some may like to speculate on why Gilmore says 'son' rather than 'daughter' or 'child', but this is immaterial. The point is that her family comes first – everything else later. Whether this is her personal viewpoint or not, the point is clearly established and the reader makes of it what he or she will.

Others may question whether such a 'simple' poem can be a 'classic'. Is 'Nationality' really poetry or just moral philosophy in disguise? Where is the imagery? Where is the 'nature'? What about the 'dark night of the soul'? Such readers overlook one (though only one) of the main functions of poetry – to distil an insight (or piece of 'wisdom') into a form that can be both clearly understood and memorised. The Latin poet, Lucretius, tried to put the whole of human knowledge, as it then stood, into poetic form for exactly this reason. Gilmore's eight lines do something comparable for the single word 'nationality'.

The poem answers, maybe once and for all, exactly what we mean by these five syllables. We do know that it was grotesquely distorted by Hitler, but we also now have Gilmore's definition as a Platonic archetype, against which to measure other lesser definitions such as 'nationalism is a matter of blood and soil' and so on. The single sentence 'This loaf is my son's bread' is as far as it goes – and no further. Of course, some (or many) may not want to go that far, but at least, after Gilmore's poem, they will know what they are refusing to sign up to.

It is worth thinking, too, about what it is exactly which helps make this short poem so memorable. It's not simply a matter of *what* it says but *how* it says it. Essentially, Gilmore is using the ballad form, that classic device of oral poetry, used for centuries before it was written down simply because it is such a good *aide memoire*. Unlike most traditional ballads, however, Gilmore's 'story' is very brief – but no less memorable.

Some painstaking readers will, no doubt, rush in to point out that line 3 in stanza 2 has only three stressed syllables instead of four normally required there ('But *this* loaf *in* my *hand*'). Gilmore could easily have slipped in an adjective in front of 'hand' – such as, say, 'loving' or 'fragile' – but it only takes a moment to see how unsatisfactory these would have been. 'Hand' is elemental and symbolic — it doesn't need any further description. It could also be argued that Gilmore's break with expectation makes this line much more memorable than one we might have slipped over mellifluously because it had the right number of syllables. Gilmore, in this case, was too skilled a poet to make such a 'mistake' without good reason.

There are other irregularities, too, which are mnemonic. The poem starts out with an extra unstressed syllable ('I have *grown*' rather than 'I've *grown*'). A couple of unstressed syllables in front of it make us come down even harder on the crucial syllable '*grown*'. Something comparable happens at the beginning of the second stanza where Gilmore reverses the stress pattern in the first foot. We read it as '*All* men/at *God's*' rather than 'All *men*/at *God's*'. The last line, too, should read 'This *loaf* is *my* son's *bread*', but we tend to hear it much more forcefully as having almost four stressed syllables rather than three, two lots of two rather than three spaced normally. '*This loaf* is my *son's bread*'. It's like a boxer hitting us with a couple of quick uppercuts.

With so much going for it technically — along with the memorable clarity of its main point (agree or disagree with it, as you will) — it's not hard to see why 'Nationality' has cropped up in nearly every anthology of Australian verse since it was written. Even if the concept of 'nationalism' were to disappear from the human vocabulary, we'd still need Gilmore's poem to remind us of what it had been (and, perhaps, what it might be better not to go back to).

'Middleton's Rouseabout'

Tall and freckled and sandy,
    Face of a country lout;
This was the picture of Andy,
    Middleton's Rouseabout.

Type of a coming nation,
    In the land of cattle and sheep,
Worked on Middleton's station,
    'Pound a week and his keep'.

On Middleton's wide dominions
    Plied the stockwhip and shears;
Hadn't any opinions,
    Hadn't any 'idears'.

Swiftly the years went over,
    Liquor and drought prevailed;
Middleton went as a drover
    After his station had failed.

Type of a careless nation,
    Men who are soon played out,
Middleton was: – and his station
    Was bought by the Rouseabout.

Flourishing beard and sandy,
    Tall and solid and stout:
This is the picture of Andy,
    Middleton's Rouseabout.

Now on his own dominions
    Works with his overseers;
Hasn't any opinions,
    Hasn't any idears.

Henry Lawson (1867–1922), 'the face on the (original) $10 note', is more highly regarded for his short stories than for his verse but it's a mistake to overlook the best of his poems, works such as 'Middleton's Rouseabout'. Written in 1890 and first published in 1896, it is very much a political poem in a very political era, but it steers well clear of the ideological simplicities prevailing at the time – and since. As a man who knew poverty well and was inclined towards solidarity with the unionists of his day, Lawson also strongly infused his own feelings into the poem.

Essentially, Lawson has little sympathy for the rouseabout ('Face of a country lout') but this does not stop him from almost admiring his social and economic progress. While Middleton himself is falling prey to 'liquor and drought', the rouseabout, previously content to work for 'Pound a week and his keep', sees his opportunity and buys his boss out. Andy, the rouseabout, however, does not make Middleton's mistakes. He moves from being 'Tall and freckled and sandy' to being 'Tall and solid and stout'. There's no evidence of his paying his own rouseabout any more than he once got himself, but it's noteworthy that the successful Andy 'Works with his overseers'. This could be taken two ways: either he rolls up his sleeves and works alongside his men in the manner of many station owners (at that time and since) or he is so successful by now that he can entrust his 'own dominions' to overseers.

One thing is consistent, however. Both as a rouseabout and as a boss, Andy is distinguished by not having any 'opinions' or 'idears'. There is an irony here. While shearers were facing off against the station owners in the great strike of 1890–91 and were fighting over the opposing merits of 'closed shop' or 'freedom of contract', Andy, the rouseabout, has his own agenda. He can't be bothered with the theories of either radicalism or conservatism. He is simply out for himself. There is no mention of any wife or child in the poem, so we may reasonably assume that his upward mobility reflects his sheer determination rather than any domestic pressures. Andy is the 'Type of a coming nation' and this will not, in Lawson's view, necessarily be a good thing. Indeed, Lawson is impatient with, even contemptuous of, the fact that Andy doesn't have any 'idears'.

While his balladeering contemporaries were inclined to cele-brations of horsemanship, humorous sporting events and the doings of bushrangers, Lawson, in 'Middleton's Rouseabout', gives us some persuasive social and political analysis. Station owners, like Middleton, whom people like Andy replace, probably deserve to be pushed aside in Lawson's view, but he has no great hopes for ex-rouseabouts who don't have 'any idears'. Lawson recognises that, given its climate and history, Australia is no place for a traditional, English-style landowning aristocracy; however, the alternative to it, he sees, is not very charming either.

So, in a very short space, Lawson has told us a great deal about life in the outback where 'Liquor and drought prevailed'. It's worth considering just how this occurs, especially since the poem uses quite a deal of repetition. Indeed, one might argue that the repeti-tion of certain phrases – and/or the slight variations between them – contribute to this compression. Take, for example, the way 'Rouse-about' initially rhymes with 'lout' before it's eventually rhymed with the more prosperous 'stout'). Such repetitions also suggest that Andy is not unique; he's a type we're going to see more of. The lack of 'idears' will be with us for a good while yet, it seems.

Perhaps equally important is the effect of Lawson's triple rhythms, the dactyllic and anapaestic feet that he uses extensively and inter-changeably throughout (though there are, admittedly, quite a few iambic and trochaic feet as well). '*This* was a *pi*cture of *A*ndy, / *Midd*le-ton's *Rouseabout*.' This rhythmic device tends to give an offhand mood to the poem, a feeling that we've seen this before and we'll see it again. The dactyls and anapaests suggest a line of dance; the waltz will go on and on with people like Andy replacing people like Middleton – and no one except the opportunists benefiting.

The poem is also tightly rhymed *abab*. There is quite a deal of repetition here, too ('sandy'/'Andy', 'dominion'/'opinions' and 'nation'/'station'), but we shouldn't object. All these repetitions have a purpose and are not a cop-out. The 'station' is a microcosm for the 'nation' – and there is, incidentally, an interesting contrast between the 'coming' nation and the 'careless' nation a little later. Andy remains 'sandy' throughout his change of fortune – and it's significant that, with or without 'dominions', he continues to have no 'opinions'.

Some readers may wish to quarrel with the syntactical awkwardness of the inversion in stanza 5 – but this also helps to set up nicely the surprise of the following line and a half where Andy abruptly buys the station. In general, the narrative of the poem develops strongly, line by line, through a flexible syntax that manages to cohere effectively despite the suspended phrases that are resolved only in the last line or two of each stanza.

Although the main interest of the poem is clearly political, sociological and historical, Lawson has more than enough poetic technique for his purpose. In just 28 lines he has given us an emblematic story for which some novelists would need 300 pages. He has left us in no doubt about his own 'opinions' and yet he has not fallen for the simplifying doctrines espoused by either side of the political debate at the time. The poem's tone may be popular, but it's really a very sophisticated work, both in its content and manner. Lawson may be best remembered these days for short stories like 'The Loaded Dog' and 'The Drover's Wife', but a poem such as 'Middleton's Rouseabout' must also be seen as an important part of his legacy.

CHRISTOPHER BRENNAN (1870–1932)

'We sat entwined an hour or two together'

We sat entwined an hour or two together
(how long I know not) underneath pine-trees
that rustled ever in the soft spring weather
stirr'd by the sole suggestion of the breeze:

we sat and dreamt that strange hour out together
fill'd with the sundering silence of the seas:
the trees moan'd for us in the tender weather
we found no word to speak beneath those trees

but listen'd wondering to their dreamy dirges
sunder'd even then in voiceless misery;
heard in their boughs the murmur of the surges
saw the far sky as curv'd above the sea.

That noon seem'd some forgotten afternoon,
cast out from Life, where Time might scarcely be:
our old love was but remember'd as some swoon;
Sweet, I scarce thought of you nor you of me

but, lost in the vast, we watched the minutes hasting
into the deep that sunders friend from friend;
spake not nor stirr'd but heard the murmurs wasting
into the silent distance without end:

so, whelm'd in that silence, seem'd to us as one
our hearts and all their desolate reverie,
the irresistible melancholy of the sun,
the irresistible sadness of the sea.

I t is strange to think of this poem being written in Australia during what historians like to call 'The Roaring Nineties' when balladists like Lawson and Paterson were at their peak and the Australian colonies were patriotically converging on federation. Of course, the scholar/poet, Christopher Brennan (1870–1932), was a very different man from Lawson and Paterson (who were different enough in themselves, of course).

Christopher Brennan, more than 70 years after his death, still divides opinion among Australian poets and academics. To some he seems our first, real 'modern' poet, a man who famously corresponded with the French symbolist, Stéphane Mallarmé. To others, he is the classic *poète maudit*, a man of great gifts who fell short of his potential. The latter group tend to see Kenneth Slessor (1901–71) as the more important founding figure.

Brennan's 'We sat entwined an hour or two together', however, remains a strangely compelling poem more than a century after it was completed in 1894. It lyrically evokes a timeless moment – and is itself somehow timeless, perhaps as a result of this accomplishment. It looks back 300 years to love poems as early as John Donne's 'The Extasie' but is not diminished or dated by such comparisons.

It is generally assumed by scholars that the lovers in the poem are Brennan himself and Anna Werth, whom he met while studying in Berlin in 1892 and married in Sydney in 1897. In 1894 Brennan was back working in the NSW public service and waiting for Anna to join him. The poem was begun the day before he left Berlin. We can only speculate on what *Fraulein* Anna thought of Brennan's version of the event described, but it is not hard to see from the poem that the marriage was likely to collapse eventually.

As with Donne before him, Brennan also describes an ecstatic episode ('an hour or two … where Time might scarcely be') but his concerns in 'We sat entwined …' seem to be with something rather larger than two lovers under pine-trees in the 'soft spring weather', pleasant though that image is. Certainly they are 'entwined an hour or two together' but they are also speechless and feel the 'trees moan(ing) for us'. In the third stanza the poet considers himself and his lover to be already 'sunder'd' and by the fourth he is saying that 'our old love (is) but remember'd as some swoon'.

It *is* a timeless moment – but time is also escaping them; the minutes are 'hasting/into the deep that sunders friend from friend'. Eventually, in the final stanza, the poet sees that the silence of the lovers' 'desolate reverie' is but a small part of some much larger desolation: 'the irresistible melancholy of the sun,/the irresistible sadness of the sea'. Brennan was born, raised and (almost certainly) died a Catholic, but it is not hard to see the influence of post-Darwinian, nineteenth-century agnostics here. The German word *Welt-schmerz* may also apply.

What is it then that makes this poem so pleasurable to read more than a century after it was written? The poem's biographical origins are interesting but increasingly irrelevant. Brennan's story, especially with its numerous setbacks in his closing years, is a sad one but this is not what we should focus on. Our concern is more with the apparent timelessness of that 'forgotten afternoon' and how the poet manages to create this impression in our minds.

A key element here is Brennan's clever use of repetition – not only the *abab* rhyme scheme adhered to throughout, but the persistence of the long 'ee' sound. It features in five out of the poem's six stanzas and is particularly important in the first two where the poet employs the exact, insistent rhyme of 'trees', 'breeze' and 'seas'. The repetitive sound of the sea is the poem's backdrop (despite the fact that he describes it three times as 'silent'). The poet makes us aware of this repetition but, increasingly, in a subliminal way.

Another important element is the juxtaposition of positive and negative imagery. We have the 'entwined' couple and the 'soft spring weather' in the opening stanza – and the memory of an earlier 'swoon' in the fourth stanza – but we also have phrases such as 'voiceless misery', 'the sundering silence of the seas' and 'murmurs wasting/into the silent distance without end'. And this is all before we reach the two climactic metaphors which so memorably conclude the poem: 'the irresistible melancholy of the sun,/the irresistible sadness of the sea'.

Yet another factor in this 'timelessness' effect is Brennan's leisurely, almost hypnotic use of the iambic pentameter. While Donne's 'The Extasie' is, by comparison, in an almost brisk tetrameter, Brennan's longer line has an expansiveness which seems to suit his emphasis on being 'lost in the vast' and on that 'far sky ... curv'd above the sea'. The poet is dealing with the illimitable here and anything shorter than a pentameter is unlikely to serve his purpose.

A further related effect is seen in the poem's syntax. In six quatrains (24 lines) there are only two sentences. This again stretches things remarkably. The almost infinite expanse of the subject matter is matched by the relative endlessness of the poem's two sentences.

With all these devices (and others such as a plentiful use of assonance and alliteration) Brennan builds up an 'irresistible' rhetorical momentum, a sustained lyrical presentation of a mental state well beyond the impress of mere diurnal concerns. We are borne along by the sadness of the young protagonists' situation, by their 'desolate reverie' – which nature itself seems to reinforce and, to some extent, explain. Their 'old love', their earlier passion, is now remembered merely as 'some swoon'. There is only 'the silent distance without end'. It's hardly a cheery poem to be thrusting upon your bride-to-be.

Literary historians have pointed to Brennan's difficulties in life as stemming from living not only with his foreign-born wife and four children (two of whom predeceased him) but with his German mother-in-law and his mentally fraught sister-in-law. It certainly must have been quite a difficult household for the scholarly symbolist poet to handle but, to judge from 'We sat entwined an hour or two together', Brennan's troubles lay deeper than that. They needn't, however, prevent us from enjoying the universality of his poem, whatever our own particular situation might happen to be when reading it.

'The Orange Tree'

The young girl stood beside me. I
    Saw not what her young eyes could see:
– A light, she said, not of the sky
    Lives somewhere in the Orange Tree.

– Is it, I said, of east or west?
    The heartbeat of a luminous boy
Who with his faltering flute confessed
    Only the edges of his joy?

Was he, I said, borne to the blue
    In a mad escapade of Spring
Ere he could make a fond adieu
    To his love in the blossoming?

– Listen! the young girl said. There calls
    No voice, no music beats on me;
But it is almost sound: it falls
    This evening on the Orange Tree.

– Does he, I said, so fear the Spring
    Ere the white sap too far can climb?
See in the full gold evening
    All happenings of the olden time?

Is he so goaded by the green?
    Does the compulsion of the dew
Make him unknowable but keen
    Asking with beauty of the blue?

– Listen! the young girl said. For all
        Your hapless talk you fail to see
There is a light, a step, a call
        This evening on the Orange Tree.

– Is it, I said, a waste of love
        Imperishably old in pain,
Moving as an affrighted dove
        Under the sunlight or the rain?

Is it a fluttering heart that gave
        Too willingly and was reviled?
Is it the stammering at a grave,
        The last word of a little child?

– Silence! the young girl said. Oh, why,
        Why will you talk to weary me?
Plague me no longer now, for I
        Am listening like the Orange Tree.

Composed some time between 1916 and 1919, but not published until 1934, 'The Orange Tree' is one of those rare poems written within their own time but which, despite that (or even because of that), seem to have a touch of eternity about them. In England and America, under the influence of Ezra Pound and T.S. Eliot (and, perhaps, the realities of trench warfare), most serious poets were abandoning the use of poeticisms such as 'ere', 'adieu', 'olden', 'affrighted' and so on. The Australian poet, John Shaw Neilson, a 'natural' if there ever was one, was working entirely outside these modernist currents, still listening to poets such as Keats – and Tennyson at the latest. Unlike Pound and Eliot, he did not feel the need to 'Make it new!', to quote one of Pound's favourite dicta.

There has been an enormous amount of bad poetry written in every age by poets and poetasters who ignored what was happening in their own time and chirped on cheerfully in a dated diction. Some of Neilson's work suffers from this, too, but the best of it, as in 'The Orange Tree', transcends the problem magnificently.

Indeed, it is possible, because of our ultra-sensitivity to poeticisms, to misinterpret 'The Orange Tree' completely. Some see it as a cute, dated exchange between a precocious young girl and a gifted 'poet', a man who is playfully trying to get her to explain herself. Such people interpret the poem as a lyrical rhapsody, full of 'nice' thoughts and little else. A closer look reveals something very different.

With 'The Orange Tree' it is important to understand the difference between the open, receptive simplicity of what the girl is saying and the standardised 'poetic' questioning of the poet. The poet is 'romantic' in the worst way and the girl romantic in the best way. The poet rushes into sentimental clichés while the girl listens, sensitively and imaginatively, to what is actually happening (even though she cannot define it or reduce it to something readily explained).

The poet's babbling covers a large and inauspicious range of clichés: the love struck adolescent playing the flute, nostalgia about the 'olden time', naive revelling in 'nature', the reversals or frustrations of young love (with the mandatory 'love'/'dove' rhyme) and even a nineteenth-century sentimental deathbed and graveside scene. Despite the seductive music of metaphors such as 'confessed/ Only the edges of his joy' and 'the compulsion of the dew', it's important to see that these are only superficial, stock responses. The real poetry is in the attitude of the girl who is watching and listening to the Orange Tree. She sees a light there 'not of the sky'. She hears something that is more mysterious than mere music or the human voice, even though it shares some of their qualities. She reprimands the silly 'poet' and says, obscurely but convincingly, 'There is a light, a step, a call/This evening on the Orange Tree.' The 'light' promises revelation. The 'step' may be a dance step or a step towards (or up to) something much more mysterious than the predictable babbling she's being plagued with. The 'call' is likewise mysterious, perhaps faintly religious, but not in any doctrinal way.

Finally, the young girl has had enough of these distractions: 'Why will you talk to weary me?' Now she has moved a step further on. Initially, she was simply looking at and listening to the Orange Tree – now she is 'listening *like* the Orange Tree.' She has become a part of nature, a part of the mysterious universe contained in the Orange Tree, rather than simply babbling about it like the 'poet'.

If one supposes that Neilson sees himself as the 'poet' (and he does use the first person), then he seems to have delivered a devastating self-critique. I think it more likely that the poem is about the contrast between the dangers of the poetic enterprise (a readiness to rush into clichés) and its ultimate purpose (to bring us closer to the instincts of the little girl). The latter is what Neilson aimed at and hoped for; the former is what sometimes got in his way if he was not careful.

Technically, the poem, though light in touch throughout, is also solidly formal with its fully rhyming (*abab*) iambic tetrameter quatrains. There are, however, several rhythmic variations that keep things more open. Lines such as '*See* in the *full gold eve*ning' move well away from iambic expectations. There are also lines where we're not sure whether Neilson's syntactical awkwardness is meant to satirise the 'hapless' poet or is merely an example of Neilson being one. 'Ere the white sap too far can climb' is surely a rather roundabout way of saying 'Before the white sap climbs too far'.

The best bits of the poem are, of course, the stanzas where the little girl talks – particularly the first one and the one that talks about 'a light, a step, a call'. Then there's also the final one, with its imperious 'Silence!' and its final revelation that she is 'listening like the Orange Tree'. All of these stanzas hint powerfully at the mysterious core of our best poetry. Not, admittedly, the satires of Pope and Swift or the sly observations of Chaucer, but certainly of the best romantic poetry, and much of the metaphysical – to cite two very different approaches. Our little girl not only uses the word 'hapless' precociously; she seems to understand Keats' theory of 'Negative Capability', too.

C.J. DENNIS (1876–1938)

'The Play'

'Wot's in a name?' she sez … An' then she sighs
An' clasps 'er little 'ands an' rolls 'er eyes.
'A rose,' she sez, 'be any other name
Would smell the same.
Oh, w'erefore art you Romeo, young sir?
Chuck yer ole pot, an' change yer moniker!'

Doreen an' me, we bin to see a show –
The swell two-dollar touch. Bong tong, yeh know.
A chair apiece wiv velvit on the seat;
A slap-up treat.
The drarmer's writ be Shakespeare, years ago,
About a barmy goat called Romeo.

'Lady, be yonder moon I swear!' sez 'e.
An' then 'e climbs up on the balkiney;
An' there they smooge a treat, wiv pretty words
Like two love-birds.
I nudge Doreen. She whispers, 'Ain't it grand!'
'Er eyes is shining an' I squeeze 'er 'and.

'Wot's in a name?' she sez. 'Struth, I dunno.
Billo is just as good as Romeo.
She may be Juli-er or Juli-et –
'E loves 'er yet.
If she's the tart 'e wants, then she's 'is queen,
Names never count … But ar, I like 'Doreen!'

A sweeter, dearer sound I never 'eard;
Ther's music 'angs around that little word,
Doreen! … But wot was this I starts to say
About the play?
I'm off me beat. But when a bloke's in love
'Is thorts turns 'er way, like a 'omin' dove.

This Romeo 'e's lurkin' wiv a crew –
A dead tough crowd o' crooks – called Montague.
'Is cliner's push – wot's nicknamed Capulet –
They 'as 'em set.
Fair narks they are, jist like them back-street clicks,
Ixcep' they fights wiv skewers 'stid o' bricks.

Wot's in a name? Wot's in a string o' words?
They scraps in ole Verona wiv the'r swords,
An' never give a bloke a stray dog's chance,
An' that's Romance.
But when they deals it out wiv bricks an' boots
In Little Lon., they're low, degraded broots.

Wot's jist plain stoush wiv us, right 'ere to-day,
Is 'valler' if yer fur enough away.
Some time, some writer bloke will do the trick
Wiv Ginger Mick,
Of Spadger's Lane. 'E'll be a Romeo,
When 'e's bin dead five 'undred years or so.

Fair Juli-et, she gives 'er boy the tip.
Sez she: 'Don't sling that crowd o' mine no lip;
An' if you run agin a Capulet,
Jist do a get.'
'E swears 'e's done wiv lash; 'e'll chuck it clean.
(Same as I done when I first met Doreen.)

They smooge some more at that. Ar, strike me blue!
It gimme Joes to sit an' watch them two!
'E'd break away an' start to say good-bye,
An' then she'd sigh
'Ow, Ro-me-o!' an' git a strangle-holt,
An' 'ang around 'im like she feared 'e'd bolt.

Nex' day 'e words a gorspil cove about
A secret weddin'; an' they plan it out.
'E spouts a piece about 'ow 'e's bewitched:
Then they git 'itched …
Now, 'ere's the place where I fair git the pip:
She's 'is for keeps, an' yet 'e lets 'er slip!

Ar! but 'e makes me sick! A fair gazob!
'E's jist the glarsey on the soulful sob,
'E'll sigh and spruik, an' 'owl a love-sick vow –
(The silly cow!)
But when 'e's got 'er, spliced an' on the straight,
'E crools the pitch, an' tries to kid it's Fate.

Aw! Fate me foot! Instid of slopin' soon
As 'e was wed, off on 'is 'oneymoon,
'Im an' 'is cobber, called Mick Curio,
They 'ave to go
An' mix it wiv that push o' Capulets.
They look fer trouble; an' it's wot they gets.

A tug named Tyball (cousin to the skirt)
Sprags 'em an' makes a start to sling off dirt.
Nex' minnit there's a reel ole ding-dong go –
'Arf a round or so.
Mick Curio, 'e gets it in the neck,
'Ar rats!' 'e sez, an' passes in 'is check.

Quite natchril, Romeo gits wet as 'ell.
'It's me or you!' 'e 'owls, an' wiv a yell,
Plunks Tyball through the gizzard wiv 'is sword,
'Ow I ongcored!
'Put in the boot!' I sez. 'Put in the boot!'
''Ush!' sez Doreen … 'Shame!' sez some silly coot.

Then Romeo, 'e dunno wot to do.
The cops gits busy, like they allwiz do,
An' nose around until 'e gits blue funk
An' does a bunk.
They wants 'is tart to wed some other guy.
'Ah, strike!' she sez. 'I wish that I could die!'

Now, this 'ere gorspil bloke's a fair shrewd 'ead.
Sez 'e 'I'll dope yeh, so they'll *think* yer dead.'
(I tips 'e was a cunnin' sort, wot knoo
A thing or two.)
She takes 'is knock-out drops, up in 'er room:
They think she's snuffed, an' plant 'er in 'er tomb.

Then things gits mixed a treat an' starts to whirl.
'Ere's Romeo comes back an' finds 'is girl
Tucked in 'er little coffing, cold an' stiff,
An' in a jiff
'E swallers lysol, throws a fancy fit,
'Ead over turkey, an' 'is soul 'as flit.

Then Juli-et wakes up an' sees 'im there,
Turns on the water-works an' tears 'er 'air,
'Dear love,' she sez, 'I cannot live alone!'
An' wif a moan,
She grabs 'is pockit knife, an' ends 'er cares …
'*Peanuts or lollies!*' sez a boy upstairs.

Some might question why a poem like 'The Play', from C.J. Dennis' *The Songs of a Sentimental Bloke*, deserves to be called a classic Australian poem. We need to remember, however, that poetry has always been a very broad church. Light verse and poems for 'mere entertainment' have always been a part of it. One doesn't have to be serious all of the time.

Although Kenneth Slessor (1901–71) is generally considered Australia's first real modern poet, room needs to be made for the vernacular poet, C.J. Dennis, who on his death was described by the Prime Minister of the time as 'the Robbie Burns of Australia'. *The Songs of a Sentimental Bloke*, in which 'The Play' is a key component, first came out in 1915 and sold more than 60 000 copies in its first 18 months. It was later filmed twice, as well as being adapted for stage and television. When 500 copies is a good run for a poetry collection in Australia today, with a population nearly seven times larger than in 1915, the success of 'The Bloke' needs some explaining.

Although popularity is no guarantee of quality, there is no doubt that Dennis, in poems like 'The Play', located and exploited something that was then – and still is – considered essentially 'Australian'. Even when roughly a quarter of our population has been born overseas, 'The Play' can still find an enthusiastic audience.

A single reading of the poem immediately gives an idea of Dennis' charm. In almost every city culture, the *cognoscente* love to laugh at the bumpkin (usually from the country, but not always so). Bill, 'the sentimental bloke', formerly with a talent for street fighting, takes his fiancée, Doreen, to see Shakespeare's *Romeo and Juliet*. In the earlier stanzas Bill wonders what all the fuss is about. Why do the Capulets and Montagues have such prestige? 'Fair narks they are, jist like them back-street clicks,/Ixcep' they fights wiv skewers 'stid o' bricks.' It doesn't take long to win us. We're already smiling at the sentimental excesses of Bill when he says: 'I'm off me beat. But when a bloke's in love/'Is thorts turn 'er way like a 'omin' dove.'

By the time we get to the point where the on-stage lovers are 'smoog(in') a treat', we know exactly where we are and what to expect. Nearly all of us know the Shakespearean original (though Shakespeare, in turn, took it from an Italian story) and we can't help but sympathise with the disbelief and impatience our hero, Bill, feels in following Shakespeare's plot. Being a sentimental man himself, Bill is given the 'Joes' when Juliet would 'sigh "Ow, Ro-me-o!" an' git a strangle-holt,/ An' 'ang around 'im like she feared 'e'd bolt.'

As Bill and Doreen take their velvet seats, we see 'high' and 'low' culture colliding while, at the same time, realising their commonality. There's a part of us that agrees with Bill when he calls Romeo 'a silly cow' for carrying on excessively and making dumb decisions. Perhaps something perverse in us also likes to see Mercurio's famously eloquent 'a plague on both your houses' speech reduced to the single line: ' "Ar, rats!" 'e sez, an' passes in 'is check.'

The confusions and misunderstandings at the end of Shakespeare's play are quickly dealt with. Juliet must wed Paris (' "Ah, strike!" she sez. "I wish that I could die!"'). After which, we have the misadventures in the tomb: first with Romeo ("'E swallers lysol, throws a fancy fit …'); and then with Juliet ('She grabs 'is pockit knife, an' ends 'er cares …'). Some in the audience may still be sitting there, stunned yet again by Shakespeare's timeless tragedy – but the sweet-seller (a mate of Bill's?) is already at his work. '"*Peanuts or lollies!*" sez a boy upstairs.'

Some critics have questioned whether Dennis' slang is the genuine article, compared, say, to the colloquial language used by 'Banjo' Paterson or Henry Lawson. It's hard to tell now. The members of the Melbourne 'push' were not known for their record-keeping. The important thing is that the language is coherent within itself. Unfamiliar words such as 'gazob' and 'glarsey' don't really need to send us off to the dictionary. We can grasp their meaning well enough from the context in which they appear. Some pronunciations, like 'ongcored' and 'minnit', may sound more Cockney than Melbourne working-class Australian, but the two dialects were probably closer in 1915 than they are now.

What many sneerers at Dennis' achievement miss is his effortless technical facility. He takes the iambic pentameter (which, in the form of *aabb* heroic couplets, goes back to Chaucer) and makes it his own vehicle entirely. Line 4 in every stanza is cut back to two stresses, thus making an effective variation from what otherwise would have been six more predictable pentameter lines. The recurrent short line reflects Bill's naivety. He's not quite 'getting it right', but on another level, of course, he's getting it more than right. He may be from the 'low' culture, but he knows how to make an 'elegant variation' when he needs one.

'I'm like all lovers, wanting love to be'

I'm like all lovers, wanting love to be
A very mighty thing for you and me.

In certain moods your love should be a fire
That burnt your very life up in desire.

The only kind of love, then, to my mind
Would make you kiss my shadow on the blind

And walk seven miles each night to see it there,
Myself within serene and unaware.

But you're as bad. You'd have me watch the clock
And count your coming while I mend your sock.

You'd have my mind devoted day and night
To you, and care for you and your delight.

Poor fools, who each would have the other give
What spirit must withhold if it would live.

You're not my slave; I wish you not to be,
I love yourself and not your love for me,

The self that goes ten thousand miles away
And loses thought of me for many a day.

And you loved me for loving much beside,
But now you want a woman for your bride.

Oh, make no woman of me, you who can,
Or I will make a husband of a man!

By my unwomanly love that sets you free
Love all myself, but least the woman in me.

Written in 1917, ten years before her death in 1927, aged 28, Lesbia Harford's 'I'm like all lovers, wanting love to be' is both curiously modern and traditional. Some aspects of it go straight back to seventeenth-century Metaphysical poets such as John Donne and Andrew Marvell. In other ways, it is so modern as to be seriously ahead of its time.

Though Harford wrote love poems to both men and women, this one is very much to a man, almost certainly the problematic artist-husband she married in 1920 and broke up with a few years later. However mixed her feelings in 'real life' might have been, Harford's poem has a structure that is neat, logical and compelling. She begins by noting how she herself is thrilled and flattered by having a lover who is so 'burnt … up in desire' that he will 'walk seven miles' 'to kiss (her) shadow on the blind'. Then she notes that the man himself is just 'as bad'. He wants a similarly undivided attention from her. So far we are in very traditional 'love poem' territory, especially as far as the woman is concerned.

Suddenly, at the beginning of stanza 7, the poet becomes quite modern in her outlook, arguing that such obsessive devotion by either or both parties is what the 'spirit must withhold if it would live'. Much better, she says, to love the other person for what they actually are rather than for their devotion to one's self; that is, to love the full complexity of their character.

Ultimately, the poet asks fiercely that her man 'make no woman of me'. Originally he loved her for 'loving much beside'. Now she wants him to stick to that. She acknowledges that, in the society of their time, the man has the power to make her behave this way but threatens that, if he does, she in turn will 'make a husband of a man', a comparably reductive process. The poet points out that it is her 'unwomanly love that sets (him) free', not her excessive devotion. It's rather neatly summed up in what must have been a shocking line for the time: 'But now you want a woman for your bride.'

Harford does admit that women have a tendency to the ultra-romantic and the devotional but recommends they suppress it. 'Love ... least the woman in me', she says to her lover. It's a little reminiscent of Lady Macbeth's 'Unsex me here' speech. She, too, wants none of women's traditional weakness.

Though all this is not exactly hard-line contemporary feminism, it is a recognition, long before its time, that long-term sexual relationships involve much more than a sentimental and obsessive devotion to the other party. 'Love all myself', Harford demands, including everything else she does with her life (not just the bits where she mends his socks and, earlier, fantasises about his watching her shadow on the blind).

Another modern dimension to this 1917 poem is the plainness of its diction. At a time when many Australian poets were still in the sway of late Victorian poeticisms (Pound and Eliot's modernism had still to be heard of here), Harford says exactly what she means, without archaisms or 'poetical' flourishes. Although the iambic pentameter, heroic couplets she uses go back at least as far as Chaucer (1340?–1400), Harford has very much adapted them to her own use. This is an ordinary, everyday woman speaking plainly and honestly to her man. She is saying no more or less than she needs to and she has found precisely the right words in which to say it. The strictness of the pentameter and the *aabb* rhyme scheme lend her arguments (controversial at the time) a sort of inevitability. The metre reaches us (and persuades us) almost before the sense of the poem catches up. Even a diehard male chauvinist (or a Mills & Boon housewife) would find the poem's logic hard to resist.

Harford's treatment of this metre is, however, mainly unremarkable. The pentameters flow very regularly (unlike those of some of her Metaphysical predecessors, 300 years earlier). Very occasionally, there are irregularities such as the extra unstressed syllable at the beginning of line 7. Harford could have said 'And *walk* ten *miles* each *night* to *see* it *there*'. The extra syllable in 'seven' rather than 'ten' suggests some particularity in the situation rather than the merely rhetorical flourish that the more regular 'ten' might have provided.

A comparable sophistication can be seen in the syntax and the use of enjambement. Most of the lines are end-stopped, but there are enough that aren't to provide variation. She uses the tension and release inherent in the heroic couplet to considerable advantage as, for instance, in stanza 7 where we need the last line of the couplet to see what exactly has been offered in the first.

The sentences, too, vary from two to several lines long – and one is stunningly short. 'But you're as bad.' Harford has gone to some trouble to avoid the sing-song effect that can result from this metre's being used too regularly and with a full stop at the end of each couplet.

Lesbia Harford led a short, difficult but relatively adventurous life. Her poetry was collected and published in 1941 by Nettie Palmer and her long-lost novel, *The Invaluable Mystery*, was discovered and published for the first time in the 1980s. 'I'm like all lovers, wanting love to be' is one of her most forceful and modern poems. In 1917 it may well have been ahead of its time (especially in Australia), but it has already long outlived that time and promises to be around for quite a while yet, steadily emerging as the classic Harford almost certainly never imagined it would become.

KENNETH SLESSOR (1901–71)

'Beach Burial'

Softly and humbly to the Gulf of Arabs
The convoys of dead sailor come;
At night they sway and wander in the waters far
    under
But morning rolls them in the foam.

Between the sob and clubbing of the gunfire
Someone, it seems, has time for this,
To pluck them from the shallows and bury them in
    burrows
And tread the sand upon their nakedness;

And each cross, the driven stake of tidewood,
Bears the last signature of men,
Written with such perplexity, with such bewildered
    pity,
The words choke as they begin –

'*Unknown seaman*' – the ghostly pencil
Wavers and fades, the purple drips,
The breath of the wet season has washed their
    inscriptions
As blue as drowned men's lips,

Dead seamen, gone in search of the same landfall,
Whether as enemies they fought,
Or fought with us, or neither; the sand joins them
    together,
Enlisted on the other front.

El Alamein.

Written in the immediate aftermath of the Battle of El Alamein in 1942, 'Beach Burial' is not only Australia's best-known war poem (or anti-war poem), it was also one of the very last Kenneth Slessor completed, even though he was not to die until 1971.

As the poetry of Wilfred Owen and Siegfried Sassoon demonstrates, there is something almost intrinsically poignant about a well-written war poem. War, to all but a few of us, is a self-evident waste of human potential even if, from time to time, we must wage it in defence of such freedoms as we have attained. What is it, then, that makes 'Beach Burial' one of Australia's classic poems?

At one level, the poem's material is simple. In a note written later, mainly for students, Slessor says 'in the morning it was not uncommon to find the bodies of drowned men washed up on the beaches. They were buried in the sandhills under improvised crosses, identification usually being impossible. Most of them were sailors, some British, some German or Italian, some of them "neutrals"'. It is the gap between this laconic, 'after-the-event' description and the intensity of Slessor's imagery and his extraordinary linguistic skill that defines the greatness of the poem.

Paradoxically perhaps, for a war poem, Slessor begins with two quiet adverbs, 'softly' and 'humbly', which set the tone for the whole poem to follow. This is not a poem of strident assertion; it is a poem of 'perplexity', of 'bewildered pity', rather than a song of praise to the 'cause' – or a denunciation of it. Ironically, the dead sailors arrive in 'convoys'. Even in death they don't avoid the regimentation of the war. At night they may 'sway and wander in the waters far under' but morning reveals their fate only too clearly.

The poet, too, is struck by how someone makes time for these burials, despite the important 'sob and clubbing of the gunfire' over the horizon. The impulse to bury the dead is as basic as the impulse to war – and in this lies, perhaps, a certain hope, suggested in the poem's closing lines. The anonymity of the sailors is doubly emphasised by the '*Unknown seaman*' label and by what the rain does to the inscriptions. Despite the individual importance of the dead to their mothers, wives, girlfriends, mates and so on, they are now 'gone in search of the same landfall', a destination where the struggle will continue but in a different form and presumably for nobler objectives.

It is the vagueness of its last phrase that gives the poem much of its strength. This is no Christian Heaven or warriors' Valhalla. It is the ultimate commonality of humanity that, perhaps ironically, the sailors have found in death but which Slessor implies would be much better addressed in life. Breaking one of the poet's most basic taboos, Slessor later spelled out (for students) what he thought he had meant by the 'other front': 'It is the idea that all men of all races, whether they fight with each other or not, are engaged together on the common "front" of humanity's existence.'

If it were only the poem's subtlety of ideas, it is unlikely that 'Beach Burial' would be seen as the great achievement it is. Poetry is more than a matter of 'great ideas'; it is their embodiment in a language that employs the full range of relevant devices that the art form has. As with most other poems by Slessor, 'Beach Burial' is something of a technical triumph.

Perhaps the most powerful of all these techniques is Slessor's use of half-rhyme. Avoiding the simplicities often associated with full rhyme (what Judith Wright called its 'resonant clang'), Slessor echoes the 'perplexity' of the poem by using rhymes that don't quite 'fit': 'come/foam', 'this/nakedness', 'men/begin' and so on. This process climaxes in the last stanza with the almost non-existent rhyme of 'fought/front'. The distance of this 'rhyme' reinforces the poet's suggestive imprecision about exactly what the 'other front' is.

Half-rhyme is also a feature of the internal rhymes in the third line of every stanza: 'wander/under', 'shallows/burrows' and so on. Indeed, the third lines of the stanzas are one of the poem's strangest and most effective features. Where most poets (except perhaps John Donne) would be happy enough to stick to an iambic pentameter throughout, Slessor uses this pattern only in the first line of each stanza. The second is a tetrameter and the third seems to be a hexameter (with an extra syllable or two thrown in). The fourth is most often a tetrameter, but it can also be a pentameter or a trimeter. Again, these changes of line length emphasise the uncertainty of the poem, its 'bewilderment', as it were.

'Beach Burial' is also marked by a wide, and well-chosen, range of sound effects – from the softness of the opening adverbs to the sad onomatopoeia of the famous image 'the sob and clubbing of the gunfire'. There is also the harsh alliteration of 'convoys … come' and 'bury them in burrows'. There is the evocative assonance of 'wavers and fades' and the short vowel sounds in 'pluck' and 'burrows' at either end of line 3, in stanza 2. Indeed, there seems to be the ghost of a rabbiter over this whole stanza.

One could go on in this vein for some time. There is not a line in the whole poem without technical interest. Even an apparently 'flat' line like the final one is seen, on further consideration, to be a clever and moving metaphor – as well as incorporating a highly memorable assonance in 'other' and 'front'. Even the relative lack of rhyme between 'front' and 'fought' can be seen as a virtue rather than a limitation.

Poems rarely come more perfect than this one. Not only do we have the subtlety of thought on a complex and recurrent issue in human history, we also have a graphic embodiment of its poignancy in language that makes the poem, and what it 'says', impossible to forget. If, as Auden wrote, 'poetry makes nothing happen', Kenneth Slessor in 'Beach Burial' certainly helped us to a much clearer understanding of what does happen in war (over and over again) and, at the least, still offers us the quiet hope of avoiding it in the future.

ROBERT D. FITZGERALD (1902–87)

'The Wind at Your Door'

(to Mary Gilmore)

My ancestor was called on to go out –
a medical man, and one such must by law
wait in attendance on the pampered knout
and lend his countenance to what he saw,
lest the pet, patting with too bared a claw,
be judged a clumsy pussy. Bitter and hard,
see, as I see him, in that jailhouse yard.

Or see my thought of him: though time may keep
elsewhere tradition or a portrait still,
I would not feel under his cloak of sleep
if beard there or smooth chin, just to fulfil
some canon of precision. Good or ill
his blood's my own; and scratching in his grave
could find me more than I might wish to have.

Let him then be much of the middle style
of height and colouring; let his hair be dark
and his eyes green; and for that slit, the smile
that seemed inhuman, have it cruel and stark,
but grant it could be too the ironic mark
of all caught in the system – who the most,
the doctor or the flesh twined round that post?

There was a high wind blowing on that day;
for one who would not watch, but looked aside,

said that when twice he turned it blew his way
splashes of blood and strips of human hide
shaken out from the lashes that were plied
by one right-handed, one left-handed tough,
sweating at this paid task, and skilled enough.

That wind blows to your door down all these years.
Have you not known it when some breath you drew
tasted of blood? Your comfort is in arrears
of just thanks to a savagery tamed in you
only as subtler fears may serve in lieu
of thong and noose – old savagery which has built
your world and laws out of the lives it spilt.

For what was jailyard widens and takes in
my country. Fifty paces of stamped earth
stretch; and grey walls retreat and grow so thin
that towns show through and clearings – new raw
    birth
which burst from handcuffs – and free hands go
    forth
to win tomorrow's harvest from a vast
ploughland – the fifty paces of that past.

But see it through a window barred across,
from cells this side, facing the outer gate
which shuts on freedom, opens on its loss
in a flat wall. Look left now through the grate
at buildings like more walls, roofed with grey slate
or hollowed in the thickness of laid stone
each side the court where the crowd stands this
    noon.

One there with the officials, thick of build,
not stout, say burly (so this obstinate man
ghosts in the eyes) is he whom enemies killed
(as I was taught) because the monopolist clan
found him a grit in their smooth-turning plan,
too loyally active on behalf of Bligh.
So he got lost; and history passed him by.

But now he buttons his long coat against
the biting gusts, or as a gesture of mind,
habitual; as if to keep him fenced
from stabs of slander sticking him from behind,
sped by the schemers never far to find
in faction, where approval from one source
damns in another clubroom as of course.

This man had Hunter's confidence, King's praise;
and settlers on the starving Hawkesbury banks
recalled through twilight drifting across their days
the doctor's fee of little more than thanks
so often; and how sent by their squeezed ranks
he put their case in London. I find I lack
the hateful paint to daub him wholly black.

Perhaps my life replies to his too much
through veiling generations dropped between.
My weakness here, resentments there, may touch
old motives and explain them, till I lean
to the forgiveness I must hope may clean
my own shortcomings; since no man can live
in his own sight if it will not forgive.

Certainly I must own him whether or not
it be my will. I was made to understand

this much when once, marking a freehold lot,
my papers suddenly told me it was land
granted to Martin Mason. I felt his hand
heavily on my shoulder, and knew what coil
binds life to life through bodies, and soul to soil.

There, over to one corner, a bony group
of prisoners waits; and each shall be in turn
tied by his own arms in a human loop
about the post, with his back bared to learn
the price of seeking freedom. So they earn
three hundred rippling stripes apiece, as set
by the law's mathematics against the debt.

These are the Irish batch of Castle Hill,
rebels and mutineers, my countrymen
twice over; first, because of those to till
my birthplace first, hack roads, raise roofs; and then
because their older land time and again
enrolls me through my forbears; and I claim
as origin that threshold whence we came.

One sufferer had my surname, and thereto
'Maurice', which added up to history once;
an ignorant dolt, no doubt, for all that crew
was tenantry. The breed of clod and dunce
makes patriots and true men: could I announce
that Maurice as my kin I say aloud
I'd take his irons as heraldry, and be proud.

Maurice is at the post. Its music lulls,
one hundred lashes done. If backbone shows
then play the tune on buttocks! But feel his pulse;
that's what a doctor's for; and if it goes

lamely, then dose it with these purging blows –
which have not made him moan; though, writhing
    there,
'Let my neck be,' he says, 'and flog me fair.'

One hundred lashes more, then rest the flail.
What says the doctor now? 'This dog won't yelp;
he'll tire you out before you'll see him fail;
here's strength to spare; go on!' Ay, pound to pulp;
yet when you've done he'll walk without your help,
and knock down guards who'd carry him being bid,
and sing no song of where the pikes are hid.

It would be well if I could find, removed
through generations back – who knows how far? –
more than a surname's thickness as a proved
bridge with that man's foundations. I need some star
of courage from his firmament, a bar
against surrenders: faith. All trials are less
than rain-blacked wind tells of that old distress.

Yet I can live with Mason. What is told,
and what my heart knows of his heart, can sort
much truth from falsehood, much there that I hold
good clearly or good clouded by report;
and for things bad, ill grows where ills resort:
they were bad times. None know what in his place
they might have done. I've my own faults to face.

First published in 1958 in *The Bulletin*, 'The Wind at Your Door',
has, despite the ups and downs of its author's subsequent reputa-
tion, become a truly canonical Australian poem. It is also, of course,
a good example of how the personal can be made universal.

R.D. FitzGerald already had a significant poetic career behind him when he wrote what is now the most widely read of all his poems. Initially associated with Kenneth Slessor and the 'Vitalism' of the Sydney 'Vision' school (which grouped around the artist, Norman Lindsay), FitzGerald in the 1930s became better known for his long, philosophical poems. By the mid-1950s, he was ready to distil a great deal of what he knew of Australia's early history into the poem that many regard as his masterpiece.

The poem moves around two figures: the first an ancestor and the second a namesake. Martin Mason was an early colonial surgeon and magistrate whose duties, as the poem makes clear, included the supervision of floggings so as to prevent unintended deaths. Morris (or 'Maurice') Fitzegarrel was the convict who, the documents tell us, endured the flogging described. As a descendant of the Irish diaspora, FitzGerald clearly feels close to both protagonists, both of whom he eventually sees as victims of the age and system in which they were caught.

Something of this point emerges in the first stanza of the poem where the poet sees his surgeon ancestor as 'bitter and hard' but perhaps made that way by the 'jailhouse yard' where he was compelled to collaborate in brutality. In the second stanza FitzGerald admits that he knows nothing of Mason's actual appearance and so, in the third stanza, proceeds to invent him: a man of 'the middle style/of height and colouring' and the 'ironic' smile of 'all caught in the system'.

In the fourth stanza we start the story proper. It's a day of 'high wind', so high in fact that it 'blows to your door down all these years' to our own day. At this stage, too, the poet begins to universalise, using the pronoun 'you' which might equally refer to himself or to the reader. Our world, he argues, was built from 'old savagery'. 'Fifty paces of that past' have become the 'vast ploughland' we now inhabit.

This is no easy patriotism, however. In the next few stanzas FitzGerald takes us straight back to the original scene with all its lacerating horror. The poet sees his surgeon/magistrate ancestor supervising there and cannot help but give us a little of his life's misadventures: the way he backed the wrong side in the Rum Rebellion and how he nobly travelled back to London to represent the interests of his Hawkesbury patients. FitzGerald concludes: 'I find I lack/the hateful paint to daub him wholly black.'

Then, at the beginning of the thirteenth stanza, we finally cross to the other protagonist, the poet's namesake, whose back is 'bared to learn/the price of seeking freedom'. In the next stanza the poet reminds us that his namesake was not a London thief but one of those Irish 'rebels and mutineers' who rose in rebellion against the British government at Castle Hill in 1804. The surgeon pays the rebel a reverse compliment by saying that this fellow Irishman 'won't yelp' and so orders the flogging to go on. The poet, in his turn, would like to prove himself a descendant of such a man. He'd be happy, he says, to take the convict's 'irons as heraldry, and be proud'.

Eventually, however, FitzGerald concedes that, for all his admiration for the convict's toughness, he 'can live with Mason'. The poet admires what he knows of his ancestor's good works and notes that '... for things bad, ill grows where ills resort'. He was a product of his times. We are then told, with a sensible caution, that 'None know what in his place/they might have done. I've my own faults to face.'

It's a caution, too, that should prevent contemporary readers from dismissing FitzGerald's account on the basis that it doesn't mention at any point an equally great example of suffering that was occurring at the same time: the dispossession of the Eora people. In 1958, to most people (FitzGerald included) that particular injustice was not of much concern. The irony may be, however, that the poet's image of the flogging with its 'splashes of blood and strips of human hide' may prove transferable. It can be taken to stand for, or imply, the other injustices of the period as well: '... they were bad times'; 'ill grows where ills resort' and so on.

It's interesting, too, to note that 'The Wind at Your Door' is dedicated to Mary Gilmore who wrote 'Old Botany Bay', a comparably famous Australian poem on a similar theme. It concludes: 'Shame on the mouth/That would deny/The knotted hands/That set us high!' Gilmore's poem runs to less than a hundred words. Fitzgerald's poem needs 133 lines of iambic pentameter to make its point.

We should not begrudge this, however. FitzGerald needs his several digressions and meditations to make the poem as psychologically convincing as it is. It's not enough for him to note merely that one of the protagonists is his ancestor and another his namesake. He needs to think more deeply on what this really means and, in the process, he has done much thinking for the reader, too. Australian sensitivity about our convict ancestry has faded considerably since the NSW governor, Earl Beauchamp, made his 1889 gaffe about the colony's 'birthstains'. These days people can be quite proud of having a convict forbear and tend to smile happily at the joke in which an Australian immigration clerk asks a British applicant: 'Do you have a criminal record?' and receives in reply the question: 'Is that still necessary?'

It is almost certainly the poem's psychological depth that explains its continuing relevance to us 50 years later – despite our views on its subject matter having changed in the interim. The leisurely pace at which FitzGerald examines his own ambivalent position is an essential part of the poem's success.

So, too, is the poet's mastery of the pentameter line and his seven-line stanza form. FitzGerald is one of those poets who, like John Donne in the seventeenth century, push the pentameter about for his own purposes. Lines as regular as 'and *sing* no *song* of *where* the *pikes* are *hid*' are unusual. More typically we have lines like the opening one where we feel three strong stresses when there are, in fact, the necessary five. 'My *ancestor* was *called* on *to* go *out*' feels more like 'My *ancestor* was *called* on to go *out*'. Some critics have found this 'unmusical' but there's no doubt FitzGerald does it deliberately. The subject matter itself mandates roughness, not mellifluousness. We also note plenty of examples of the 'inverted foot' where the stress is put on the first syllable for emphasis rather than on the second where it should be. '*Splash*es of *blood* and *strips* of *hum*an *hide*' is just one.

And, of course, graphic imagery of the kind just quoted is another reason for the poem's persisting impact. FitzGerald finds the images with which to convey the violence and cruelty that were so much a part of the convict system. The black humour of the cat-o'-nine tails as a 'pampered knout' or a 'clumsy pussy' are just two examples. 'Have you not known it when some breath you drew/ tasted of blood?' is another. There is nothing gratuitous here either. The poet is just reminding us of how terrible things were. They are the bloody instances from which he derives the generalisations 'they were bad times' and 'ill grows where ills resort'.

The relentlessness of FitzGerald's seven-line stanzas may also be part of this effect. Through all this savage detail and all his ruminations, the poet keeps his *ababbcc* rhyme scheme going. The reiteration of the three '*b*'s' and the two '*c*'s' in each stanza has a cumulative effect. Like the man at the post, we are not going to be let off lightly.

As the definitive poem about Australia's convict past, R.D. FitzGerald's 'The Wind at Your Door' is going to be around for as long as we are willing to recognise that part of our history. Indeed, it remains a powerful instrument against our forgetting it. While brutal treatment of the convicts may not have been the only injustice of the period, the poem reminds us only too well of an essential part of our complex national origins.

A.D. HOPE (1907–2000)

'The Mayan Books'

Diego de Landa, archbishop of Yucatan
– The curse of God upon his pious soul –
Placed all their Devil's picture-books under ban
And, piling them in one sin-heap, burned the whole;

But took the trouble to keep the calendar
By which the Devil had taught them to count time.
The impious creatures had tallied back as far
As ninety million years before Eve's crime.

That was enough: they burned the Mayan books,
Saved souls and kept their own in proper trim.
Diego de Landa in heaven always looks
Towards God: God never looks at him.

Canberra poet, A.D. Hope, wrote several of Australia's (and possibly the language's) classic poems. These are normally said to include 'Australia', 'Imperial Adam', 'The Death of the Bird' and 'Moschus Moschiferus'. 'The Mayan Books', published in the early 1970s and collected in his last book *Orpheus* (1991), may at first glance seem slighter than the works listed above, but it deserves to be considered with them.

Just 12 lines long, 'The Mayan Books' is one of those poems that goes straight in to make its point and then gets out again. There is no unnecessary elaboration or scene-setting. It is surprising how much information is pressed into so few lines. We meet the lamented archbishop; we hear outlines of his two-step crime and we have the final, ironic result. A book on Central American history will hardly tell us anything more important about Diego de Landa than we already know from Hope's poem.

The achievement of 'The Mayan Books', however, is much more than a mere demonstration of the aphorism that 'Brevity is the soul of wit'. It is also one of tone and viewpoint. The narrative voice, at one level, seems to be Hope's own, that of a bemused, white-haired English professor with a very idiosyncratic turn of mind. At another level, though, it also seems to be that of an enlight-ened monsignor with inside knowledge of who's in heaven and who's not and how the furniture is arranged. It's the monsignor who makes the oxymoronic comment: 'The curse of God upon his pious soul'; it's he who recites the jargon of the day, adjudging the Mayans to be 'impious creatures'. On the other hand, it is probably Hope himself who talks of 'Eve's crime', an episode he is concerned with in quite a few of his other poems – 'Imperial Adam', to name just one. Conversely, it is the monsignor rather than the professor who is in a position to tell us that, through all eternity, God never looks at Diego.

The tone thus created is a sly, mock-ingenuous one that, in satirical poetry, goes all the way back to Swift and Pope and, beyond that again, to Roman satirists like Horace and Martial. It's a highly effective tool and anyone or anything ridiculed with such a weapon tends to stay wounded – there are no second chances. If we ever read anything good about Diego de Landa elsewhere we will be most unlikely to believe it.

Classics like 'The Mayan Books' have a way of floating into and out of focus, according to how much we seem to need them at the time. Hope's poem, 'Australia', with its caustic reference to the 'chatter of cultured apes/Which is called civilisation over there', was more necessary in the 1950s than it is now. In these days of wall-to-wall fundamentalisms and unquestioning self-righteousness, 'The Mayan Books' is increasingly relevant. The religious and cultural self-confidence (let's say it, 'arrogance') of the God, Gold and Glory seeking imperial Spanish is a mind-set quite familiar to us today, right across the spectrum from Osama bin Laden to George W. Bush. The exasperation contained in the simple phrase 'That was enough' is something that we well recognise – the sense that one has given one's enemy his chance and there's an end to it. You're either 'for us or against us'. Hope's poem keeps reminding us that things were never that simple. Although the Mayans' 'ninety million years' speculation about the earth's beginning is neither here nor there, it's a lot closer to the mark than the famous 4004 BC date for the Garden of Eden.

'The Mayan Books' is written in Hope's favourite form, the iambic pentameter quatrain with an *abab* rhyme scheme. If it has a slightly eighteenth-century flavour that doesn't make it any less useful as a vehicle in the late twentieth. Just to advance an opinion in such a strict and assertive form often gives it a kind of *ipso facto* credibility. The form makes its own argument and, before we realise, we have been carried along and converted – ironically, in this case – to a sceptical viewpoint. The initial pentameter is just the right length to accommodate the full name and title of our protagonist (though there are a couple of extra unstressed syllables in there just to loosen it slightly). The next pentameter neatly contains our monsignor's slightly blasphemous aside. The next two lines continue the story with the sentence hopping across the stanza gap to finish halfway through the next stanza. The tetrameter would be too short a line, perhaps, to carry the poem's rather relaxed tone. Free verse, unthinkable for Hope, would be much less likely to work in this context. How, with free verse, would we get the neatly ironic rhyme of souls' 'trim' and God's never looking at 'him'?

The syntax, too, is no less important. The first sentence is six lines long; the other three, just two lines each. Six lines are needed to establish the situation – after which ensue three snappy, two-line comments, culminating with the final cosmic irony still being suffered by the unfortunate Diego. Hope even uses the gap between stanzas 1 and 2 to create the sensation of a snide addendum. Diego keeps the calendar just in case it might be useful. After all, it was the Pope who made the rulings on such things in those days.

'The Mayan Books' will continue for quite some time to remind us that keeping one's (bigoted) soul 'in proper trim' and burning what we don't understand may well be counterproductive. It also continues to insist that God is a much larger concept than numbskulls like the archbishop can imagine. By never looking at Diego, the Almighty is not particularly punishing his self-appointed lap-dog. He is merely preoccupied with much bigger things than small minds like Diego's will ever be able to accommodate.

'The Commercial Traveller's Wife'

I'm living with a commercial traveller;
He's away, most of the time;
Most I see of him's his wife; as for her:
I'm just home from a show,
And there I am undressing, in my shirt;
I hear midnight chime,
And up flares the curtain at the window;
The door's opened; it's Gert,
That's the wife; her hair's hanging down;
She's only got her nightgown
Blowing up against her in the wind;
She's fat, and getting fatter;
I said, 'What's the matter?'
'Jack,' she said, 'now's your chance';
'What chance?' I said. 'You out of your mind?'
She goes over to the bed;
I grab my pants;
'That's enough of that,' I said. 'Now, go on; you get
    out.'
'But, Jack,' she said, 'don't you love me?'
'I don't know what you're talking about,'
I said, 'besides, Jim –
'What about him?'
'Yes; Jim,' she said; 'there's always Jim, but he's
Always away; and you don't know
What it's like. I can't stand it. And anyhow,
Jack, don't you want me?' 'Oh, don't be an ass,'
I said; 'look at yourself in the glass.'

She faced the mirror where she stood
And sort of stiffened there;
Her eyes went still as knots in a bit of wood,
And it all seemed to sigh out of her;
'All right,' she said; 'all right, all right, good-night,'
As though she didn't know if I heard,
And shuffled out without another word.
Well, I was tired; I went to bed and slept.
In the morning
I thought I'd dreamt the whole thing;
But at breakfast, I could have wept;
Poor Gert, clattering the dishes
With a dead sort of face
Like a fish's.
I'll have to get a new place.
I'm going out today to have a look.
Trouble is, she's a marvellous cook.

At one level 'The Commercial Traveller's Wife' is a useful re- minder of how strong the demotic strand in Australian poetry has been. At another, it is also a subtle morality tale. Its author, Ronald McCuaig, was perhaps the first urban Australian poet to use language in this way. Previously, of course, the bush balladists had used colloquial language for humorous effect, as had C.J. Dennis in *The Sentimental Bloke,* but McCuaig was almost certainly the first literary poet to have seen its potential.

The story of the poem seems simple enough. Neglected older woman makes unsuccessful pass at younger gent. Younger gent unceremoniously knocks her back and looks for new lodgings. Its morality, however, is much more complex than that. To start with, who is the 'I' in the poem? Is this a dramatic monologue or a personal anecdote? As Kenneth Slessor made clear in some of his poems, the mores of 1920s Sydney were more adventurous than we might care to remember. In 'The Commercial Traveller's Wife' the morality is ultimately quite complex.

The narrator (let's agree he's a creation of McCuaig's and not the poet himself) assumes he's boarding with the commercial traveller rather than with his wife – who is actually there much more than her husband is. The young man is clearly something of a chauvinist, a man-about-town who's 'just home from a show'. He might almost be telling this as a yarn to a friend in the pub. '… it's Gert,/That's the wife'. He doesn't say *his* wife; that is, the commercial traveller's wife. Gert, at this stage, is just an auxiliary figure who comes with board and lodging at so much a week. He's hardly noticed her before – other than to savour her cooking, it seems.

Now, in the context where she's come into his room uninvited, the narrator notes that 'She's fat, and getting fatter'. His response to her approaches is to 'grab (his) pants' rather than commit the adultery she's proposing. It's interesting that the narrator's apparent misgivings about the husband ('besides, Jim –/'What about him?') come only after he's said no and told her to get out. Already the morality is confused. It becomes even more complicated when the narrator, with unnecessary cruelty, tells her to look in the mirror. By this stage the reader is probably feeling that, despite the seventh commandment, this narrator is a rather paltry young man.

Improbably, however, the narrator does seem to show some remorse for what he's done. He's sensitive enough to notice how 'it all seemed to sigh out of her' and that next morning she is 'clattering the dishes'. He even says 'I could have wept' (though we do notice the somewhat undercutting rhyme of 'slept' three lines earlier). He realises that not only has the wife done something problematic but so has he by so unfeelingly knocking her back. On the other hand, at the same time and with much less compassion, he compares her 'dead sort of face' to a 'fish's' (rhyming callously with 'dishes') and finishes off by lamenting self-interestedly: 'Trouble is, she's a marvellous cook'.

All this perhaps explains why the average reader will probably feel a bit queasy about this poem. Despite the biblical injunctions against adultery, we can see that it's a sad and rather cruel thing that's happened. We don't very much identify with the narrator, but we can see he's not totally insensitive. We're far from convinced, however, that he would have rejected her advances if she had not been 'fat, and getting fatter'. 'Jim', the absent husband, has been only a secondary reason, we can see.

In addition to being intrigued by the poem's psychology and morality, we are also struck by McCuaig's mastery of the colloquial. It's not just his use of everyday phrases such as 'Most I see of him's' and 'That's the wife'; it's the way he integrates these elements into what is a very cleverly written poem by any standard. At first, with its irregular line lengths and colloquial rhythms, we might almost think the poem is written in free verse; however, it's not long before we start to notice the extensive use of rhyme, despite the unevenness of line length. Indeed some of these odd lengths are a part of the humour (as, for instance, when he uses the short line 'Like a fish's' to get a rhyme with 'dishes' only two lines earlier). There's a sort of false naivety about this. It's as if McCuaig wants us to think that he can't quite get the pentameter right so needs to take (literal) short-cuts.

A similar effect can be seen in the poem's metre. There are quite a few standard iambic lines ('She *faced* the *mirror where* she *stood*/ And *sort* of *stiff*ened *there*'), but there are many where the need to be idiomatic produces convincing irregularities. The first line is an excellent example: 'I'm *living* with a com*mer*cial *trav*eller'. It could have been 'I'm *living with* a *married couple*', but that would not have had the flatness McCuaig has deliberately achieved with the line as it is. It's this sort of thing which gives the poem its slightly disconcerting 'pub anecdote' feeling. We see it again in 'I *thought* I'd *dreamt* the *whole thing*', which could easily have been the more regular 'I *thought* I'd *dreamt* it *all*'. McCuaig can also push his metre towards the anapaestic to get a slightly different effect, as in 'With a *dead* sort of *face*/Like a *fish*'s'. Ironically, there is no suggestion of any waltz here, for all the triple rhythms.

It's worth having a closer look at McCuaig's rhyming, too. There are very few lines in the poem that don't at least half-rhyme though sometimes the rhyming sound may be several lines distant. Sometimes it can be humorously close, as in the adjacencies of 'Jim' and 'him' and 'fatter' and 'matter'. These close rhymes can also suggest the narrator's callowness – as also in the closing couplet which, incidentally, has a nice contrast between the regular iambic pentameter of the penultimate line and the extra unstressed syllable 'a' in the last line which makes us land so decisively on the key syllable of '*marvellous*' ('*Trouble is*, she's a *marvellous cook*').

On balance, 'The Commercial Traveller's Wife' reminds us what a many-roomed mansion poetry can be. It doesn't have to consist of deathless sentiments in impeccable syntax. It can also be about the everyday – and the shoddy moral compromises made by people who are fully human but have no particular claim to fame. Similarly, it can use totally colloquial language and be quite unelevated in its tone. The dictions of Milton, Wordsworth – or even Wallace Stevens – are not the only possibilities. There's also room for phrases like 'I grab my pants' and the rhyming of 'dishes' with 'fish's'.

ELIZABETH RIDDELL (1910–98)

'The Children March'

The children of the world are on the march
From the dangerous cots, the nurseries ringed with
    fire,
The poisoned toys, the playgrounds pitted
With bomb craters and shrapnel strewn about;
From the whips, the iron bars, the guns' great shout,
The malevolent teachers and the lethal sports
Played on the ruined fields fenced by red wire.

The children of the world are on the march
With the doll and the schoolbag to safe quarters,
The temporary haven, the impermanent home;
Nightly turning their thoughts to the forsaken
    hearth
The wandering, wondering children of the world
March on the sea and land and crowded air –
The unsmiling sons, the sad bewildered daughters.

Elizabeth Riddell came to Australia from Napier, New Zealand, to start a life in journalism with the Sydney *Truth* at the age of eighteen. During World War 2 she spent considerable time in Britain when it was under attack and in Europe towards the end. This experience shows through strongly in her remarkable sonnet, 'The Children March'.

Though much of Riddell's relatively small output (five books) was more cheerful and more lyrical than 'The Children March', it is in this poem that she has caught and distilled one of the eternal truths of any war – that it is never started by children but it is children (almost as much as soldiers) who become the main sufferers.

This tends to be the case whether one considers a particular war 'justified' or not.

Riddell begins the poem with her insistent line 'The children of the world are on the march', thus emphasising that she is talking about a universal experience, not just the children of one side or one nation. She goes on to list the various things that not only threaten their childhood as it might normally have been experienced, but their very lives. The details cover everything from the blitz ('the nurseries ringed with fire') to the Jewish holocaust ('whips, the iron bars'). They include, too, accidental deaths from mines while playing on 'the ruined fields fenced by red wire'. The 'malevolent teachers' are more obscure perhaps and could refer either to the more brutal teaching methods of those days or to totalitarian indoctrination.

In the second stanza Riddell is more concerned with the impact of the various evacuations endured by the children in an attempt to save them from physical destruction. She pictures their home-sickness as they go from a 'temporary haven' to an 'impermanent home'. Each night their thoughts return 'to the forsaken hearth'. In the third line from the end, the poet reiterates her phrase 'children of the world' – and neatly sums up their sense of being lost with the two related participles 'wandering, wondering'. In the penultimate line she introduces a note of surrealism, which serves also to emphasise the children's huge numbers. They march not only on 'the sea and land' but on, or in, the 'crowded air'. This could conceivably refer to various airlifts (of which there weren't many), but it's more probably designed to give us a sense of the children as disembodied spirits, still fleeing the violence even in the 'crowded air' – 'crowded' not only with themselves but with all the bombers and fighters flying through it.

Finally, in the last line, Riddell pins things down a little. These are not just generalised 'children' of no particular sex or origin. They are both male and female – and they are someone's sons and daughters. Realistically, we don't see the idealised happy child (so often seen in the propaganda of both sides) but 'unsmiling sons' and 'sad bewildered daughters'. It's not likely either that Riddell is being sexist in drawing such distinctions. It seems probable somehow that the impact of the war should have a slightly different effect on either sex – the sons 'unsmiling' and the daughters 'sad' and 'bewildered'.

To some readers, 'The Children March' may have a slightly 1930s, 'dated' air. Its debt to Auden is clear enough and it echoes, probably unconsciously, Wallace Stevens' poem of the '30s, 'Dry Loaf', which features lines such as ' ... the dry men blown/Brown as the bread, thinking of birds/Flying from burning countries and brown sand shores ...' and so on. It might have been better for us if the poem had in fact been dated, if its subject had become irrelevant – but no one needs reminding that wars continue and that their impact on children is undiminished (even, in some cases, with children being forced to take up arms).

A further reason for this poem's durability is not just its continuing relevance but its technical skill. Riddell has taken the 600-year-old sonnet form and turned it to her own purposes. Instead of the normal eight and six lines – or the three lots of four plus a couplet (as used by Shakespeare) – Riddell uses two stanzas of seven lines. Her rhyme scheme is unusual, too, with the rhyming sound for the seventh line of each stanza occurring six lines earlier. She puts the couplet we might expect in lines 13 and 14 in the middle of the first stanza ('about/shout'). In the second stanza, she takes further liberties, with her rhyming restricted to the 'quarters/daughters' of lines 2 and 7 – though 'hearth' in line 4 is certainly a half-rhyme with 'march' in line 1.

With rhythm, also, Riddell makes some productive variations. Though the opening line for each stanza is a perfect iambic pentameter, there are quite a few other lines where she introduces extra syllables or puts two stressed syllables next to each other for emphasis. The poem's second line, for instance, has 13 syllables rather than the normal ten. Quite a few others have extra syllables, which somehow has the effect of extending the range and dimensions of what she is talking about. 'The *wandering, wondering children of the world*' is one such. The two-stress phrases '*Bomb craters*' and '*red wire*' are, on the other hand, clear examples of where the stress pattern reflects the harshness of what is being described.

Elizabeth Riddell is a perfect example of the sort of poet whom a tradition may easily lose track of. Not prolific and something of a 'poet's poet' in that she was admired more by other poets than by the general public, Riddell deserves to have the best of her work preserved for generations who will not have known her personally and will be unfamiliar with the journalism for which she was better known. While 'The Children March' is not especially typical of Riddell's poetry, it is an example of her craftsmanship at its best and a poem of powerful emotional impact, both when first published and decades later.

WILLIAM HART-SMITH (1911–90)

'Baiamai's Never-failing Stream'

Then he made of the stars, in my mind,
pebbles and clear water running over them,
linking most strangely feelings of im-
measurable remoteness with intimacy,

So that at one and the same time I
not only saw a far white mist of stars
there, far up there, but had my fingers
dabbling among those cold stones.

First published in Meanjin Papers in 1944, William Hart-Smith's 'Baiamai's Never-failing Stream' remains at once one of the high points of the Jindyworobak movement and one of the few examples where a non-Aboriginal writer has successfully caught at least a part of the Aboriginal cosmos. The Jindyworobaks flourished from the mid-1930s to the early 1950s and aspired to incorporate what they knew of Aboriginal culture and religion into the mainstream of Australian poetry. Like Roland Robinson, William Hart-Smith (who came to Australia from England via New Zealand in 1936) was identified with this group initially but soon outgrew its limitations.

Although Aboriginal creation stories differ widely, Baiamai (variously spelt) is usually considered an over-arching creative figure whom missionaries could usefully compare with the god of Genesis. As the poem implies, however, Baiamai lacks the jealousy and the tribalism of Jehovah and seems content to be a background figure for more specific ancestor spirits who created various features of the Australian landscape as they travelled through it.

William Hart-Smith, in his rendering of this figure, begins by establishing the limitations of his own situation. The poem is not a dramatic monologue from an Aboriginal viewpoint but is written from a European (and perhaps secular) viewpoint. The poet admits that it is all 'in my mind' and continues to emphasise the subjectivity of his experience of what we take to be the Milky Way. He implies, too, that this is but a fragment of something larger by starting the poem with 'Then' as if the Milky Way or the 'never-failing stream' was but one in a succession of Baiamai's creations.

The poem moves on to emphasise the similarities and disparities of scale between the cosmic 'stream' that Europeans know as the Milky Way and the literal stream of 'clear water' in which the poet has '(his) fingers/dabbling'. One is a thing of unthinkable immensity; the other is down here running over 'cold stones'. It's the intersection of 'remoteness' with 'intimacy'. The specificity of the cold water over the dabbling fingers helps us understand what would otherwise be beyond us.

This, Hart-Smith seems to imply, is the genius of Aboriginal creation stories: that they enable us to understand the macro through the micro. The landscape, even the cosmos, is assimilated and taken into oneself through the stories told about it. Baiamai's story is told so that the narrator may see that the 'far white mist of stars' is something as close to him as the creek water running through his fingers and over 'cold stones'. Baiamai has given us this insight for our own benefit. It is a revelation every bit as real as those we are accustomed to in the New Testament (or Genesis, for that matter).

It is Hart-Smith's achievement to have distilled all this (and more) down to two quatrains. Like many other writers of free verse, Hart-Smith was also influenced by the Imagist movement (circa 1912) and by American poets such as William Carlos Williams (with whom he corresponded). Like Hart-Smith's poem, 'Full Moon', 'Baiamai's Never-failing Stream' is a definitive Imagist poem. A single comparison is made: 'A white mist of stars' becomes the creek running over 'cold stones'. This is at the root of the poem's extreme compression and implications radiate out from it, as always with successful poems of this kind.

Another of this poem's distinctions is its pioneering use of free verse. In 1944 (and for another 20 years or so) Australian poets without exception were still using traditional metres (even those few who, like Kenneth Slessor, had absorbed, at least to some extent, the modernism of Ezra Pound, T.S. Eliot and others). Ironically, but appositely, Hart-Smith uses the free-verse rhythms of the King James Bible for his Aboriginal creation story. 'Then he made of the stars, in my mind' could almost be a quotation from one of the psalms. It also uses the triple rhythms, and those extra unstressed syllables, which are so often a mark of free verse. 'Then he *made* of the *stars*, in my *mind*'.

Likewise, there are plenty of two (or more) stressed syllables adjacent to each other, another free-verse technique. '*clear water*' and *far white mist*' are just two examples. The most memorable of these is the poem's final image, the '*cold stones*', syllables which are not only of equal stress but assonantal as well.

Interestingly, Hart-Smith did not suddenly abandon traditional aspects of poetry altogether. He had a lingering affection for rhyme, especially half-rhyme, and quite often used it to tie a poem together. Thus we get the half-rhyme between 'them' and 'im' and also between 'im' and the stressed '*in*' in '*in*timacy'. The alliteration between '*st*ars' and '*st*ones' in the second stanza is also a kind of rhyme. The 'mind' and 'I' assonance which finishes the first line of the first and second stanzas is yet another linking device.

Something of this same sense of transition can be felt with the poem's use of enjambement. Although most of the lines are end-stopped (as was normally but not always the case in more traditional poetry), on two occasions the poet employs an extreme enjambment – ending a line with the pronoun 'I' in one case and with the hyphenated syllable 'im-' in the other. Again, Hart-Smith was well ahead of his time.

'Baiamai's Never-failing Stream' thus exists on two levels: as a convincing (and useful) insight from one worldview to another; and as a fine example of craftsmanship in a form which many readers at the time considered to involve no craft at all. They were all too ready to speak of 'chopped prose' and so on. It's interesting, however, that they rarely said the same thing about King David's Psalms or the Song of Solomon.

ROLAND ROBINSON (1912–92)

'Mapooram'

(related by Fred Biggs, Ngeamba tribe, Lake Carjelligo)

Go out and camp somewhere. You're lying down.
A wind comes, and you hear this *Mapooram*.
'What's that?' you say. Why that's a *Mapooram*.
You go and find that tree rubbing itself.
It makes all sorts of noises in the wind.
It might be like a sheep, or like a cat
or like a baby crying, or someone calling,
a sort of whistling-calling when the wind
comes and swings and rubs two boughs like that.

A *wirreengun*, a clever-feller, sings
that tree. He hums a song, a *Mapooram*:
a song to close things up, or bring things out,
a song to bring a girl, a woman from that tree.
She's got long hair, it falls right down her back.
He's got her for himself. He'll keep her now.

One evening, it was sort of rainy-dark,
they built a mia-mia, stripping bark.
You've been out in the bush sometime and seen
them old dry pines with loose bark coming off.
You get a lot of bark from those old dry pines,
before they rot and go too far, you know.
That woman from the tree, she pulled that bark.
It tore off, up and up the tree. It pulled
her up, into the tree, up, up into the sky.

Well, she was gone. That was the end of it.
No more that *wirreengun* could call her back.

'*Mapooram, Mapooram.*' 'What's that?' you say.
Why, that's two tree boughs rubbing in the wind.

While collaborations are inevitable in the performing arts, they are much less common in literature – especially in poetry, the most personal of literary genres. Roland Robinson was known initially as a member of the Jindyworobaks, a group that in the 1930s and 1940s attempted (with insufficient research and experience) to incorporate elements of Aboriginal culture into mainstream Australian poetry. Robinson soon transcended the category and is now best remembered for his vivid, romantic nature poetry set in some of Australia's more remote areas.

It may seem unfair, then, to take one of Robinson's collaborations as an index to his work more generally, but 'Mapooram' (written from material provided to him by Fred Biggs) is a difficult poem to go past. Unlike many white writers sympathetic to Aborigines, Robinson actually had considerable contact with them at various points in his life. From these came a book (in 1970) called *Altjeringa and other Aboriginal Poems.* 'Mapooram' is one of its most memorable.

'Mapooram' is a work that neither Roland Robinson nor Fred Biggs could have written by himself. The story is deeply Aboriginal (though no less universal for that) and its iambic pentameter form is profoundly English (though there is no reason why Biggs could not have learned it if he'd wanted to). The poem has, within itself, a necessary tension between these two worlds, even as it tells a story that is clearly meaningful to both.

Let's look at the story from Biggs' point of view initially. Biggs is telling Robinson, whom he knows as something of a bushman, to 'Go out and camp somewhere.' When he does he will most likely hear a 'Mapooram' (pronounced '*Mapooram*', it would seem from the scansion), the sound of a tree rubbing against itself. The typical European might, at best, hear in this noise something reminiscent of a sheep, a cat or a baby. The Aborigine, however, hears much more than that. He hears the ancient tribal story of the *wirreengun*, the 'clever-feller', who sings a woman out of that tree to have 'for himself'.

In the penultimate stanza, Biggs seems to become side-tracked, talking on to Robinson about the 'loose bark' of those 'old dry pines'. But, of course, like all good storytellers, he is merely setting up the climax – when the woman, ripping down strips of the dry pine bark, is 'pulled … up, up into the sky'. Interestingly, and significantly, the *wirreengun*'s powers do not extend to getting her back.

Unlike Greek myth, where hubris is clearly punished, the Aboriginal myth seems to view the woman's disappearance as a faintly humorous irony. The 'clever-feller' is not quite as smart as he thought he was (though still smart enough, of course, to sing a woman out of a tree in the first place). Interestingly, at the end, Biggs anticipates Robinson's predictable European scepticism and slyly seems to agree with it, admitting, 'Why, that's two tree boughs rubbing in the wind.' But, of course, the white-feller is not going to forget the story – as the existence of the poem shows.

From Robinson's point of view, however, the situation is rather different. Fred Biggs, who obviously knows a fair bit of Ngeamba lore (more than he'd ever be likely to reveal to a white man), has told Robinson a sly, unforgettable story in Aboriginal English. The poet in Robinson recognises the story as great material but is immediately confronted by several problems. Does he retell it in grammatically 'correct' English? Does he just transcribe the exact words of Fred Biggs and so risk caricaturing him as uneducated? Or does he make the story sound like a bush tale by Henry Lawson (if the writers of that period had paid any serious attention to Aboriginal culture)?

In fact, Robinson decides to use one of the oldest narrative devices known in our language (iambic pentameter blank verse) to recast the story in a mixture of his own words and those of Fred Biggs. Thus we have the Aboriginal English (and, admittedly, rural working-class English) of '*them* old dry pines' and the 'standard' English of '*those* old dry pines' in the succeeding line. We have deeply resonant phrases, such as 'it was sort of rainy-dark', in which we're not sure whether we're hearing the 'conscious' poetry of Robinson or the 'natural' poetry of Biggs.

Certainly, there's a fair bit of parallelism through the poem – a grammatical feature of many Aboriginal song cycles (but also, of course, the Hebrew psalms). Stylistically, Robinson (with the indispensable assistance of Fred Biggs) has combined these very different elements into a seamless whole – an example of functional Aboriginal/European reconciliation long before the term had any currency.

Doctrinaire readers, on both sides of the racial divide, might see Robinson's 're-write' of Biggs' story as an 'appropriation', as yet another European rip-off. This was certainly a risk Robinson took, and was aware of, but ultimately the poem is its own justification. If it had been badly written, as many of the Jindyworobaks' poems were, 'Mapooram' could deservedly (if uncharitably) be dismissed along these lines. Fortunately, the poem turns out to be a great story, subtly retold by Robinson in a style entirely appropriate to the purpose, a language that is at once his own and, in a different way, Fred Biggs' too.

Some may complain that the poem is rather lean on imagery, that there's not as much metaphor as we see in Robinson's more exalted nature poetry. That's true, but such readers would also be missing the point that the whole poem is a metaphor. What is the woman who is sung from the tree and then pulled 'up, up into the sky' if not a metaphor? The interesting thing is that we can't say exactly what she's a metaphor for – though it's pretty clear she is one. If we were able to pin her down more precisely, we'd be losing the poetry – not to mention the relative 'strangeness' of Aboriginal culture (as it must seem to non-Indigenous readers).

And Fred Biggs, of course, wouldn't explain the metaphor; he'd just smile and say again, 'Why, that's two tree boughs rubbing in the wind.'

JOHN BLIGHT (1913–95)

'Death of a Whale'

When the mouse died, there was a sort of pity:
the tiny, delicate creature made for grief.
Yesterday, instead, the dead whale on the reef
drew an excited multitude to the jetty.
How must a whale die to wring a tear?
Lugubrious death of a whale: the big
feast for the gulls and sharks; the tug
of the tide simulating life still there,
until the air, polluted, swings this way
like a door ajar from a slaughterhouse.
Pooh! pooh! spare us, give us the death of a mouse
by its tiny hole; not this in our lovely bay.
– Sorry we are, too, when a child dies;
but at the immolation of a race who cries?

Between 1954 and 1973 the Queensland poet, John Blight, wrote over 160 sonnets about the sea. 'Death of a Whale' is probably the most famous of them, having been republished in anthologies in Britain and the United States as well as in Australia. Most of these sonnets look hard at some aspect of the sea or its littoral and then move on to more universal implications. After a couple of readings, it is not hard to see why 'Death of a Whale' should have been so successful in making this sort of movement.

The poem begins with the huge contrast in scale between the whale and a mouse, suggesting right there the overwhelming diversity in macroscopic life, if not the microscopic. It also suggests from the start how the human capacity for compassion and grief is determined more or less by size (and, perhaps, by implication, proximity). A 'tiny, delicate creature' elicits in us an immediate sympathy. The big (dead) whale draws a big crowd, moved more by idle curiosity than by grief. It's a 'lugubrious' phenomenon we can't quite take in. The poet asks the rhetorical question 'How must a whale die to wring a tear?' and, of course, there is no answer. Suddenly however, with a change of wind, there is a childish revulsion instead. 'Pooh! Pooh! spare us, give us the death of a mouse/… not this in our lovely bay.'

In the sonnet's closing couplet the wind changes again. We are taken from the superficiality of the crowd's reaction to the much more universal and important issue (which the twentieth century witnessed several times over): '… at the immolation of a race who cries?' The leap from the 'Pooh! Pooh!' to this has been a risky one but all the more effective for that risk having been taken. One moment we are given the juvenile reaction of a crowd; the next we are considering, arguably, the Holocaust in World War 2.

Of course, like most good poems, Blight's sonnet raises more questions than it answers. There *are* plenty of people who cry at the 'immolation of a race' – their family and friends for a start and then many others who realise the complexity and value of what has been lost. Some readers may argue that Blight is referring only to the destruction of the whales as a genus rather than the genocide inflicted on any group of humans from the Armenians onwards. Certainly some species of whales were closer to extinction in the 1950s when the poem was written than they are now. To see the poem as being merely about whales, however, is to sell it short. It's all a matter of scale and our human reaction to such differences. We can pity the mouse but the whale is too big and lugubrious for compassion. Similarly, Blight seems to be saying, when humans are confronted by the extermination of hundreds of thousands, or millions, of people not known to them personally, their capacity for grief is numbed rather than aroused.

Again, it is possible to quarrel with this. Successive twentieth-century genocides have been variously remembered, ignored or gone unprevented. Debates have raged over exactly what genocide is (were nineteenth-century Australian Aborigines, for example, victims of genocide or not?) but it is much less often the case than it was perhaps in the 1950s that people fail to cry at 'the immolation of a race'. Indeed, it may well have been works of art like 'Death of a Whale', as well as a range of other historical factors, which have made this so. Certainly the systematic destruction of European Jews by the Nazis in Europe from 1942 to 1945 has been extensively written about and fiercely remembered by relatives and descendants of the victims.

At a technical level, of course, 'Death of a Whale' has much more to commend it than the sudden but successful shifts of tone already discussed. Its rhyme scheme follows the Shakespearean or Elizabethan model with three lots of four (*abbacddceffe*) and a final couplet (*gg*), carefully designed to make the emotional and intellectual impact it does here. More significant again is the mixture of full rhyme and half-rhyme used throughout. Half-rhyme has become a clever way for modern poets to gain the benefits of traditional form without being too obvious about it. Blight has been smart here, too, in keeping the balance of rhymes and half-rhymes more or less equal. The final couplet, arguably, needs to be a full rhyme, however, to have its full effect.

The sonnet is likewise traditional in having a turn of thought or *volta* at the end of line 8; in this case with a literal change in wind direction to bring on the crowd's revulsion. The poem is traditional, too, in its use of the classic iambic pentameter but, like many sonneteers before him, Blight is happy to vary the pattern considerably with forceful double stresses such as '*mouse died*', '*dead whale*' and '*big/Feast*'. He can also play freely sometimes with line length. An iambic pentameter normally has nine, ten or eleven syllables (five of them stressed), but Blight chooses to finish the poem with 'but at the immolation of a race who cries?' – which actually has twelve syllables and reads more like a hexameter than a pentameter. By placing four strong stresses in a line where we can more or less hear six, Blight creates a context in which they can operate. In terms of its sense, we hear the line as 'but at the *immolation of a race* who *cries*?' but know, subliminally perhaps, that its underlying pattern is 'but *at* the *immolation of* a *race* who *cries*?'

Whatever one's view on such technical issues – or one's overall interpretation of the poem (is it a race of whales or a race of people being referred to?) – there is little doubt that 'Death of a Whale' is a masterful sonnet and that its overall point (whatever you take that to be) has not become less relevant in the 60 or so years since its composition. John Blight was not only expert on the history of the English sonnet and the details of the Queensland coastline, he knew quite a deal about the human heart as well.

DOUGLAS STEWART (1913–85)

'Leopard Skin'

Seven pairs of leopard-skin underpants
Flying on the rotary clothes-line! Oh, look, look,
    virgins,
How with the shirts and pyjamas they whirl and
    dance.
And think no more, trembling in your own
    emergence
Like butterflies into the light, that tall soft boy
Who nightly over his radio crooned and capered
Alone in his room in weird adolescent joy
Is mother's boy, softy: has he not slain a leopard?

But more than that: does he not wear its skin,
Secretly, daily, superbly? Oh, girls, adore him,
For dreaming on velvet feet to slay and to sin
He prowls the suburb, the wild things flee before
    him,
He miaous at the leopardesses, and they stop:
He *is* a leopard – he bought himself in a shop.

At first glance it may seem strange to place such a 'light' poem as Douglas Stewart's 'Leopard Skin' in a book of 'classics', but we need to remember that the slyness and satire seen in 'Leopard Skin' have always been part of our tradition. The eighteenth-century poets, Alexander Pope and Jonathan Swift, would have had a good chuckle at this poem, too, for all of its mid-twentieth-century Australian detail.

And some may consider it strange to select a poem such as 'Leopard Skin' from Stewart's work, seeing he was so much better known for his verse plays and nature lyrics such as 'The Snow-Gum' and 'Brindabella' (with lines such as 'Once on a silver and green day, rich to remember'). He was also respected as a great editor of poems at *The Bulletin* and of poetry collections at Angus & Robertson, a man who selflessly advanced the careers of others. Although originally from New Zealand, Douglas Stewart lived in a Sydney suburb and knew only too well what a Hills Hoist was despite his love of trout-fishing in the Monaro and so on.

Arguably, in 'Leopard Skin', Stewart is dealing with a different sort of lyricism, the lyricism of the self-invented adolescent, the fantasy world of the male teenager – though perhaps the fact that the protagonist is buying his own underwear makes us suspect that he may be older than he seems. In any case, it just goes to show how mundane a poem's origins can be – in this case, a quick glance at somebody else's washing over the back fence.

From the 'virgins'' point of view, however, the leopard-skin underpants wearer (LSUPW) is a fairly pathetic figure, a 'tall soft … mother's boy' who spends too much time in his room, imagining that he is Perry Como or Frank Sinatra. In his own opinion (or fantasy) the LSUPW is prowling the suburb 'on velvet feet', making 'the wild things flee before him' and stopping the leopardesses in their tracks. The virgins may be 'trembling in (their) own emergence', but there's not much about the LSUPW to make them alarmed – or much interested, for that matter. The situation is neatly summed up when the LSUPW 'miaous' rather than 'growls' at the leopardesses. He is still a junior tom with a lot to learn. And, of course, the naive foundations of his fantasy are brutally summarised in the last phrase of the poem, 'he bought himself in a shop'.

At the level of literal meaning (like most satires) 'Leopard Skin' presents no problems. It's like a good cartoon. We laugh as soon as we get the point. And then we laugh again every time we go back to it. What is less obvious is the craftsmanship involved – the skill that has already given the poem most, but not all, of its durability (since the posturings of male adolescents are, after all, eternal).

The poem is, of course, a sonnet – in the Elizabethan (or Shakespearean) manner with its concluding couplet. With its division into eight and six lines and its *volta* (or turn of thought) at the end of line 8, it also echoes the earlier Petrarchan form. Both varieties normally call for iambic pentameter, but it is here that Stewart has taken the liberties that reveal (along with its 'rotary clothes-line') the poem's modernity. Like its adolescent protagonist, the poem does not want to fit into the cage designed for it. It wants, at least partially, to break free. Hence while each line has its clearly stressed five syllables ('*How* with the *shirts* and py*jam*as they *whirl* and *dance*'), there are also quite a number of extra unstressed syllables – two extra in the line just quoted. The record is probably the second line, which has 14 syllables altogether instead of the usual ten. It's as if the poem is continuously threatening to break into anapaestic but, like its protagonist, it never quite does so.

Some ultra-conservatives may see all this as a simple failure to meet the requirements of the iambic, but, in reality, it's an example of how modern poets can take an old inheritance and adapt it for their own purposes. Stewart's LSUPW is not just patrolling the perimeters of his cage; he wants to break free of it. One can see something comparable in Stewart's varying use of rhyme. Sometimes we have the traditional full rhyme ('joy' with 'boy'), but we also have quite a number of tentative half-rhymes such as 'virgins' with 'emergence' and 'capered' with 'leopard'. In addition, we have the so-called 'feminine' rhymes 'adore him' with 'before him', always a good way of signalling that a poem is less than serious. And, of course, the final couplet does brilliantly what it should do – it brings the poem to a snappy end by somehow summarising all that has gone before.

A further thing that this freedom with metre and rhyme contributes to – but does not, in itself, create – is the poem's distinct sense of a narrator. There seems to be someone in there insisting we look at the 'Seven pairs of leopard-skin underpants', someone telling the 'virgins' to 'look, look' and 'adore' the LSUPW as he 'prowls the suburb'. There is someone there asking mockingly, 'has he not slain a leopard?' and making the (somewhat bitchy) remark that the LSUPW has 'bought himself in a shop'. The personality of this narrator has something in common with the amused, sardonic narrator of Byron's *Don Juan* or Chaucer's *The Canterbury Tales*. It's an archetypal voice we recognise instantly, a voice reminding us of how important a figure he (it's mostly a 'he') has been in our long poetic tradition. Poetry is not all a matter of nobly described heroic events and sublime enjoyment of nature – or love at a distance. It's also about rotary clothes-lines and somewhat pathetic wearers of leopard-skin underpants.

JOHN MANIFOLD (1915–85)

'On the Boundary'

Young McIvor jackarooing
        on his uncle's western run
Found it lonely riding boundaries
          lonelier still at set of sun.

By the creek he found a lubra
        baiting yabbies on a line:
'Come along o'me, I'll give you
        tucker, baccy, drink of wine.'

'I'll be no worse off by staying
        here, I've all the food I need;
'I don't fancy wine or baccy,
        thank you very much indeed.'

'Come along and don't be cheeky,
        you shall have a yellow dress.'
But she shook her head in silence
        and it nettled him no less.

'I don't have to give you presents,
        if you scorn 'em that's your loss.
'I could tow you on a halter
        just to show you who's the boss.'

'Who's the boss, you boundary-rider?
        I'm of better blood than you!
'I was sired when Boss McIvor's
        brother was the jackaroo.'

Young McIvor stared his sister out of sight,
                and off he rode
Muttering, 'Lecherous old bastard!
                Who'ld have thought it? I'll be
                blowed!'

'On the Boundary' might seem a perverse choice to make from the work of a man who also wrote such canonical poems as 'The Tomb of Lt. John Learmonth A.I.F.' and 'Fife Tune'. The highly comic bush ballad, 'Incognito', might well have been another option. 'On the Boundary', however, at a distance of 50 years or so, runs deeper than it might appear on first reading.

When approaching this poem, it helps to remember that John Manifold, known as a communist for most of his life, was born into Victoria's western district pastoral elite. It helps to remember, too, that some of the fiercest conflict on the nineteenth-century frontier took place in that area. This poem is 'On the Boundary' in more ways than one. Jackarooing, too, was a curious business in which younger men from the gentry class worked on other people's properties to 'learn the ropes', as it were. Sometimes they were sons of friends of the pastoralist; sometimes they were the sons of less fortunate relatives; they were even, at times, from the English aristocracy. The tasks themselves, however, could often be boring and humiliatingly menial. Riding the boundaries to check on fences was just one of them.

It's significant, too, in this jackaroo context that we're not given the Christian name of any of the poem's characters – though the surname McIvor does serve to remind us of how important the Scots were in Australia's nineteenth-century pastoral industry. The jackaroo himself is just 'Young' McIvor. To the girl, the man employing the jackaroo is simply 'Boss' McIvor. The girl, in turn, is not asked her name; nor does she give it. The whole story is a tableau of frontier life with its diverse and complex interactions between Aborigines and Europeans – and the double standards, or 'humbug', which were so often a part of it.

Essentially, the story we're told is humorous but we soon sense some serious undertones, some of which even the poet himself may have been unaware of. At one level 'On the Boundary' is simply an account of an arrogant young whitefella trying to seduce a girl from the local Aboriginal tribe which, we may assume, is still surviving on its traditional land – now 'owned' by the McIvors. As might be expected from a man of Manifold's convictions, the girl displays a spirited resistance to the jackaroo's propositioning. She doesn't need his 'wine or baccy' – or the 'yellow dress' he offers when he thinks she's just playing hard to get. Upon being further rejected, the jackaroo reminds the girl of the impunity with which he could, if he chose, take her by force. This 'ups the ante' as far as the girl is concerned. She angrily and somewhat disdainfully points out to the jackaroo that she is in fact the niece of Boss McIvor and that he'd better be on his way and mind his own business.

Beyond this comedy, however, there are several serious, even tragic implications. The jackaroo is genuinely 'lonely'; we need not doubt that. The girl, in other circumstances, might well have been interested – if he had used more subtle methods that took her true humanity into account rather than simply trying to bribe her or threaten force. The power relationships whereby the jackaroo can tell her not to be 'cheeky' is a barrier that needlessly separates them. And all this is before she reveals, without knowing it, that she is, in fact, the jackaroo's half-sister. This would not only, in itself, rule out a sexual relationship; it also reminds us of the sadness in the situation wherein he can't simply jump down off his horse and embrace the girl as his sister – a parallel, it seems, to how the jackaroo's father wasn't prepared to recognise the girl's mother or acknowledge his daughter. The 'lubra' in stanza 2 has become the 'sister' in stanza 7, but nothing can be done about it. The secret must he kept.

Of course, there are many ironies in all this. Some of the less obvious include the way the Aboriginal girl uses 'posh' phrases like 'thank you very much indeed' and declares that 'I'm of better blood than you!'. She's picked up something from her gentry half, too, it seems. On the other hand, there's a sense of the pedigree and the stud about her unapologetic reference to her being 'sired' by

Boss McIvor's brother. She hasn't transcended her situation but her 'cheekiness' suggests that she might well do so.

Though apparently within the ballad tradition which Manifold so much admired (partly for political reasons), 'On the Boundary' makes some interesting variations to it which lend the poem a certain distinction – and reveal it to be a literary ballad rather than one composed anonymously by the campfire. Most ballads used the iambic metre; though a few employed the anapaestic from time to time. Very few employed the trochaic metre used by Manifold here. The stressing of the first syllable of each line throughout the poem seems to give it a false naivety or even a childlike quality. It's as if the poet were telling a story to a niece or nephew and insisting that he or she pay close attention. '*Young* McIvor *jackarooing/on* his *uncle's western run* …'. One almost sees the wagged finger. Paradoxically, of course, this is perhaps not a story one should be telling children.

For all of the poet's cleverness in this regard, it's still possible that some readers might be disconcerted by the metre in the last stanza where the tetrameter seems to be abandoned in the first two lines. On a closer look, however, we realise that the six stresses of line 1 and the two stresses of line 2 add up to the normal eight for any two lines. Manifold is emphasising here the humiliation of the jackaroo by truncating his line, as it were. So, too, in the first line of this stanza, where the six stressed syllables underline how long the jackaroo is watching his sister (formerly his potential seducee) walk proudly away.

'On the Boundary' is not only on the literal boundary ridden by the jackaroo. It's on the boundary of decent human behaviour (for at least two generations, it seems) – and it's on the boundary of the ballad form it purports to be using. It's also on the boundary of the comic and the tragic, reminding us how poets since ancient Greek playwrights like Aristophanes have used comedy to make serious points about human (or inhuman) behaviour.

JUDITH WRIGHT (1915–2000)

'Remittance Man'

The spendthrift, disinherited and graceless,
accepted his pittance with an easy air,
only surprised he could escape so simply
from the pheasant-shooting and the aunts in the
    close;
took to the life, dropped easily out of knowledge,
and tramping the backtracks in the summer haze
let everything but life slip through his fingers.

Blue blowing smoke of twigs from the noon fire,
red blowing dust of roads where the teams go slow,
sparse swinging shadow of trees no longer foreign
silted the memory of a greener climate.
The crazy tales, the hatters' crazy secrets,
the blind-drunk sprees indifferently forgiven,
and past them all, the track to escape and nowhere
suited his book, the freak who could never settle.
That pale stalk of a wench at the county ball
sank back forgotten in black Mary's eyes,
and past the sallow circle of the plains' horizon
faded the rainy elms seen through the nursery
    window.

That harsh biblical country of the scapegoat
closed its magnificence finally around his bones
polished by diligent ants. The squire his brother,
presuming death, sighed over the documents,
and lifting his eyes across the inherited garden
let a vague pity blur the formal roses.

Although Judith Wright was to publish ten more collections after her first book, *The Moving Image* (1946), there are several poems in it which she was destined never to excel: 'Brother and Sisters', 'South of My Days', 'Bora Ring', 'Nigger's Leap, New England' – and, arguably, 'Remittance Man'. Many readers would also include 'Bullocky' in that list, but its author, in her closing years, considered the poem to have had far too much exposure and to be too easily taken over by the 'white triumphalist' view of Australian history.

'Remittance Man', another poem about an archetypal Australian rural figure, has no such difficulties. At one level it is simply a character sketch of someone she knew about. At another, it is a microcosm of how British 'settlers' came to terms emotionally with Australian landscapes (particularly those of the interior) as well as being, to a lesser extent, a portrait of the incomprehension of those who stayed at 'Home'.

Perhaps not everyone would now know that a 'remittance man' was someone from a 'good' family who had 'disgraced' himself and been sent off to the colonies where he would receive a regular 'remittance' for the rest of his life. It was normally enough to keep a man alive but not in any comfort, hence the need to keep moving in search of casual employment.

Wright's remittance man is both an individual and a type. He has wasted his credibility back in England and been disinherited. His being 'graceless' refers primarily to his unwillingness to conform to the stifling manners of his class and time, but may also indicate a kind of sulky disregard. He is positively relieved to escape the 'aunts in the close' and the no less tiresome aristocratic business of shooting birds for sport. In the poem's first sentence our hero has, by implication, already experienced a three-month sea voyage and is now relishing the 'backtracks in the summer haze'. By the end of the second sentence he is fully acclimatised and forgetful of his origins.

The third sentence details the remittance man's 'lifestyle' and it is important to note how it culminates in the assertion that he is a 'freak who could never settle'. Of course, as at the end of the poem, this is essentially the view of those who have stayed behind, those who would never be able to appreciate how the disinherited brother might actually prefer 'black Mary's eyes' to those of that 'pale stalk of a wench', that girl whom his brother may well have gone on to marry.

In the poem's final stanza, Wright sees Australia, particularly its inland areas, as 'harsh' but also magnificent. We are a little less romantic these days about the so-called 'Dead Heart', having finally noticed that it has been inhabited by humans for thousands of years. We don't need to see it as 'biblical'. Wright, to be fair, is, however, primarily supporting the view of the 'naturalised' remittance man – as against the soppiness of his brother, still in a sense standing at his 'nursery window'. The brother, to be sure, is 'lifting his eyes' but all he sees is an 'inherited garden' and some 'formal roses' – which, in turn, are just slightly blurred by the sentiment he feels, or imagines he feels, towards his vanished sibling, the emigrant brother whose bones are, at that very moment, being 'polished by diligent ants'.

The poem, ironically perhaps, is written in one of English poetry's oldest forms, blank verse – which goes back at least as far as Milton. At the same time, however, it is 'loosened up' by the colonial experience; it is no longer being written to match the 'formal roses'. Right from the start we can sense that Wright's iambic pentameters are rarely going to be a simple matter of five unstressed syllables and five stressed syllables alternating. The first line seems to have only three strong stresses – '*spend*', '*dis*' and '*grace*' – even though the underlying metre is still faintly heard as 'The *spend*/thrift, *dis*/in*her*/*ited*/and *grace*less'. We note how '*her*' and '*ed*' get much less stress than the other three stresses in the line – and how 'less', the eleventh syllable in a ten-syllable line, is casually allowed to hang on at the end.

Similarly, we see quite a few examples of that irregularity where two stressed syllables are placed next to each other: '*pale stalk*' and '*vague pity*' are just two of the more memorable ones. Wright implies that Australia's 'harsh biblical country' has little time for the niceties of traditional English prosody – and yet, importantly, she doesn't abandon it altogether. Our swaggie-protagonist remains English in certain ineluctable ways, especially when contrasted, for example, with 'black Mary' and her relations.

'Remittance Man' is a poem whose technique effortlessly supports the main thrust of its meaning. Judith Wright is describing a symbolic character and situation, but she is also reinforcing her portrait with suitably flexible rhythms and evocative sound effects' (too numerous to list here, though the assonance in 'go slow' is an obvious one). It is impossible to imagine this poem's being written in England during the period in which it is set. Nor can we imagine either of those two great 'English' near-contemporaries of Wright – Eliot and Auden – telling the story in anything like the same way. Their rhythmic subtleties were harnessed to other, different, purposes.

In 'Remittance Man' Judith Wright has written a classic poem out of our own landscape (or one of our key ones anyway). At a distance of 60 years or so, Wright's poem can still make us wonder about the extent to which most of us in this country have quite a deal in common with the remittance man and rather less with 'the squire his brother'. For us, too, the 'trees (are) no longer foreign' and 'the view through the 'nursery window' is substantially forgotten.

DAVID CAMPBELL (1915–79)

'Windy Gap'

As I was going through Windy Gap
A hawk and a cloud hung over the map.

The land lay bare and the wind blew loud
And the hawk cried out from the heart of the cloud,

'Before I fold my wings in sleep
I'll pick the bones of your travelling sheep,

'For the leaves blow back and the wintry sun
Shows the tree's white skeleton.'

A magpie sat in the tree's high top
Singing a song on Windy Gap

That streamed far down to the plain below
Like a shaft of light from a high window.

From the bending tree he sang aloud,
And the sun shone out of the heart of the cloud

And it seemed to me as we travelled through
That my sheep were the notes that trumpet blew.

And so I sing this song of praise
For travelling sheep and blowing days.

'Windy Gap' is one of David Campbell's earliest and most anthologised poems. It is perhaps the classic lyric of the Monaro plateau, evoking, as it does, the clear air and the high vistas of the region. Students who know very little about poetry are quick to see it as the genuine article, a poem that seems to fulfil all their expectations of what a poem might be. Strangely, despite his prominence, there has been relatively little academic discussion of Campbell's work, possibly because his pure lyricism escapes the scholar's various tools. It is much more congenial to expatiate on the mythological background to Eliot's 'The Waste Land' than to search for the more abstract and elusive essence of a lyric like 'Windy Gap'.

What then makes this one of Australia's most memorable poems? What can be said about the 'pure lyric' that is not already said in the poem itself? It is not so much a matter of vivisecting a beautiful little creature and leaving it dead on the table, as some students (and readers) are prone to think. A close look can deepen appreciation. We can internalise what we have noticed about the poet's technique and then read the poem again just for its sheer lyric force.

Perhaps the most striking thing about 'Windy Gap' is how it holds both the visual and the aural in a kind of balance, and the way it describes one in terms of the other in a kind of synaesthesia. We have the noise of the wind in the first line and the image of the plain below as a map in the second, and then the combination of the two in the third. We hear the hawk and the magpie, and we see the 'tree's white skeleton', revealed by the wind blowing back the leaves and the wintry sun illuminating its stem.

The process becomes even more pronounced later in the poem where the magpie's song is a 'shaft of light' and the narrator's sheep are notes blown by the 'trumpet' of the magpie's song. Even in the last line we have, in summary, the sound of the 'blowing days' and the vision of the 'travelling sheep'. It is in the combination of these two senses, sound and sight, that most of the poem's energy derives. If it were confined to one or the other sense only, the poem would be much less powerful.

Another dimension of this visual side that is also important is how the poet manages to combine the stylised, archetypal ingredients that we see in many poetic traditions with something much more specifically Australian. The hawk and the magpie are found elsewhere, as are the sheep and the tree. The sheep are not named as Merino; the tree is not classified as a Snow Gum (or something taller); and yet, as Australian readers at least, we have no doubt where the poem is located and what aspects of the landscape, climate and so on Campbell is celebrating. It is a definitive example of how a skilled poet can take an already existing tradition and renew it with a local twist – but without over-using 'local colour', as it were. Campbell admired balladists like Paterson, but he stopped short of using their more obvious techniques.

Equally visual are Campbell's images throughout the poem: the plain as a 'map'; the 'skeleton' of the tree; the 'shaft of light' of the magpie's song; the sheep as trumpet notes. The positive, celebratory images are nicely offset by the skeleton of the tree and the potential skeletons of the sheep. It is a whole, living world Campbell is talking about here, not just a storybook one.

A further key element in the success of 'Windy Gap' is its rhythm. Based on the iambic tetrameter couplets used by poets like Swift for satirical purposes, 'Windy Gap' has many unstressed syllables added to the mix, which perhaps help to give it that feeling of lift-off associated with high places and windy days. A few lines are purely iambic as in 'And so I *sing* this *song* of *praise*', but most have two or three extra unstressed syllables, creating the feeling that the poem might almost be in a triple metre. In line 4, for instance, there are three additional unstressed syllables (see brackets): 'And (the) *hawk* cried *out* from (the) *heart* of (the) *cloud*'. And yet this is followed by the purely iambic line: 'Be*fore* I *fold* my *wings* in *sleep*'.

Something analogous is happening with the rhyme scheme too. Clearly it is *aa, bb, cc* and so on as used by the satirists, but Campbell tosses in a few half-rhymes to disconcert us and avoid any sing-song effect. 'Sun' and 'skeleton', for instance, where the lightly stressed, indeterminate vowel at the end of 'skeleton' is made to half-rhyme with 'sun'. In stanza 6, Campbell pushes his luck even further by rhyming '*win*dow' with 'be*low*', seemingly a full rhyme admittedly but with the stress falling in the 'wrong' place.

It's a strange poem. You can almost see the Akubra, the Driz-abone and the R.M. Williams boots; you can practically smell the horse sweat though none of these is mentioned. You can feel seventeenth- and nineteenth-century English verse in the background, but you don't doubt for a minute it's Australian. You see a couple of 'doubtful' technical effects but you're still quite certain that 'Windy Gap' was written by a true poet at the top of his form. It's not hard to see why anthologists have so often chosen it – and perhaps why academics have so rarely written about it. It has spoken for itself already and needs no further assistance.

JAMES McAULEY (1917–76)

'Because'

My father and my mother never quarrelled.
They were united in a kind of love
As daily as the *Sydney Morning Herald*,
Rather than like the eagle or the dove.

I never saw them casually touch,
Or show a moment's joy in one another.
Why should this matter to me now so much?
I think it bore more hardly on my mother,

Who had more generous feelings to express.
My father had dammed up his Irish blood
Against all drinking praying fecklessness,
And stiffened into stone and creaking wood.

His lips would make a switching sound, as though
Spontaneous impulse must be kept at bay.
That it was mainly weakness I see now,
But then my feelings curled back in dismay.

Small things can pit the memory like a cyst:
Having seen other fathers greet their sons,
I put my childish face up to be kissed
After an absence. The rebuff still stuns

My blood. The poor man's curt embarrassment
At such a delicate proffer of affection
Cut like a saw. But home the lesson went:
My tenderness thenceforth escaped detection.

My mother sang *Because*, and *Annie Laurie*,
White Wings, and other songs; her voice was sweet.
I never gave enough, and I am sorry;
But we were all closed in the same defeat.

People do what they can; they were good people,
They cared for us and loved us. Once they stood
Tall in my childhood as the school, the steeple.
How can I judge without ingratitude?

Judgment is simply trying to reject
A part of what we are because it hurts.
The living cannot call the dead collect:
They won't accept the charge, and it reverts.

It's my own judgment day that I draw near,
Descending in the past, without a clue,
Down to that central deadness: the despair
Older than any hope I ever knew.

James McAuley was a controversial figure in Australian poetry, politics and culture. He was one of the two hoaxers in the Ern Malley affair (1944) and later a founder of *Quadrant* magazine. While many people are still arguing about the man 30 years after his death, there are few who dispute the merits of his best poems. Among these certainly is 'Because' from his collection, *Surprises of the Sun* (1969).

Although McAuley was a Catholic convert (or perhaps because of that), 'Because' is a classic statement of 'secular Protestantism', a widely prevalent belief system in Australia, especially among those who grew up in the shadow of two world wars and the Great Depression of the 1930s. It's all about restraint, duty, self-discipline and repeated patterns. Sometimes it's called 'strength of character', but McAuley correctly sees that, in his father's case (and perhaps in many others), it was 'mainly weakness'. Of course, McAuley, in this explicitly autobiographical poem, cannot escape it himself either – for all of his Catholicism: 'How can I judge without ingratitude?' 'But we were all closed in the same defeat.'

It is paradoxical, then, that out of such a 'defeat' McAuley has wrought the triumph of this poem. It's a triumph not only of technique (with its seemingly effortless *abab* iambic pentameter quatrains, so beloved by Australian poets of his generation) but of tone. McAuley has caught the exact resonance of the worldview he's describing: its greyness, its dryness, its extraordinary containment. A love as 'daily as the *Sydney Morning Herald*' is just the first of its features. Not for these people the soaring of the eagle or the cooing of doves.

In the poem's final stanza this bleakness becomes unbearable: 'Descending in the past, without a clue,/Down to that central deadness: the despair/Older than any hope I ever knew.' Written by a Catholic, supposedly certain of resurrection, these lines seem even more depressing – but they are also deeply convincing. A miserable childhood is not easily recovered from.

Of course, McAuley does more than offer merely tone as an explanation for the way things were. He understands only too well his father's reaction to 'drinking praying fecklessness' and how damaging such behaviours often were in the 'Irish blood' in which Protestants of the period thought they were so prevalent. The tragedy is that such caution and good sense led, not to something like the eagle or the dove, but merely to 'stone and creaking wood'. This stiffness is shown most memorably in the poem's central episode where the young boy is refused his father's kiss. Note, too, in passing, the brutal rhyme of 'kissed' with 'cyst'. We see from this that yet another lifetime of containment will follow: 'My tenderness thenceforth escaped detection.'

It's important to note that, although McAuley is more sympathetic to his mother (on whom 'it bore more hardly'), he does not unreasonably blame his father. 'People do what they can; they were good people,/They cared for us and loved us.' And, in any case, what would be the point? 'The living cannot call the dead collect'.

The fact remains, however, that the poet is still 'Descending ... to that central deadness.' There seems to be no escape, despite what we may know of the poet's life and beliefs from outside the poem.

Other factors in the triumph of 'Because' are its conversational leisureliness and its sincerity. McAuley seems almost to be musing to himself – or, perhaps more accurately, confiding to a trusted friend about the limitations of his childhood and their permanent impact. The poem starts with a plain statement ('My father and my mother never quarrelled') and continues with several others ('I never saw them casually touch', 'I never gave enough, and I am sorry' and so on). McAuley is in no hurry. He is going to give us all the relevant information in his own time, using his leisurely pentameters rather than anything shorter or tighter.

Conversely, however, he is also going to display the same self-discipline with his *abab* rhyme scheme that his parents imposed on themselves. There are, admittedly, some half-rhymes here and there, but, in a way, these serve perversely to remind us of the rigidity of the others. It's only fair, after all, that the son of a father who 'dammed up his Irish blood' should allow himself a few half-rhymes.

It's interesting, too, to see how the *abab* rhyme scheme seems to strengthen the way everything (all this 'stone and creaking wood') fits into place. The poem does not have the light, satirical touch of Pope or Swift with their *aa, bb, cc* couplets. Nor does it have the exalted license of Walt Whitman with his free verse. It is something shaped into just the right degree of containment to suggest the beliefs of the two (or three?) people at the poem's core.

And one can't close, of course, without noting the irony in the poem's title. At one level it's a song title, but it also has something of young children's refusal to explain when they, on being asked why they misbehaved, just say 'because ...' But, on the other hand, the whole poem is also an explanation of why the poet is the way he is – proceeding 'Down to that central deadness' – and why his father before him had 'stiffened into stone'. It's a further irony that nothing can be done with such knowledge anyway – but there is surely a sense in which we are better off for having had the realisation. Philosophers, theologians and historians have all written books about 'secular Protestantism' (giving it one name or another), but no one has reduced it to its essence as powerfully and poignantly as James McAuley does in this poem.

GWEN HARWOOD (1920–95)

'Suburban Sonnet'

She practises a fugue, though it can matter
to no one now if she plays well or not.
Beside her on the floor two children chatter,
then scream and fight. She hushes them. A pot
boils over. As she rushes to the stove
too late, a wave of nausea overpowers
subject and counter-subject. Zest and love
drain out with soapy water as she scours
the crusted milk. Her veins ache. Once she played
for Rubinstein, who yawned. The children caper
round a sprung mousetrap where a mouse lies dead.
When the soft corpse won't move they seem afraid.
She comforts them; and wraps it in a paper
featuring: *Tasty dishes from stale bread.*

First published in the mid-1960s, Gwen Harwood's 'Suburban Sonnet' (along with its companion piece, 'In the Park') has become the yardstick against which any vaguely comparable Australian poem is measured. There is a rich vein of 'suburban disillusionment' running through our poetry and 'Suburban Sonnet' by Gwen Harwood is its definitive expression.

Though the poem is astonishing on the technical level, that is not what we notice first. Far more relevant is the situation of the fugue-playing mother with her side-tracked aspirations. It's not that she doesn't want the kids or that she had hugely unrealistic musical ambitions. She remembers, after all, that Rubinstein yawned. The children irritate her; they wear her out but she doesn't 'lose it'. When they are alarmed by the dead mouse she 'comforts them' and very practically disposes of it. And this in a period when women were meant to be afraid of mice.

The woman is also forced to do and be everything at once. We see her rushing from the piano stool to quieten the squabbling children, and thence to the stove with its pot boiling over. Then, as she is scouring the pot and losing track of her fugue, she is called out on 'mouse duty'. There is no way she is going to be able to make a 'tasty dish from stale bread'. Her life will go on for years, yet with its aching veins, fighting children, snatches of music and mouse disposals. It's impressive how much telling detail Harwood has crammed into her 14 leisurely lines.

If the poem were simply a prose paragraph containing all this detail (say, for instance, a column in one of our daily newspapers) it would not have outlasted the disposable paper it was written on. Harwood, ironically herself in the same situation at its time of writing, has created here a work of art with the same intricacies as those found in the fugue her protagonist is forced to abandon. Like Bach, Harwood has to follow the rules. It is even more ironic that the rules for the Petrarchan sonnet were formulated almost 800 years ago and yet here we have Harwood using them for entirely contemporary purposes.

Like Petrarch, she starts with an octave (though not quite his rhyme scheme with her *abab, cdcd* rather than his *abba, abba*). She does, however, wind up with a Petrarchan sestet (*efg, efg*), even if she doesn't make the traditional turn of thought or *volta* at the end of line 8. Indeed, she deliberately jaywalks the corner, as it were, with her phrase '… scours/the crusted milk'. This is about as far as one can get, subject-wise, from a Petrarchan love sonnet.

Harwood's artistry here exists at both the micro and the macro level. Though the whole poem is in the traditional iambic pentameter, Harwood varies this in a number of places for particular effects. The phrase 'veins ache', for instance. Not only does it consist of two assonantal, stretched diphthongs (very Australian), it also seems to put them together as two stressed syllables. According to the iambic pattern 'ache' should not be stressed – but how can we resist doing so? The words, the syllables, seem to have exactly equal value.

She does something similar with the phrases 'soft corpse' and 'stale bread'.

Another skill that Harwood seems to have had more of than almost anyone else (English-wide) is her use of enjambement. Only five out of her 14 lines end with a punctuation mark. This is no series of plodding couplets with neat rhymes and commas. This is a complex rhyme scheme that is set down easily over sentences that run on and often finish in mid-line. The most obvious case of this is the phrase 'A pot' at the end of line 4. It gives a nice sense of tension and release. 'A pot?' we ask, 'What pot?' – until it boils over on us at the beginning of the next line.

To go further in this vein is unnecessary. Most readers understand the poem very well at first reading, but it is the cleverness of Harwood's technique that makes them remember it as well as they do. The same or similar content can be seen in dozens of newspaper columns every week – but Gwen Harwood's 'Suburban Sonnet' is a poem you can memorise and bring back when you need it – which could be quite often.

'The Three Fates'

At the instant of drowning he invoked the three
    sisters.
It was a mistake, an aberration, to cry out for
Life everlasting.

He came up like a cork and back to the river-bank,
Put on his clothes in reverse order,
Returned to the house.

He suffered the enormous agonies of passion
Writing poems from the end backwards,
Brushing away tears that had not yet fallen.

Loving her wildly as the day regressed towards
    morning
He watched her swinging in the garden, growing
    younger,
Bare-foot, straw-hatted.

And when she was gone and the house and the
    swing and daylight
There was an instant's pause before it began all over,
The reel unrolling towards the river.

First collected in Rosemary Dobson's 1984 volume of the same name, 'The Three Fates', this deceptively simple poem has already become something of a classic in Australian poetry. Dobson, at the time of writing, is the last living member of an outstanding generation of Australian poets who emerged during and just after World War 2. They include Judith Wright, David Campbell, Douglas Stewart, A.D. Hope, James McAuley and R.D. FitzGerald. Poems such as Dobson's 'The Three Fates' demonstrate only too clearly that she deserves her place among them. Unfashionably for many of us, but not for her own generation, Dobson assumes a knowledge of Greek mythology – especially, in this case, the three goddesses (Clotho 'the spinner', Lachesis 'the measurer' and Atropos 'the cutter') who, collectively, control our thread of life.

Sensibly, in case we miss the point, she refers to the protagonist's coming up 'like a cork' and being reeled in until his (now suspended) fate sets him again 'unrolling towards the river'. As with many poets before her, Dobson has taken a Greek myth and given it a new and insightful twist. Numerous poets before her have emphasised how unavailing it is to try to escape the fate the three sisters have in store for us. Sophocles' *Oedipus Rex* is the classic example. Dobson makes a rather different point.

In her case, the three sisters relent and give our hero what he thinks he's asked for. He wants to reverse the fate that has brought him to the river-bank. Unfortunately, he doesn't realise the implications of his request. He has made a 'mistake', has committed an 'aberration' and must, it seems, be punished appropriately.

Though certain philosophers and scientists have tried to wean us from a linear conception of time, it does seem to fit the evidence of our senses. We are born, we grow old, we die – in that order. Dobson, in 'The Three Fates', cleverly asks the 'what-if?' question. What if this direction were reversed, how would we feel? Almost humorously, she takes us through the sequence.

The lover puts his clothes back on 'in reverse order' (quite a task when you think about it) and then experiences his love affair backwards until his girlfriend recedes, not only into the attractive woman he first loved, but also, by turn, into her own childhood and pre-existence. Even the 'daylight' is gone – hers and his own. At that point, as with the myth of Sisyphus, his fate begins all over again.

The moral of the story is apparent and is, unusually, stated clearly in the first stanza: it is a 'mistake … to cry out for/Life everlasting'. By implication, it is better to accept our mortality, to make the most of what we are given and leave it behind uncomplainingly. Some readers might take this line even further to imply a critique on promises of an afterlife, but this would be hard to prove.

At one level, the poem is simply a parable – indeed, almost a homily. Why, then, should we call it a classic? The point it is making, of course, is at once a simple and complex one. But the story of the bobbing 'cork', the 'clothes in reverse order' and the disappearing 'straw-hatted' girl is not a classic narrative in itself. It's the way the story is told that's important.

Dobson has achieved an unusually distinctive tone in this poem and has a highly personal way with rhythm. The tone is wry, almost humorous, but also a little *faux naïf*. The period details help, too – 'the swing', the 'straw-hatted' girl, even the invocation of 'the three sisters'– but they are not essential. There is the humour of someone who is drowning suddenly bobbing back up 'like a cork'. There is the almost slapstick cinema of (hurriedly?) getting back into one's clothes; not to mention the paradox of 'Brushing away tears that had not yet fallen.' We can imagine, too, what sort of poems they were – forwards *or* backwards. And yet, by stanza 5 the humour has vanished. Everything's gone – 'the house and the swing and daylight' – and our hero is forced, through his own mistakenly uttered wish, to begin all over again.

At first glance, the poem seems to have a certain formality. Its three-line stanzas and frequently truncated third lines lead one to expect something like iambic pentameter with perhaps a trimeter in the last line of the stanza. In fact, the poem is written in a leisurely, even ironic, free verse (unlike the locked-in situation of the protagonist). We readers have the luxury of sitting back safely and learning from the story. In the first line there's a rough sense of the anapaestic: 'At the in/stant of *drown*/ing he in*voked*/the three *sis*ters.' In the corresponding line in stanza 2 we have a countervailing sense of the iambic: 'He *came*/up *like*/a *cork*/and *back*/to the *riv*/er-*bank*.' The narrator is locked into his (iambic?) fate, despite the extra unstressed syllable in the second-last foot.

It is not for nothing that 'free' verse is sometimes called 'mixed' verse. The opening line of the third stanza could, in this context, be seen as a hexameter, a metre notorious for being one foot longer than the standard pentameter – and, so, clearly appropriate for the excesses being endured: 'He *suff*/ered *the*/*enorm*/ous *ag*/onies/of *pass*ion.'

As with many free-verse writers, Dobson also includes a little rhyme to give a sense of continuity or suggest finality. We have the echo of the 'or' vowel throughout in 'for', 'order', 'enormous', 'fallen', 'pause' and 'towards' – and, of course, the closing half-rhyme of 'over' and 'river'.

Another device that helps the sound of the poem resonate in the mind is Dobson's alliteration in, for example, the almost playful 'came up like a cork' and particularly in the insistent last line: 'The reel unrolling towards the river'.

But, of course, the poem is more than the sum of its devices. They simply serve to provide aesthetic satisfaction and to make the poem's moral more memorable. The two aspects are inseparable – which is as it must be if a poem is to outlive the period in which it was written. Paradoxically, though we must all make our journey to the river-bank, some of us, like Rosemary Dobson in 'The Three Fates', may leave something behind more durable than our clothes.

'Gifts'

'I will bring you love,' said the young lover,
'A glad light to dance in your dark eye.
Pendants I will bring of the white bone,
And gay parrot feathers to deck your hair.'

But she only shook her head.

'I will put a child in your arms,' he said,
'Will be a great headman, great rain-maker.
I will make remembered songs about you
That all the tribes in all the wandering camps
Will sing forever.'

But she was not impressed.

'I will bring you the still moonlight on the lagoon,
And steal for you the singing of all the birds;
I will bring down the stars of heaven to you,
And put the bright rainbow into your hand.'

'No,' she said, 'bring me tree-grubs.'

Kath Walker's *We Are Going* (1964) was the first collection of poetry by an Aboriginal person published in Australia. In later years Kath Walker used the name Oodgeroo Noonuccal and by her death in 1993 she was easily the best known and most widely respected Aboriginal poet in the country. The title poem of that first collection is often anthologised and her sardonic poem, 'No More Boomerang', is also widely known and has been several times set to music. It is in 'Gifts', however, that her talent is seen at its most sophisticated.

In this short account of a tribal courtship, Oodgeroo has written something which is specifically concerned both with traditional Aboriginal life (there is no mention of anything subsequent to the white man's arrival) and with differences between the sexes world-wide. It is also, perhaps incidentally, a sardonic put down of long-held attitudes towards poetry as a seduction device.

Oodgeroo's young would-be lover proceeds in three steps – and their order is important. In the first stanza he offers the girl jewellery and adornments – and, of course, a love that will cause 'A glad light to dance in your dark eye.' Note that he offers his love first and then backs it up, as necessary, with something he assumes is more substantial. The girl's reaction, by contrast, is not even verbal: '… she only shook her head'.

In the second stanza, the young lover becomes more ardent and eloquent. He appeals to her nascent maternal instincts by saying 'I will put a child in your arms' and, typically for a male perhaps, tells her how she will be able to live vicariously through her husband's achievements as he becomes a 'great headman, great rain-maker'. In addition, he offers to immortalise her in song, a blandishment employed by poets in European culture as far as, at least, the ancient Greeks. It seems to have had a similar or even greater durability in Aboriginal culture. Needless to say, the girl again is 'not impressed'.

In the third stanza, and more urgently now, the young lover offers her poetry itself – romantic poetry, that is. He will bring her 'the still moonlight on the lagoon'. He will 'steal for (her) the singing of all the birds'. If these are not successful he will give her 'the stars of heaven' and even put 'the bright rainbow' in her hand. It's notable that, in the ordering of the young lover's powers and skills, poetry is accounted the highest. Some may argue that what the young man is offering is not so much poetry as magic. Perhaps he's boasting that he'll become a 'clever-feller', a great 'lore man' who will have supernatural powers. The point remains, however, that all of these magical offerings take 'poetic' expression. Moonlight on water, birdsong, stars and rainbows are standard 'poetic' ingredients across the cultures.

At last, in response to poetry, his ultimate weapon, she does deign to reply verbally. Not only is this reply a great undercutting of the 'sublime' ('moonlight on the lagoon' and so on), it also shows that she's keeping her options open. The extravagances she's heard are fine as far as they go, but tree-grubs in her (and her children's) belly are more essential. It may be that tree-grubs are food traditionally gathered by men, but there can be no doubt that she prefers their flavour and their sustenance to stars, rainbows and moonlight. We note that the young girl doesn't reject the man outright; she just makes a more important demand. It's quite possible that, with tree-grubs, the romance could proceed.

We may assume that Oodgeroo, as a female, identifies with the practicality of the girl's preference, but it's also possible that, as a poet, she might be implying that the audience for poetry, rather depressingly, is more often inclined to tree-grubs than to the fineries of blank verse (or song cycles, for that matter).

In any case, it's blank verse that Oodgeroo uses throughout most of the poem – and skilfully, too. Kath Walker, as she was then, was forced to leave school at 13 and work as a domestic. In lines such as 'A glad light to dance in your dark eye' there is no trace of under-education. The adjacent stresses on 'glad' and 'light' and on 'dark' and 'eye' emphasise all the key ideas, as does the alliteration from 'dance' through to 'dark'. It's a very sensuous image. One almost wonders why it didn't win the girl after all.

In other poems, particularly her explicitly political ones, Oodgeroo quite often used rhyme. Here she prefers the blankness of blank verse (though there is some echoing between 'lover' and 'hair' in the first stanza and a half-rhyme between 'you' and 'lagoon' in the second-last one). Perhaps with the ultra-romantic ingredients used already, Oodgeroo felt she had gone far enough in that direction without resorting to rhyme, as well.

One can't finish without emphasising, too, the 'anti-poetic' qualities of the girl's replies (both verbal and non-verbal). The poem is, in fact, built around these contrasts: the grandiloquent promises and their anti-romantic reception, culminating with the demand for tree-grubs rather than 'moonlight' and so on. There are three questions and three responses, each in high relief. Like a European folk tale, the poem has an archetypal narrative structure – in addition to the metrical structures we've been noting line by line.

One might consider, too, where 'Gifts' fits into the Aboriginal struggle for survival and equality, the cause to which Oodgeroo devoted so much of her life and her poetry. Surely, more direct poems like 'No More Boomerang' are more important? 'Gifts', however, and a few other poems of comparable sophistication, play an even more important role by effortlessly demonstrating how an Aboriginal poet may transcend the more simplistic of political messages and suggest instead the internal coherence of Aboriginal culture and its universality. It's easy enough to imagine a story like this told in another culture, but to hear it narrated so convincingly within Aboriginal culture ensures mainstream Australian readers are more inclined to transcend the condescending prejudices they might previously have harboured.

DOROTHY HEWETT (1923–2002)

'The Witnesses'

This is the wide country
I lived in when I was young,
The great clouds over it,
The hawk in the high sky hung ...

Hung upside down like a metal bird,
Fixes time in his fatal eye.
The mice run circles, the plovers cry,
Till I hardly know in that hurtling sky
Which of the three wild things am I ...
Murderer, victim, recorded cry.

The hawk spins round like a weather vane.

The seed spills bitter, the hawk turns slow.
Under the rainbow arch will lie
The girl with the haystack hair awry,
Her legs outflung and her brief blood dry,
While the bumpkin boys go whistling by
with gravel rashed knees and weeping eye ...

And the hawk in the high sky hung.

Although first collected in Dorothy Hewett's controversial book, *Rapunzel in Suburbia* (1975) (banned from distribution in Western Australia for several years), 'The Witnesses' has the flavour of a rather earlier period. The adventurous rhetoric and the poem's insistent rhymes tend to remind us of Dylan Thomas – and the 'New Apocalypse' school with which he was loosely associated in the 1940s.

The hawk which hangs over the beginning, middle and end of the poem is not only an effective dramatic device but a symbol for something important, indeed unavoidable, in human life and that of the natural world. Hewett's hawk is no mere lazy wedge-tailed riding the thermals but a 'metal bird' with 'time ... in his fatal' eye, a bird who can hang 'upside down' and turn 'like a weather vane'. His shadow disturbs the mice and the plovers below him – and proves a considerable point of identity for the poem's narrator. Indeed, she hardly knows 'Which of the three wild things am I .../Murderer, victim, recorded cry.'

The answer may be established by tracing the narrative line of the poem as a whole. Initially, we have the 'wide country' and the 'great clouds' of the poet's youth. In the second stanza, the hawk, already sighted in the first, is seen as a primeval threat. The narrator feels herself to be up in the 'hurtling sky' with the hawk. Like the hawk, she knows she's a 'wild thing' but where exactly does she fit? Is she, as a poet, just a recording 'witness' of nature's brutal ecology or is she, in fact, a participant? A 'victim' perhaps – or, even, like the hawk, a 'murderer'?

In the fourth stanza, the answer becomes clearer. 'Victim' seems to be the most probable of the three roles. We're in the wheat country, so the phrase the 'seed spills bitter' has, at one level, a literal suggestion of waste but it also foreshadows the ejaculate involved in the rape which the 'girl with the haystack hair awry' is to suffer a few lines later. It somehow preconditions us to see this brutal event in a wider context, as part of some larger cycle which can't be easily avoided. Hewett's two-line description of the rape is as graphic as we're ever likely to get: 'The girl with the haystack hair awry/Her legs outflung and her brief blood dry'. There is no doubt that the girl has been damaged (her virginity taken by gang rape), but no less significant is the behaviour of the 'bumpkin boys' who did it. Like the hawk, they don't seem able to recognise clearly their part in the cycle. They seem almost sheepish, as if they don't really understand what happened – or are in the grip of something larger than themselves. We note, too, incidentally that the girl has fought back. Their eyes are 'weeping' from where she has scratched them.

Finally, the poet brings us back to the 'hawk in the high sky hung', the predator who has seen all this happen and understands that brutality such as we've seen is a precondition of life – and almost impossible to avoid. In some ways it's a strange poem for a woman, widely viewed as a feminist, to have written. The 'hawk in the high sky hung' is a dispassionate witness to the savagery but also, at other times, a participant. Hewett's feminism can be seen chiefly in the way the girl, courageously but unavailingly, fights back. The child from the 'wide country', like the hawk, realises that this is all part of some larger cycle which has somehow to be endured – though not without protest.

To better understand how the poem delivers this unwelcome news so forcefully we need look no further than the insistent rhyme pattern in those two key stanzas, two and four. Each of these starts with an unrhymed line, but after that the 'eye' sound is heard at the end of every single line of both stanzas. The effect is to reinforce the sense of inevitability leading up to the rape in the middle of the fourth stanza. The regular iambic (sometimes trochaic) tetrameters of these two stanzas add further to the effect. We are being marched off to witness something we may not want to see but the metre reminds us we've run out of options. 'The *mice* run *circles*, the *plovers* *cry*, / Till I *hardly know* in that *hurtling sky* …' The occasional extra unstressed syllable in these lines seems merely to enhance the effect. By the time we come to 'The girl with the haystack hair awry' we know that the same rhythm is going to run over her too.

Dorothy Hewett was also successful as a playwright, autobiographer and novelist, but it is in a poem like 'The Witnesses' that we come closest to the essence of her worldview. The boys are 'bumpkins'; the girls are (or should be) 'wild things' with 'haystack hair awry', but all are inevitably caught up in something larger than themselves, an existential cycle to be endured rather than complained about. It's significant, too, to note that the girl's humiliation takes place under a 'rainbow' arch of sky – which suggests something redemptive, or at least colourful, in the suffering over which it is arched. The girl who stayed inside and never went out into the 'wide country' to see the 'hawk in the high sky hung' may not have encountered the 'bumpkin boys' but she would also know less about life.

FRANCIS WEBB (1925–73)

'Harry'

It's the day for writing that letter, if one is able,
And so the striped institutional shirt is wedged
Between this holy holy chair and table.
He has purloined paper, he has begged and cadged
The bent institutional pen,
The ink. And our droll old men
Are darting constantly where he weaves his
    sacrament.

Sacrifice? Propitiation? All are blent
In the moron's painstaking fingers – so painstaking.
His vestments our giddy yarns of the firmament,
Women, gods, electric trains, and our remaking
Of all known worlds – but not yet
Has our giddy alphabet
Perplexed his priestcraft and spilled the cruet of
    innocence.

We have been plucked from the world of
    commonsense,
Fondling between our hands some shining loot,
Wife, mother, beach, fisticuffs, eloquence,
As the lank tree cherishes every distorted shoot.
What queer shards we could steal
Shaped him, realer than the Real:
But it is no goddess of ours guiding the fingers and
    the thumb.

She cries: *Ab aeterno ordinata sum.*

He writes to the woman, this lad who will never
    marry.
One vowel and the thousand laborious serifs will
    come
To this pudgy Christ, and the old shape of Mary.
Before seasonal pelts and the thin
Soft tactile underskin
Of air were stretched across earth, they have sported
    and are one.

Was it then at this altar-stone the mind was begun?
The image besieges our Troy. Consider the sick
Convulsions of movement, and the featureless baldy
    sun
Insensible – sparing that compulsive nervous tic.
Before life, the fantastic succession,
An imbecile makes his confession,
Is filled with the Word unwritten, has almost
    genuflected.

Because the wise world has for ever and ever
    rejected
Him and because your children would scream at the
    sight
Of his mongol mouth stained with food, he has
    resurrected
The spontaneous thought retarded and infantile
    Light.
Transfigured with him we stand
Among walls of the no-man's-land
While he licks the soiled envelope with lover's
    caress

Directing it to the House of no known address.

'Harry' is a part of Francis Webb's 'Ward Two' sequence, based on his time as a patient in Parramatta Psychiatric Hospital in 1960–61. Webb's situation as an inmate is inseparable from the poem's force. It could not have been written by a merely sympathetic observer. To say this is not to glamorise mental illness, however. Webb's suffering was very real and it limited his career as a poet, even while it informed it.

To understand the poem adequately (though never completely) it is important to keep in focus not only the young man writing (or attempting to write) his letter but the poet and other inmates who surround him. Something about the almost religious concentration with which this 'moron' is trying to compose his letter affects the onlookers, those 'droll old men', those spinners of 'giddy yarns' about their condition and the behaviours that brought them here. They are 'Transfigured with him' as he solemnly writes, or imagines he writes, to 'the House of no known address'.

This final transfiguration is the culmination of a series of religious, specifically Catholic, symbols which prepares us for such a revelation throughout the poem. It is, after all, a 'holy holy chair and table' on which the young man with his 'mongol mouth' weaves the 'sacrament' of his letter. Is this a sacrament, Webb wonders. Of 'Sacrifice?' Of Propitiation?'. Not exactly – but they are part of what is 'blent/In the moron's painstaking fingers'. He has been perplexed and surrounded by his fellow inmates' talk of 'Women, gods, electric trains, and remaking/Of all known worlds' but has not yet mastered the 'giddy alphabet' with which he might write down actual words. The 'priestcraft' of his concentration remains unperplexed by such complications.

The fourth stanza introduces us, eventually, to the letter's addressee. Her name appears to consist of 'One vowel'. She may assume something of the shape of the Virgin Mary. We are told that before 'seasonal pelts …/Of air were stretched across the earth, they have sported and are one.' Like the Virgin, she was 'set up from eternity', but that perhaps is where the comparison stops. To the 'pudgy Christ' writing (or attempting to write) his letter, she is unreachably remote.

In the fifth stanza the poet, the letter-writer's fellow inmate, begins to speculate on whether the human mind began in such inauspicious terrain. Perhaps what the boy is doing is 'Before life', back when 'the Word' was still unwritten (despite John's assertion that 'In the beginning was the Word, and the Word was with God, and the Word was God' [John 1:1]).

For all of the young man's unattractive appearance, the 'mongol mouth stained with food', he has by his sincere and unselfconscious devotion to his task somehow 'resurrected/... the infantile Light', the light back there at the beginning, before all the complications of the human mind. Those 'darting constantly' about him are eventually 'transfigured' by what they have seen. Although the poem is fiercely Catholic in its imagery, it does conclude, however, with the reminder that the 'soiled envelope with lover's caress' (like our prayers perhaps?) is directed to 'the House of no known address'. It's an image which continues to remind us that, for all their 'transfiguration' these inmates, so busy 'remaking/... all known worlds', are still isolated, still set apart from 'the world of commonsense' out of which they have been 'plucked'.

All this is not necessarily apparent on a first consideration of the poem. 'Harry' needs, and deserves, several concentrated readings to yield its full force. Without being too 'biographical', one can see clearly how it adds to the poem when we realise that when Webb talks of 'we' he is including himself. The poet, too, has been 'plucked from the world of commonsense' and is creating, like the others, 'giddy yarns' to explain his situation. We can think of Webb, too, working on the detail of the poem, devising its Donne-like stanzaic form and its curious rhyme scheme where the unrhymed word at the end of each stanza becomes the first rhyming word of the next. Likewise with the short penultimate line in each stanza which precedes the last line's unique hexameter. We can sense the struggle (as we do in John Donne's verse) that Webb has had with the poem's rhythm. There are no neatly turned tetrameters and pentameters as we find in, say, the work of Ben Jonson or Robert Herrick. Webb's rhythms are knotty and irregular, mimicking perhaps the difficulty the illiterate young man is having with his 'writing' – those 'thousand laborious serifs'.

It's impossible to find an accurately metrical line here. We feel instead the cramped irregularity of lines such as 'And so the *striped institutional shirt* is *wedged*', which graphically suggests the physical awkwardness of what it describes. Some lovers of euphony and strict metricality may find such distortions almost amateurish, but there is no doubt they work very well towards the poem's final effect – that being, of course, the overwhelming compassion we feel, as readers, for the 'mongol' – and for his fellow inmates who are moved despite themselves and for reasons they don't quite understand.

In the decades since this poem was first published terms like 'moron', 'mongol' and 'imbecile' have, understandably, become politically incorrect yet, paradoxically perhaps, such terms do nothing to undermine the effectiveness of 'Harry'. These are the words that the nurses, no doubt, use and what the inmates bandy about among themselves. They are rough points of identity and only help to make, for us more fortunate readers, the poem more poignant. Though Francis Webb wrote quite a few more 'ambitious' poems (which persuaded the English critic, Sir Herbert Read, that his work was equivalent to that of Rilke, Eliot, Pasternak and Robert Lowell), it is ultimately in a poem like 'Harry', with its deeply felt religious imagery – and its 'laborious serifs' – that we see Webb at his most moving and most interesting.

'Experiment'

Picking apples, they talked about the bible
and Jesus. They were atrocious. The fruit was superb.
The exegetist kept silent on the subject
and would not suffer fools at all preferring
to run a tight dairy. It was a community
of profits dispersing Christian Pacifists,
of twenty families and thirty children,
sixty acres of orchards and five hundred
of amateurishly utilised farmland. The apples
attracted itinerant pickers in the sappy season,
eccentrics and nomads who came among the
    residents
as slightly exotic entities until
the regimen of picking was established,
the rhythmical rapacity and the trees'
numb flow of colour under the cobalt sky.
Day after brilliant day as though ensconced
within a Van Gogh painting in the midst
of vibrant leaves and fruit of gold and crimson,
of green and russet, swallowing the sunlight,
plumping it back in juice and frost-white flesh,
the pickers moved through argosies of effort.
The talk among the trees was minimal;
there were few members, fewer labourers
who held an interest in the experiment
they worked for. But the individual thinker
who happened among them was welcomed as a
    talking point,

and so, in turn, became a passive witness
of their recidivism to the stultified
norms of dank suburbia: the hidden hunger
for prestige and possessions, the impatience
and bleak competitiveness with one another
surfacing and submerging, the inevitable
sexual attractions and adulterous
inclinations fulfilled and unfulfilled.
The most that could be done was to pick well,
endeavour to bruise no apples, talk and listen
dispassionately and find no cause for wonder
at such good intentions coming at best
to a fair yearly crop of splendid apples
from an emotional concentration camp.
It wasn't the straightjacket of their religion
but the rack of their emotions pulled them out of
    shape
and made them as crippled as the township's worst.
They brought the suburbs with them in their hearts.

Before the Australian poet, Bruce Beaver, dedicated the rest of his, often very sick, life to poetry, he worked in a variety of manual jobs. Many of these experiences ran deep and surfaced, sometimes decades later, in his poems. 'Experiment' from *Charmed Lives* (1988) is one of the best of them.

Of course, Beaver's blank verse (as well as the importance of apples in the poem) reminds us of the American poet, Robert Frost, and his classic poem 'After Apple Picking'. Both poems have a religious dimension, but Beaver has a very different feeling from Frost's satisfied exhaustion (Frost is on his own farm, for a start). The narrator of 'Experiment' is, we sense (but can't prove), a young man in the process of informally educating himself, a bemused seasonal worker in the orchard of a religious sect that has withdrawn from town life to maintain the purity of their convictions and work together for the communal good.

The underlying paradox of the poem is established, very explicitly, in its second line: 'They were atrocious. The fruit was superb.' Beaver then goes on to give us the details: number of families, number of children, number of acres and so on – even the personalities of the other workers and the 'community' members in charge. Some might see this information as excessive, but Beaver wants to, and needs to, recapture the literal truth of his memory, to recall things exactly as they were.

Among the most dominant of these memories are the apples themselves and the weather in which they were picked. The fruit was 'gold and crimson,/... green and russet'. The apples seemed to be 'swallowing the sunlight,/plumping it back in juice and frost-white flesh'. The weather was similarly idyllic: 'Day after brilliant day'; 'the cobalt sky' and so on. Though the poem is totally realistic, we can't help thinking a little of the Garden of Eden and the Adam and Eve narrative. They, too, were originally surrounded by abundant and generous nature – until they ate (without approval) the apple from the tree of knowledge. It's a little ironic then that these religious enthusiasts are back in the Garden and still bent down by Original Sin; for example, 'the hidden hunger/for prestige and possessions'; the 'adulterous/inclinations fulfilled and unfulfilled'. Though the community members like to talk about 'the bible/and Jesus', they don't seem to see the parallels – and, to give the young narrator full credit, he refrains from pointing it out to them (or to us). He merely resolves to 'pick well' and 'endeavour to bruise no apples'. Even a suggestion about how the community might make more money from dairying is clearly going to be unwelcome.

We are used to the 'suburbs' being disdained by poets, whether they be inner-city cosmopolitans or romantic lake-dwellers. Beaver here makes the suburbs stand for all that is dreary and inescapable in humanity's make-up. The 'Christian Pacifists' have consciously – and unsuccessfully – tried to escape these things by moving into the Edenic isolation of the countryside, but, somehow, the 'frost-white flesh' of the apples hasn't been enough. They are still subject to 'the inevitable/sexual attractions' and the complications that flow from them; 'prestige and possessions' are probably even more of a problem. The narrator, as a seemingly unspoiled young man, observes all this but is content to work through his 'argosies of effort' – though we may suppose he was also the 'individual thinker/who ... was welcomed as a talking point'. It is certainly he who makes the final and most despondent observation of the poem: 'They brought the suburbs with them in their hearts.'

In 'Experiment' we can see a relatively recent example of how effectively blank verse may be used for narrative poetry, whether it be Milton's *Paradise Lost* or Bruce Beaver's 44-line realistic parable. A few lines may exceed the pentameter's 10- or 11-syllable limit, but most fit the pattern easily enough, particularly the last line, which is so memorably regular: 'They *brought*/the *sub*/urbs *with*/ them *in*/their *hearts.*'

The sentences, too, are generally long and relaxed. The story is being told by a narrator who takes his time and wants us to have all the details we need in order to understand things properly. Bruce Beaver was always known as a 'talkative' poet who was happy enough to run the risk of being called 'prolix' and this poem well illustrates how a poem may be both compressed – and leisurely. Some poets might have cut back Beaver's 44 lines to 30 or so and changed neither the essence nor point of the story, but there are not too many people who, reading 'Experiment' a second or third time, would want to cut much out. Some may prefer less directness of imagery – and want to delete phrases such as a 'crop of splendid apples/from an emotional concentration camp' or 'the stultified/ norms of dank suburbia' though expressions like these are part of the poet's character as a narrator. He's just a bit opinionated and he doesn't care if you know it.

Though 'Experiment' may not endear itself to members of communes and/or religious sects (or even to idealists generally), there would be few, even of them, who could deny that Beaver has a point here; that 'good intentions' are easily 'pulled ... out of shape' by the emotions people inescapably carry with them in the 'suburbs' of their hearts.

'Mort aux chats'

There will be no more cats.
Cats spread infection,
cats pollute the air,
cats consume seven times
their own weight in food a week,
cats were worshipped in
decadent societies (Egypt
and Ancient Rome), the Greeks
had no use for cats. Cats
sit down to pee (our scientists
have proved it). The copulation
of cats is harrowing; they
are unbearably fond of the moon.
Perhaps they are all right in
their own country but their
traditions are alien to ours.
Cats smell, they can't help it,
you notice it going upstairs.
Cats watch too much television,
they can sleep through storms,
they stabbed us in the back
last time. There have never been
any great artists who were cats.
They don't deserve a capital C
except at the beginning of a sentence.
I blame my headache and my
plants dying on to cats.
Our district is full of them,

property values are falling.
When I dream of God I see
a Massacre of Cats. Why
should they insist on their own
language and religion, who
needs to purr to make his point?
Death to all cats! The Rule
of Dogs shall last a thousand years!

'*Mort aux chats*' by expatriate Australian poet Peter Porter is, despite its supposedly domestic subject matter, one of the great satirical poems in twentieth-century English. In most, but not all, of his work Porter is a poet who owes more to Swift and the Augustans than to Wordsworth and the Romantics. He is interested in how we interact socially rather than in transcendent matters of the soul.

In '*Mort aux chats*' he has nailed down xenophobic paranoia so conclusively that one would think it might never raise its head (or bark!) again. It would be cheering to think of this poem as being of historical interest only, but a cursory reading of the newspapers or five minutes with the television news show that it has, alas, lost none of its relevance in the years since it was first published in *Preaching to the Converted* (1972).

The poem begins and ends with two extreme statements: 'There will be no more cats' and 'The Rule/of Dogs shall last a thousand years!' In the 33 or so lines between lies an encyclopaedia of all the irrational accusations ever levelled at any one of the several groups in world history which have become scapegoats. It's ironic that the term 'scapegoat' was originally Jewish (see Leviticus 16) since they themselves have been the ones who, throughout history, have been 'scapegoated' most. Who would have thought a poet could compress so much paranoid nonsense into so few lines and send it up so mercilessly?

Porter has obviously read his Goebbels. He knows how the

propagandist can start with a small untruth (or even a disadvanta-
geous fact) and build a whole structure of lies upon it. A cat *can*
spread infection (if you are scratched by it). Cats *do* make a noise
while mating. Cat piss *can* be problematic in the garden. And yet,
in no time at all, our Hitlerian orator is crying for 'a Massacre of
Cats' and 'The Rule of Dogs' for a thousand years. How has he
moved from one point to the other? Is there a logical progres-
sion? Certainly, there's not much logic in Hitler's *Mein Kampf* – and
(appropriately) there's not much in '*Mort aux chats*' either.

Let's look at some of the (pseudo) arguments more closely. We
have the bogus use of statistics about how greedy cats are. We have
historical references to 'decadent societies' (with the assumption that
the speaker's society is completely pure); we have the back reference
to preferred ancient societies (Greeks for our canine orator; Aryans
for Hitler). We have the sinister markers of physical difference – cats
'sit down to pee' (or male circumcision for the Jews).

Then we move on to the sexual paranoia that is so often part
of bigotry (most obvious in the attitude of whites in the US Deep
South towards black males). There is even the suggestion of lunacy
– 'they/are unbearably fond of the moon'. And then comes the
generous appearance of rationality or pseudo-compromise (the
'good cop/bad cop' routine): '... they are all right in/their own
country but ...'. They *do* have 'traditions', he concedes, *but* they are
'alien to ours'.

Soon, though, we are back to cheap jibes about smell, followed
up quickly with an intellectual insult: 'Cats watch too much tele-
vision'. Towards the end we have a couple of the time-honoured
Nazi lies about Jews: they made Germany lose World War 1 and
German-Jewish artists like, say, Mendelssohn, were somehow infe-
rior to 'truly' German ones such as Beethoven or Wagner. Even the
capital C issue is raised. Anti-Semitic writers of the 1920s and 1930s
often made a point of not giving Jews their capital letter.

Finally, in the poem's last quarter, we have the eternal paranoia
of the majority being 'bred out' by a fertile minority. And, of course,
though Hitler was pretty severe on most brands of religion, God
gets His look in: 'When I dream of God I see/a Massacre of Cats.'

There is, alas, no shortage of fundamentalists around the world who are ready to enlist God on their side through selective quoting of holy texts.

Porter concludes by having his deranged orator ask the dumbest question of all: 'Why/should they insist on their own/language and religion ...?' As if this were not exactly what the majority has been happily doing all along! The last two lines, of course, refer deliberately to the Nazis, to their slogan 'Kill all Jews' and to Hitler's boast that his Reich would last a thousand years (it lasted twelve).

Through all this it's hard to think of anything a 'scapegoated' minority has been accused of which the poet has left out. He's got the lot – not logically arranged, of course, but when were such prejudices ever logical? Although the poem grows out of the Nazi experience, Porter is careful to widen its application with contemporary references to television and to a few things that even Jews were never accused of – 'sleep(ing) through storms', for instance. He gives his poem a French title, too, to suggest that bigotry is not confined to any one nationality, though it is often nationalistic. Importantly, too, Porter keeps his focus on cats as animals, their actual habits and so on, so that the cat-as-symbol can retain its wide applicability.

Written in a kind of free verse, close to the hectic speech rhythms of a Hitler or a Goebbels, '*Mort aux chats*' is lineated as a 'thin' poem rather than a long-lined one like those of Walt Whitman (or Allen Ginsberg). Perhaps this narrowness tells its own tale, suggesting the 'thinness' of the arguments. Maybe, also, the extensive use of enjambement reflects the slippery way the argument moves on to another point before the previous one is in any way 'proved'. 'Cats/sit down to pee ...' or 'the Greeks/had no use for cats'. We also have quite a deal of alliteration to make phrases more memorable: 'The *c*opulation/of *c*ats' and 'who/needs to *p*urr to make his *p*oint'. We notice, too, that, for all the poem's free verse, it ends with a resonantly Shakespearean iambic pentameter: The *Rule*/of *Dogs*/shall *last*/a *thous*/and *years*!'

One is tempted to e-mail this poem to some of the burgeoning hate-sites around the world in the hope that it might do some good – and prove Auden wrong when he said that 'poetry makes nothing happen'. The problem is that the bigoted (and that includes most people, at one level or another) are notoriously immune to irony. The bigots so targeted would probably take the poem as a vote of support. 'The Rule/of Dogs shall last a thousand years!' Let's hope not.

'Secret Policeman'

Pledge me: I had the hangman for a father
And for my mother the immortal State;
My playground was the yard beside the lime-pit,
My play-songs the after-cries of hate.

Admire me: I fill these shining boots,
I am soul expanded to a uniform;
A hired world glitters at my senses,
The smell of blood keeps my blood-stream warm.

Pity me: from a world ruddy with flame
I am tugged in dreams to the first cave again,
And in that humid soil and atmosphere
Lie down each night beside the murdered men.

The dead eyes point the way I go,
The dead hands presage me in air.
I run on shifting pavements, by fired walls
Falling, and weighted lamp-posts everywhere.

Though not collected until *Arcady and Other Places* (1966),
Vincent Buckley's 'Secret Policeman' seems very much writ-
ten out of the failed Hungarian Uprising just ten years earlier.
Its author was a key member of Melbourne's Catholic intellec-
tual community – which was fiercely anti-communist. Photos and
newsreel images of secret policemen hanging from lamp-posts in
Budapest, or people said to be informers and secret policemen,
were circulated widely around the world, including Australia. Many
intellectuals across the political spectrum were drawn vicariously

to these events, considering from the relative safety of Sydney's or Melbourne's streets and cafés what they might or might not have done in similar circumstances.

'Secret Policeman' is actually poem VIII of a sequence called 'Eleven Political Poems'. The sequence is often described as 'satirical' in intent. This is certainly true of a poem such as 'Poetry and the Party Line', where Buckley humorously outlines how a totalitarian regime may co-opt everyone (often without too much effort) into its service. The last field to be mentioned is 'Poetry, our most respected corpse'. Buckley imagines the poet, entombed like Lenin in a glass case, 'One soldier at the feet, and one at the head'.

'Secret Policeman' is slightly different. Here Buckley is speculating on the background and on the motivations a secret policeman in a dictatorship might have. As potential members of the totalitarian society we are given three successive instructions: 'Pledge me', 'Admire me' and 'Pity me'.

In the first stanza, following the first of these injunctions, we are given some explanations of how such a man might end up so ruthlessly devoted to the state. His father has been an executioner before him; he's been brought up in a state orphanage (subject to its unrelenting propaganda); he was underprivileged as a child (playing 'beside the lime-pit') and grew up with propaganda songs rather than nursery rhymes. It's not an auspicious beginning. We may not be prepared to forgive him but we can see 'where he's coming from', as they say.

In the second stanza, the ego arrives, probably in compensation for the hardships endured in the first. His soul is a 'uniform'; his world is only 'hired' (as he is) and somehow the smell of other people's spilt blood is what keeps his own circulating.

In the third (and, in a sense, the fourth) stanza we are asked to 'Pity' him. At night he is forced to revisit in dreams the cave in which the men he has murdered (or informed on) have been buried. The cave, of course, also has something of Plato about it, a cave where what one sees on its walls are but shadows of what really exists outside.

In the last stanza the policeman's victims point the way towards his own death; their dead hands 'presage' him in air. In the last two lines, we are running with him as he seeks to escape being lynched by the partisans after someone has recognised him as a secret policeman. He can expect no fairer trial than he gave others. A lamp-post in the street will soon be 'weighted' with his corpse.

All this may seem some distance from the literal truth of Australian politics in the years 1956 to 1966, but it's not at all far from the rhetoric used in the metaphorically bloody battles within the Australian Labor Party during its 'split' in the mid-1950s. The Hungarian Revolution of 1956 was the first clear (as opposed to cloudy) sign that Stalin's empire was not a workers' paradise but a repressive tyranny. Many previously devoted Australian communists left the party at this point; and many of its fellow travellers ceased supporting it. Today, with the Soviet empire collapsed in 1989, this may all seem remote, but Buckley in this poem has captured the Australian political atmosphere of the time very convincingly (albeit metaphorically).

Of course, the poem would have only limited merit if it merely portrayed particular political atmospheres with verisimilitude. Unfortunately Buckley's poem has not gone out of date. There are still plenty of regimes around the world where secret police (and their attendant torturers) are employed. 'Secret Policeman' continues to remind us of the ordinariness of the origin of such people, their egoistic delusions and, finally, their vulnerability, if not their pitiability. One continues to hope that when they go to bed with their guilt they 'Lie down each night beside the murdered men'.

The four-square quatrains of *abcb*-rhymed pentameters are much less fashionable today than they were in the 1950s and early 1960s, but they easily work well enough for Buckley's purpose. They seem to shape his argument – even as, by their regularity, they appear to confirm it. Once, in the opening lines of the final stanza, Buckley cuts his line short to a tetrameter, seeming to hurry the policeman along to his fate ('The *dead* eyes *point* the *way* I *go*'). On another occasion he presses three stressed syllables together ('A *hired world glitter*s *at* my *sen*ses'), but there's no doubt about the function the iambic pentameter performs in the poem overall.

To those who celebrate the Irish element in Vincent Buckley's work (seven of his eight great-grandparents were Irish), 'Secret Policeman' may seem a perverse choice by which to remember him. Buckley had much to say about Ireland, too, though some of it seems less essential now that peace in the north appears to have been reached. The scenario in 'Secret Policeman' has not gone away, however; nor has our need for such a compressed and evocative portrayal of its threat. Buckley's 'Secret Policeman' is no mere 'noir' scene from a movie. It's something people in countries around the world are living with right now as you're reading this analysis (and re-reading the poem).

BRUCE DAWE (1930–)

'Drifters'

One day soon he'll tell her it's time to start packing,
and the kids will yell 'Truly' and get wildly excited
    for no reason,
and the brown kelpie pup will start dashing about,
    tripping everyone up,
and she'll go out to the vegetable-patch and pick all
    the green tomatoes from the vines,
and notice how the oldest girl is close to tears
    because she was happy here,
and how the youngest girl is beaming because she
    wasn't.
And the first thing she'll put on the trailer will
    be the bottling-set she never unpacked from
    Grovedale,
and when the loaded ute bumps down the drive
    past the blackberry-canes with their last
    shrivelled fruit,
she won't ask why they're leaving this time, or
    where they're headed for
– she'll only remember how, when they came here,
she held out her hands bright with berries,
the first of the season, and said:
'Make a wish, Tom, make a wish.'

It's important to remember that not all classics were written centuries ago and in other countries. 'Drifters' by Bruce Dawe, written in Melbourne in the 1960s, will most likely be around for a very long time. It's not a triumph of metrical arrangement or a stunning succession of images. It's not about some major figure in our political landscape or a moment of blazing spiritual insight. It is, however, a masterpiece of tone and understatement – and a striking example of what free verse can do at its most subtle.

The poem starts getting things right from the first line. Though embodying, to us now, an outmoded way of living (where the husband can simply tell his wife 'to start packing'), Dawe, ironically, sets his poem in the future. It's all about to happen and even the poignant flashback at the end is, in fact, a prediction. It's all happened before and it will happen again and there's nothing, it seems, that the wife (or girls) can do about it. We're not told why the man has to move and we don't need to know.

In the second line, Dawe's ear for the colloquial picks up the excitement in the one word 'Truly?', and his quiet eye for detail is soon seen in the wife's noticing that one of her daughters is happy to be going and the other isn't. It's all still understated, though. The older girl is only 'close' to tears rather than crying; the younger one is merely 'beaming' rather than cheering.

A similar understatement is seen in the symbolism towards the end of the poem when the family drives past the 'last shrivelled fruit' of the blackberry-canes and the wife remembers how her hands were 'bright with berries' when they first arrived. We don't need a prize for guessing what the wish is. One of Dawe's particular gifts is to effortlessly and accurately draw a clear line between sentimentality and genuine poignancy. Indirection, of course, as in the poem's last line, is part of his secret.

There are many other details that also make the poem both convincing visually and profoundly moving. The kelpie pup, for instance. It senses something is wrong but doesn't quite know what. The green tomatoes have to be picked and taken – they can't be wasted. The 'ute' (not a 'utility') 'bumps' down the drive, giving us a good idea of the rented house they've been living in. Then, of course, there is the optimistic handful of berries, so much in contrast to the 'last shrivelled fruit'.

All these details are strung together in just two loosely constructed sentences and we note that seven of the poem's 13 lines start with 'and'. The items run on rather in the manner of a primary school student's composition. They also emphasise, but not unkindly, the characters' relative lack of sophistication. The technique, rather democratically, puts everyone and everything on the same level, from the kelpie pup 'dashing about' and the bottling-set 'never unpacked from Grovedale', right through to the close-to-tearful, or beaming, daughters and the wordless wife being carried off down the drive. Even what is not described is significant. The husband is referred to in the first line but is actually named only in the last. The family's location is not given, though their previous one is. Dawe shows a tremendous tact about what to mention and what not to – an ability that clearly comes from his real knowledge of the subject.

Another element that helps make this poem a masterpiece is its long, loose, free-verse lines, each one at liberty to do what it has to. The best example is line 3, where the rhythm of the pup's 'dashing about' is also caught in the line's almost anapaestic metre: 'and the *brown* kelpie *pup* will start *dash*ing a*bout* …'. One can get a sense of how important this quasi-anapaestic rhythm is by notionally rewriting the first line as trochaic: '*One* day *soon* he'll *say* it's *time* to *pack.*' If one re-reads the original now one can see just how important those extra unstressed syllables are in creating both the mood of the poem and its meaning.

Above all these factors, and partly because of them, is the skill with which Dawe has allied his tone to his subject. His colloquial language is effortless, unobtrusive, and very close to what the family itself might use in its more articulate moments or in its interior monologues. Standard phrases such as 'get wildly excited' or 'close to tears' are not clichés here; they are indicators of the reality of the poem's subjects. This is just the diction such people would use. They mightn't be quite up to a phrase like 'bright with berries', with its alliteration and buried metaphor, but they would know exactly what Dawe means by having used it – and be grateful he did.

Unlike some middle-class poets writing about 'the workers', Dawe is not talking down or making some abstract doctrinal point. He is right in there with them, as bemused as they are. The poem thus transcends, and will probably outlive, the ideologies that purportedly make sense of, and sympathise with, their plight.

DAVID MALOUF (1934–)

'The Year of the Foxes'

for Don Anderson

When I was ten, my mother, having sold
her old fox-fur (a ginger red, bone-jawed
Magda Lupescu
of a fox that on her arm played
dead, cunningly dangled
a lean and tufted paw)

decided there was money to be made
from foxes, and bought via
the columns of the *Courier Mail* a whole
pack of them; they hung from penny hooks
in our panelled sitting-room, trailed from the backs
of chairs; and Brisbane ladies, rather
the worse for war, drove up in taxis wearing
a G.I. on their arm
and rang at our front door.

I slept across the hall, at night hearing
their thin cold cry. I dreamed the dangerous spark
of their eyes, brushes aflame
in our fur-hung, nomadic
tent in the suburbs, the dark fox-stink of them
cornered in their holes
and turning ...

Among my mother's show pieces –
Noritaki teacups, tall hock-glasses
with stems like barley-sugar,
goldleaf demitasses –
the foxes, row upon row, thin-nosed, prick-eared,
dead.

      The cry of hounds
was lost behind mirror-glass,
where ladies with silken snoods and finger-nails
of chinese lacquer red
fastened a limp paw;
went down in their high heels
to the warm soft bitumen, wearing at throat
and elbow the rare spoils
of '44: old foxes, rusty-red like dried-up wounds,
and a G.I. escort.

There have been many accounts of war childhoods, some more harrowing than others. Quite often those from the periphery of a war, such as David Malouf's 'The Year of the Foxes', can be as moving or as instructive as those caught under the bombs. As he says in the poem, in 1944 David Malouf was ten, an age when one sees that the world is much more complex and elusive than one had previously thought.

The complexities of the fox-fur business are definitely the concern of the mother's. The father is unmentioned throughout. The son, the poet-to-be, watches precociously but with little real understanding as yet of what is going on between the women who return to the 'warm soft bitumen' with their newly acquired fox-fur and those G.I. escorts who have provided the cash.

The boy himself, having more imagination than any of the adults involved, is more concerned with the animals who once lived in the furs. He imagines, in one instance, that the fox is only 'play(ing) dead'. At night, across the hall from his mother's merchandising, the boy seems to hear the foxes' 'thin cold cry'. He sees them at the point of death, 'cornered in their holes/and turning …'. Even for him, however, 'The cry of hounds/was lost behind the mirror-glass.' By the end of the poem he is watching events almost dispassion-ately – though he does still describe the red fox-furs as being 'like dried-up wounds'.

And, of course, there is another dimension to the boy's side-long observations of what transpires in his mother's house. He is fascinated by the detail: 'Noritaki teacups, tall hock-glasses/with stems like barley sugar,/goldleaf demitasses'. The fox-furs hanging on 'penny hooks' or 'trail(ing) from the backs of chairs' are part of a total visual effect – as are the 'Brisbane ladies, rather/the worse for war'. Even the 'G.I. on their arm' fits into the picture, anony-mous though he remains. These are all part of something larger, which he doesn't yet understand but which is indubitably interest-ing. One almost sees him lurking in the doorway as he observes the ladies with 'silken snoods and finger-nails/of chinese lacquer red/fasten(ing) a limp paw' and going back down to the 'warm soft bitumen'.

As mature readers, we fill in the blanks the ten-year-old's mind leaves for us. We now know what these G.I.s were going off to; we know some of the moral compromises the women 'rather/the worse for war' had to make. We know how war can create opportu-nities for some (such as the poet's mother) even as it destroys them for many others. The war is very much offstage but its impact is felt nevertheless – even on a ten-year-old boy who knows very little about it really.

Of course, we're also aware that this ten-year-old mind is being filtered through the consciousness of a mature poet, some 25 or so years later (the poem was first collected in *Bicycle and Other Poems*, 1970). This maturity enables another level of cleverness in the poem. It's not just the slight precocity of the ten-year-old observer, it's the ironic asides of the poet decades later. It's the poet surely and not the ten-year-old who notices that the ladies are 'rather/the worse for war'. It may have been a joke of the mother's perhaps, but it is still the adult who has remembered it. It is the same adult who calls his mother's clients, with some irony, 'Brisbane ladies'. Pretty clearly these women of elastic virtue and their G.I. escorts are not 'ladies' as we might normally understand the term. It is the poet, too, who sees that these 'ladies' wear the G.I. on their arm as a sort of trophy, showing them off to other women who haven't been so lucky or clever. It is the poet, too, who sees the 'warm soft bitumen' as something additional to a good road surface.

Yet, the irony of the poem remains that all these things were first seen by the ten-year-old, who may not have fully comprehended them but was nevertheless aware that he would need to store them for later processing. It is in this doubleness that much of the poem's charm, and its significance, resides. It is the adult poet who has provided the sophistication foreshadowed by the boy.

This sophistication is intensified by Malouf's playfulness with his poem's rhythms and lineation. The first line is a classic iambic pentameter ('When *I* was *ten*, my *moth*er, having *sold*') and seems to promise the steady blank verse of a Robert Frost (or a Wordsworth before him). Malouf, almost immediately however, undercuts this expectation with a short third line of two stresses only ('*Mag*da Lu*pes*cu') and then goes on to an almost humorous enjambement at the end of the fourth line ('played/dead'). We think at first the fox might just be 'play(ing)' but suddenly it's 'dead'. We can see something similarly ironic in the gap between the widely separated internal rhyme of 'war' in stanza two's antepenultimate line and the word 'door' at its end. One hears the same sound again right at the end of the poem as a sort of closure, the 'or' of ''44' and the 'or' in 'G.I. escort'.

Essentially, the poem is written in free verse – but it's the free verse employed also by the American poet, Robert Lowell, in his *Life Studies* book of just a few years earlier (1959). There, too, we can hear the echo of an original iambic pentameter before the demands of a precise memory, similar to Malouf's, seemed to require a loosening of the form, a move that has the effect of paring away any remaining rhetoric and concentrating on the details themselves. The 'goldleaf demitasses' and the 'high heels' in the 'soft warm bitumen' are left to do their work unassisted.

David Malouf is, of course, much better known these days as a fiction writer but it is as a poet that he began – and with poems of high quality, as the early poem, 'The Year of the Foxes', demonstrates. He has continued to write poetry throughout his career as a novelist and has recently published the collection *Typewriter Music* as well as a new book of selected poems, *Revolving Days*.

CHRIS WALLACE-CRABBE (1934–)

'Other People'

In the First World War they …
Who were *they*? Who cares anymore? …
Killed four of my uncles,
So I discovered one day.

There were only four on that side of the family
And all swept away in a few bad years
In a war the historians tell us now
Was fought over nothing at all.

Four uncles, as one might say
A dozen apples or seven tons of dirt,
Swept away by the luck of history,
Closed off. Full stop.

Four is a lot for uncles,
A lot for lives, I should say.
Their chalk was wiped clean off the slate,
The War meant nothing at all.

War needs a lot of uncles,
And husbands, and brothers, and so on:
Someone must *want* to kill them,
Somebody needs them dead.

Who is it, I wonder. Me?
Or is it you there, reading away,
Or a chap with a small-arms factory?
Or is it only *they*?

First collected in Chris Wallace-Crabbe's *Where the Wind Came* (1971), 'Other People' has remained ever since one of the crucial latter-day poems about World War 1 – and war more generally. At the time of its first publication, controversy was raging about Australia's involvement in the Vietnam war and many poets, Wallace-Crabbe included, were looking back to World War 1 as a paradigm for war's wastage of lives more generally.

A lot of these poems, in retrospect, seem simplistic and overly dogmatic, but 'Other People' over nearly 40 years has retained its force – and its charm. 'Charm' may seem a strange word in relation to a successful anti-war poem, but that is what the poem has – and in abundance.

The source of this is almost certainly the *faux-naiveté* of the poem's narrator. At one level, the speaker is, of course, a Melbourne *littérateur* in his mid-thirties at the time. At another, clearly, he is the small boy deprived of uncles who might have taken him for walks and made him interesting playthings in their garden sheds. For readers who bothered to check the book's biographical note (or knew the poet personally), the awareness that Wallace-Crabbe was born a full 20 years after 1914 adds an extra poignancy. 'Their chalk was wiped clean off the slate' well before the poet emerged.

On the other hand, of course, the poem is clearly much more than a cry of anguish for the loss of four uncles, painful though that must be. It is also a serious meditation on exactly who or what caused their death? From the very first line, the poet rehearses the possibilities. The ubiquitous and anonymous 'they' is his first – and final – surmise. Other possibilities include 'you there, reading away', 'a chap with a small-arms factory' and even the poet himself. As readers, we have no trouble dismissing ourselves as the cause – and being born 20 years or so too late more or less lets the poet off. The 'chap with a small-arms factory' is a more likely suspect, but the offhanded tone in which he is mentioned suggests somehow that it can't be that simple. If it were, the poet would surely have given him more than his one line.

Thus we are brought back to the 'they'. 'They' seems to embody amoral historical forces beyond our control; all those old reasons for conflict that now mean 'nothing at all'. And yet, can it be really so vague? As the poet says, 'Somebody needs them dead.' Since no one living now was in a position to influence events leading up to World War 1, we may well feel safe in declaring that 'they' caused it; however, Wallace-Crabbe's tone in the final stanza seems unwilling to let us off so lightly. How could it have been only 'they'? Maybe it was 'me' after all. Or 'you there, reading away' (and feeling so innocent). Maybe it was the 'chap with a small-arms factory' after all.

However it was, the poet makes it only too clear that 'Four is a lot for uncles'. This is the fact that we can't get away from. We can't just speak of uncles as we might of a 'dozen apples or seven tons of dirt'. They were living people, albeit unknown to us (and to their nephew, frustratingly). 'Their chalk was wiped clean off the slate.'

The *faux-naiveté* mentioned earlier as part of the poem's charm is also reinforced, perhaps even created, by the various rhythmic tensions in the poem. At one level, the poem seems to want to be in iambic tetrameter or trimeter quatrains but, at another, there are numerous additional unstressed syllables pushing it towards a triple rhythm – anapaestic, probably, or dactyllic. A few lines seem solidly iambic ('War *needs* a *lot* of *un*cles', for instance), but the majority have a triple rhythm which gives them an offhand or almost childish quality. Lines such as 'In a *war* the histo*ri*ans *tell* us *now*/Was *fought* over *no*thing at *all*' seem to echo, in their lilting quality, the fatuity of the original propaganda. This 'doubleness' of effect is a difficult one to bring off. The war is a serious topic, after all. Why are we reading about it, we might ask, in such light-hearted metres?

A similar point can be made about the poem's relative lack of rhyme. With the *abca* pattern established in stanza 1, we're expecting some fairly traditional quatrain rhyming – probably *abcb* but *abca* if that's what suits the poet. First up then we have four unrhymed stanzas before we reach our *abcb* expectation in the final stanza. Admittedly, there are a couple of 'ay' rhymes along the way to go with 'they' and 'day' in the first stanza and 'away' and 'they' in the last. It's as if the little boy in the poem refuses to give us the rhymes that might make the whole pressure of the poem easier to bear. He's refusing to be as clever as we need him to be.

This all takes us back then to the false naivety mentioned already. We have that sense of both a little boy deprived of his uncles and the disillusioned and mature poet who understands that the war 'Was fought over nothing at all.' Some historians, since 'Other People' was written, have revised the 'revisionists' and now argue that the territorial ambitions of Wilhelmine Germany presaged those of Hitler and that stopping the first aggression was no less important than stopping the second. These are complex issues and cannot be resolved here. They do little, however, to undermine the artistic and moral success of 'Other People'. 'Four is a lot for uncles' – and will remain so.

THOMAS SHAPCOTT (1935–)

'Flying Fox'

She tosses and rumples alone on the double bed:
when, damn him, when will his car cringe in
through their gate and clatter over the one loose
    stone
to announce his coming? Her life has become a
    code
of sound, a mesh of reassurances
and locks. She wills herself still and tight. No use,
each minute drums with the wrong silence, the
    wrong noise
on the rigid tendons of her own unease.

And still she waits, as tensely she listens, and hears
in the rank-growing neighbour papaw tree outside
a marauding flying fox circle and flap and cling
scooping the ripe air, gripping with clawed wings
at its easy quarry, the fleshy neglected fruit,
and tear through its shallow skin, and feast on it.

Thomas Shapcott has been publishing poetry since the mid-1950s. 'Flying Fox', first collected in his volume, *Inwards to the Sun* (1969), is still one of the poems he is best known for. In it he shows not only his feeling for the tropical luxuriance of Brisbane, near which he grew up, but a clear mastery of the modern sonnet.

More important than either of these, perhaps, is Shapcott's understanding of the tensions and frustrations involved in many marriages. The husband, awaited by his wife, is not especially unpleasant, it seems. His car will 'cringe in' eventually – though he is, of course, rather unwisely neglecting her.

The wife 'tosses and rumples'; she is imprisoned in her situation, her 'mesh of reassurances/and locks'; she is a captive of her 'own unease'. She is a victim, too, of repetition; she awaits the sound of the 'one loose stone' that always signals his arrival. The line 'She wills herself still and tight' is less than definitive; it could refer to her determination to freeze her husband out when he arrives or it could refer to her efforts to maintain morale under pressure. Whatever the woman's intention, it seems she is unsuccessful. The slow lapse of time is drumming 'on the rigid tendons of her own unease.'

Thus in the octave of Shapcott's sonnet we have the woman's situation clearly, if ambiguously, established. The sestet introduces a new element into the situation – and intensifies the atmosphere. The papaw tree next door is 'rank-growing'; the air is 'ripe'; the fruit is 'fleshy' and protected by only a 'shallow skin'. Into the papaw trees flaps the 'marauding flying fox' – or fruit bat, to give it another, more accurate and less dramatic name. We know the wings of flying foxes are leathery and 'clawed'. It is thus not hard to imagine the noise of the animal's disconcerting flapping in the papaw leaves or the sound of its feasting on the 'fleshy neglected fruit'. Some poets, such as T.S. Eliot in 'The Waste Land', have emphasised the threatening and grotesque appearance of bats ('Bats with baby faces in the violet light/Whistled and beat their wings …'), but Shapcott is more concerned with the symbolic impact the sound the fruit bat makes on the stressed and neglected wife.

Like the papaw, she too is a 'fleshy neglected fruit' vulnerable in the 'ripe air', an 'easy quarry' tossing inside her 'shallow skin' and, in a sense, waiting to be feasted on. Whether her consumer will be her husband or an interloper is unclear, but there is no mistaking her sense of vulnerability. In stanza 1 we saw her frustration; in stanza 2 we feel her fear.

It's significant that at no point does Shapcott use an explicit comparison. There is no simile or metaphor. He simply presents the woman in her situation in the first stanza and describes, with extraordinary sensuousness, the fruit bat and its feeding in the second. Readers may fill in the rest for themselves. This is the differ-ence between drama and melodrama. If the poet had written 'she lay there like a fleshy neglected fruit' the gesture would have been excessive, even tasteless. Leaving it to readers to make their own comparison is a much better strategy.

A similar level of understatement is seen in the poem's title. Shapcott could have had a title like the one Robert Lowell gave his sonnet on a comparable theme, 'To Speak of the Woe that is in Marriage'. He could have given it a soapie title like 'Desperate Housewives', but he prefers the obliqueness of naming the only new element in the situation, the flying fox. Of course, the two words themselves, in combination, are essentially poetic. Foxes are marauders, after all, and if they are airborne, so much the more disturbing. The effect would be very different if the poem were simply called 'Fruit Bat' or tagged with its Latin genus *Pteropus*.

Something comparable happens, too, with Shapcott's use of rhyme. Instead of giving us the three fully rhyming quatrains and the final couplet we'd normally expect in an Elizabethan sonnet, Shapcott uses a series of half-rhymes. In the first quatrain we have 'bed/code', 'in/stone' in an *abba* arrangement. The second quatrain becomes *cdcd* or possibly *ccdd* (one could argue about this). At the beginning of the last stanza, however, the rhyme seems to disappear altogether for a moment before returning with a pair of couplets to finish ('cling/wings' and 'fruit/it'). Thus, as Eliot recommended in 'The Music of Poetry', rhyme is used more for musical purposes than for structural ones. In this way 'Flying Fox' is a gesture back to a long-established tradition rather than a literal re-use of it.

It's a nice paradox, then, that these sorts of freedoms can only be taken because generations of earlier poets refused them and so left to the last 100 years or so the option of playing with these 'shadow-ing' effects. If we weren't already familiar with regular full rhymes we wouldn't be able to enjoy these subtle allusions to them. 'Flying Fox' shows Shapcott taking full advantage of this somewhat luxu-rious situation and, in the process, underlining his contemporary analysis and treatment of what is a timeless situation, a neglected wife who 'tosses and rumples alone on the double bed'.

'There Was a Time: The Youth'

There was a time, but I do not remember,
when this warm-reeking woolshed was a fortress,
the wall-slits slits for muskets, and my parents
sentries alert against the shadowy clans.
I remember only peace, the predicted harvests,
the shadows dwindling beneath our ascending sun.

There was a time of shepherds on heath-wild hills,
uncleared, unfenced; a rough camp at the homestead
where there were always strangers whose names
    were suspect
and screeching laughter of gins from the dying
    horde.
I remember only this cool stone house in the
    paddocks,
raised among olives and palms to my father's name.

The penned sheep wait for the shears, and the drays
    depart
weighed down with bales for the white coast and
    the steamer;
the May rains come and the harrows pursue the
    seeding,
the harvest winds ripen orchard and corn alike.
Grain, tree and beast bring forth in their proper
    season,
and overnight parsons give thanks in the candle-
    light.

My father has faltered in nothing: his hearth is
    established,
his sons are grown; we shall reap the predicted
    harvests.
Only I, riding the flat-topped hills alone,
feel in the inland wind the sing of desert,
and under alien skin the surge, the stirring,
a wisdom and a violence, the land's dark blood.

Though Randolph Stow is generally seen these days as an expatriate novelist, there was a time in the 1960s when he was equally considered a rising star of Australian poetry. This view derived mainly from a single volume, *A Counterfeit Silence*, which came out in 1969. The poem chosen here, 'There Was a Time: The Youth', is a monologue from 'Stations: A Suite for Three Voices and Three Generations', a central sequence in that book. The poems as a whole present the evolving thoughts of the youth's parents as well as those of the youth himself. It is not hard to sense that Stow, a somewhat rebellious scion of a Western Australian landed family, identifies with the youngest of the three voices, the young man 'riding the flat-topped hills alone' and sensing as he rides 'the land's dark blood'. Indeed, this is very much a poem of what Chris Wallace-Crabbe has called 'squattocratic guilt', the second- or third-generation awareness in pastoral families of how their forbears came to acquire the land they themselves will inherit (or, in some cases, refuse to inherit). Such poems, with their relatively impractical feelings of guilt, can sometimes appear sentimental, but Stow avoids this in a number of ways to emerge with a convincing evaluation of all that has taken place – and its continuing significance for both victors and vanquished.

He starts by admitting that it all happened in a time which he 'do(es) not remember', a time when his parents waited 'alert against the shadowy clans'. The vagueness of the latter, the absence of a tribal name, emphasises the relative ignorance of the first generation about the people they were fighting against. The youth, on the other hand, has had an easier time of it, remembering only 'peace', 'predicted harvests' and the 'dwindling' shadows of the defeated.

In the second stanza, Stow (or his young narrator) goes into more detail, recalling a time of shepherds before fences and perhaps their interbreeding with the 'gins from the dying horde', to produce 'strangers whose names were suspect'. The narrator has been told of such things but personally remembers only 'this cool stone house …/raised … to my father's name'. Everything is so much better ordered these days, it seems. The sheep 'wait' for the shears, the 'drays depart/… with bales for the white coast' (an interesting ambiguity, since the coast is white with surf as well as with political domination). Everything occurs in its 'proper season' and the 'overnight parsons' bestow a religious aura of approval to the bargain.

The youth recognises that, unlike him, his 'father has faltered in nothing'. The parent has done what had to be done. He hears no 'sing of desert' in the 'inland wind'. It is only the speaker, he of the second generation, who feels that the skin of the land is 'alien' to him, who recognises in the desert wind 'the surge, the stirring,/a wisdom and a violence'. It is almost as if the land itself will belatedly fight back. The land (together with its first inhabitants) has both a 'wisdom' and a potential for 'violence'.

Conversely, this could be seen as contrasting with the Aborigines' 60 000 year wisdom about the land which, by violence, the Europeans took from them. Either way, the result is uneasy. He who rides 'the flat-topped hills alone' as a member of the second or subsequent generations is more than likely to feel disconcerted by the 'land's dark blood' – 'dark', of course, in the double sense of the black skin which contains the blood and the 'dark' deeds which were done to get the land in the first place. It is worth noting, however, in this context, that the speaker also has a brother who seems, like the father, to be quite untroubled by what has occurred.

Written in the mid-1960s, 'There Was a Time: The Youth' was certainly, at least a little, ahead of its time. Now, after the apology of early 2008, the poem's 'time' may be considered by some to have passed. Most Aboriginal people and their leaders are no longer calling for the unequivocal 'guilt' that Stow displays here, but the 17-year gap in life expectancy between Aboriginal and non-Aboriginal people still demonstrates that all is not well and that the unease felt by Stow, or his narrator, is (or should be) still very much with us. The 'land's … blood' is still 'dark' and we are still some distance from any substantial resolution/s to the problem.

How is it then that Stow's poem avoids the aesthetic pitfalls endemic to much political poetry and to this issue in particular? One technique, perhaps, is the combination of literal description of the West Australian pastoral landscape and the biblical resonances of phrases such as 'predicted harvests', 'proper season', 'bring forth', the 'olives and palms to my father's name' and so on. There is an ironic echo of the way the Jews in the Old Testament were 'given' the 'promised land' (see Joshua 2:9, for a start). God seems to smile down on the success of the narrator's parents; their 'sun' is 'ascending' (even if their son is troubled). 'Grain, tree and beast' are all equally fecund in their 'proper season'. The father has no misgivings; he has 'faltered in nothing'.

The metre in which all this is expressed is an appropriately irregular and attenuated iambic pentameter – with extra unstressed syllables added. Quite often we feel ourselves approaching the free verse of the King James Bible. One sees the additional syllables, for instance, in 'the *shadows dwind*ling be*neath* our a*scend*ing *sun*' or '*raised* among *ol*ives and *palms* to my *fath*er's *name*'. This slow-moving and somewhat unpredictable rhythm helps establish the mood of the poem as a whole, both in the calm self-assurance of the narrator's father (and brother) and in the more agitated questioning of the narrator. A snappier or more regular rhythm would have less gravitas – less of both the falsely based pride of the unthinking pioneer and less of the desperate seriousness shown by the poem's speaker.

Other Australian poets in the mid-1960s, under the influence of poets such as A.D. Hope and James McAuley, might have been tempted to employ the resonant rhyming pentameter quatrains so beloved of both these poets, but Stow, in 'There Was a Time: The Youth', has wisely abjured rhyme, being content with a few (almost accidental?) half-rhymes such as 'clans' and 'sun' in stanza 1 and 'seeding' and 'season' in stanza 4. Such echoing contributes to the overall, rather Old Testament-like, musical effect of the poem. It doesn't use rhyme to establish a structure of thought. In some ways, it's what Stow hasn't done more than what he has done that is important here. The poet avoids being too 'four-square' and thus allows the poem to 'spread' a little, to expand with the land itself and the size of the questions raised.

'There Was a Time: The Youth' raises and examines a classic theme in Australian poetry – and in Australian culture generally. With its Old Testament echoes it also treats the theme in a classic way. It should be no surprise then to find it in a collection of our country's classic poems – nor to find it in subsequent anthologies down the years (even if, and/or when, the plight of the 'shadowy clans' is properly addressed).

JUDITH RODRIGUEZ (1936–)

'In-flight Note'

Kitten, writes the mousy boy in his neat
fawn casuals sitting beside me on the flight,
neatly, *I can't give up everything just like that.*
Everything, how much was it? and just like what?
Did she cool it or walk out? loosen her hand from
   his tight
white-knuckled hand, or not meet him, just as he
   thought
You mean far too much to me. I can't forget
the four months we've known each other. No, he won't
   eat,
finally he pays – pale, careful, distraught –
for a beer, turns over the pad on the page he wrote
and sleeps a bit. Or dreams of his Sydney cat.
The pad cost one dollar twenty. He wakes to write
It's naive to think we could be just good friends.
Pages and pages. And so the whole world ends.

Poems such as 'In-flight Note' are a necessary reminder that the business of poetry is not always serious, that there should always be room for lightness and satire. We don't have to be mourning endlessly over elegies or relishing moments of romantic transcendence.

The somewhat malicious slyness in Judith Rodriguez' poem begins with the title. The sonnet itself is an 'In-flight Note' but so, too, is the missive being penned by the 'mousy boy'. Paradoxically, too, the 'mousy' boy is writing to his 'kitten' and is dreaming, perhaps, of his 'Sydney cat'. He's a mouse who, for all his pretentions, has met his match. His seemingly fatal colourlessness is emphasised by his 'neat/fawn casuals' as well as the faux sophistication with which he can write of the naivety of the proposal that he and his 'ex' could ever be 'just good friends'.

By line 4 we are starting to register the impatience of the poet herself. She is sceptical about just 'how much' 'everything' might have been. She doesn't approve of the boy's slack similes either ('and just like what?'). She continues to speculate, uncharitably, about exactly how the girl might have ended the relationship. 'Did she just cool it or walk out?' Rodriguez, or her narrator, imagines the somewhat pathetic possessiveness with which the boy's 'tight/white-knuckled hand' held the girl's and the expression with which she might have (must have?) spurned it. This is somehow confirmed by the apparent pathos of '*I can't forget/the four months we've known each other*' – though it feels more like bathos than pathos.

The poet then continues to observe the boy's petulant and self-absorbed behaviour as he travels beside her. He won't eat (too stressed, presumably) but he will have a beer – and is careful to look romantically 'pale, careful, distraught' as he pays for it. Unsympathetically, the poet watches him sleep for 'a bit' (and dream perhaps of his 'Sydney cat'). This incidentally implies, almost effortlessly, that the youth's disdainful 'ex' is almost certainly from Melbourne – as is, we may suspect, the poet. There seems to be a little bit of provincial rivalry here. One must concede, however, that the plane could be flying south from Brisbane, a city with which Rodriguez was once associated.

The poet notes, too, that the pad costs $1.20 – rather more in 1988 when the poem first appeared in book form than it is now, but still an unremarkable sum. It seems, somehow, to re-emphasise the relative smallness of the affair. Nevertheless, the 'mousy boy' continues ('pages and pages') unabashed – thus offering the poet the opportunity for one final wisecrack at her fellow traveller's expense: 'And so the whole world ends.' It may have ended, she suggests, for this self-dramatising, self-deceiving boy – but for the rest of us it just keeps right on going. The sardonic observation is further reinforced by the realisation, or at least the implication, that in a few weeks the 'mousy boy', too, will have forgotten his 'kitten' and be no longer 'pale, careful, distraught'.

Of course, Rodriguez risks offending her readers, most of whom will remember that 'young love' is serious stuff and not to be joked about. On the other hand, we have no difficulty in accepting the poet's version of events; the boy does seem to 'deserve' everything he gets, not only from his 'ex' but from the poet and from us readers too. Anyone who can write so naively about naivety seems to deserve whatever ill-fate overtakes him.

This perception is further intensified by the cleverness with which the poet has composed her sonnet (a form itself associated with love since the beginning). Rodriguez ends with the neat couplet we expect in Elizabethan sonnets but she rhymes and half-rhymes rather freely on her way to that point – ignoring, too, as she goes the mandatory turn or *volta* at the end of line 8. The fact that 12 of the poem's 14 lines all end with a 't' sound seems only to reinforce the bathos of the protagonist's self-absorption. It's as if he can't break out of his own rhyme scheme (or the one the poet has unkindly imposed on him).

The rhythm, too, has a resolute refusal to meet the strictures of the pattern underlying it. This is not a bad thing, however. Rhythmically speaking, there are almost no regular lines and it's no accident that the final one is pretty much as close as we get to the normal iambic pentameter ('*Pages* and *pages*. And *so* the *whole* world *ends.*') Such a delayed predictability reinforces the pseudo-bathos of the whole situation. Of course this isn't the end of the 'whole world'! How could anyone ever have thought so, implies the poet – unkindly.

It is through all these sorts of devices then that the poet has persuaded us to connive at her ungenerous view of the 'mousy boy'. She leaves us no room to escape. Luckily, the poet doesn't say anything to the boy himself so we don't have to be cowardly witnesses to a bullying, even though we do seem to have observed (with the poet) something vaguely humiliating going on, even if it is self-inflicted. Fortunately, as indicated earlier, poetry does not always have to be about spiritual uplift. There are many other rewards, some of them more than a little unworthy perhaps.

'The Mitchells'

I am seeing this: two men are sitting on a pole
they have dug a hole for and will, after dinner, raise
I think for wires. Water boils in a prune tin.
Bees hum their shift in unthinning mists of white

bursaria blossom, under the noon of wattles.
The men eat big meat sandwiches out of a
    styrofoam
box with a handle. One is overheard saying:
drought that year. Yes. Like trying to farm the road.

The first man, if asked, would say *I'm one of the*
    Mitchells.
The other would gaze for a while, dried leaves in
    his palm,
and looking up, with pain and subtle amusement,

say *I'm one of the Mitchells.* Of the pair, one has been
    rich
but never stopped wearing his oil-stained felt hat.
    Nearly everything
they say is ritual. Sometimes the scene is an avenue.

Les Murray's 'The Mitchells' is a masterpiece of the laconic. It is about a particular Australian style, originating in the bush but also to be found in the city (though perhaps less often now than when the poem was first published in the mid-1970s). Murray is famous for having asserted that the only class is those who speak of class and this poem is a perfect illustration of his argument.

Of the two Mitchells, one has been rich but 'never stopped wearing his oil-stained felt hat'. The other, by implication, is and has been poor. They are both working uncomplainingly at this manual but reasonably skilled task – and neither of them makes any fuss about which one of them has been rich. It is irrelevant (though pleasant enough at the time, presumably). One of them declares '*I'm one of the Mitchells*', but so does the other one, 'looking up, with pain and subtle amusement'. The pain would seem to be at his having been asked at all, rather than from any recall of a past differential – which generates only 'subtle amusement' anyway.

The poem, however, is no mere piece of sociologising. Murray has closely observed the men's behaviour (and the values it implies) – and then proceeds to render it exactly. Their 'dinner' is, in fact, what most of us now call 'lunch'. They boil water in a 'prune tin', not because they can't afford an aluminium billy, but because a prune tin is good enough for the job so why waste money? They eat 'big meat sandwiches' rather than, say, delicate cucumber or asparagus ones. And they have kept them cool in a 'styrofoam/box with a handle' – not an 'Esky' as a reviewer once berated Murray for not saying.

Right throughout, Murray resists any temptation to simplify his protagonists. The 'prune tin' could have been a 'billy', much loved by the balladists. The 'Yes' in line 8 would have been, in most other hands, a self-consciously ocker 'yeah'. Murray observes, truthfully enough, that 'Nearly everything/they say is ritual', but note that it is only 'nearly' and not 'everything'. They are also capable of quoting, if not themselves inventing, a forcefully poetic phrase: '*Like trying to farm the road.*' This is the sort of vernacular poetry to which men like the Mitchells can effortlessly rise. These are people of some sophistication, capable of 'subtle amusement' and able to appreciate a 'noon of wattles' and the 'unthinning mists of white//bursaria blossom', even though they are unlikely to use such language to describe them. This sort of beauty, for them, would normally remain unspoken but would be no less appreciated for that. Some might think Murray is just showing off his lyrical talent but the 'unthinning mists of white//bursaria blossom' have, one could argue, a much deeper and more generous purpose.

Murray neatly avoids any sense of his simply barracking for his 'home team' (what some would call the 'rural working class') by leaving us with the reminder that 'Sometimes the scene is an avenue'. In other words, the Australian laconic is not only to be found in the country, where it almost certainly originated, but also in the cities where most Australians live. The 'avenue' phrase works well, too, as a framing device. The poem begins with 'I am seeing this' and ends with the assertion that the scene can be replicated throughout the whole nation. A measure of just how Australian this poem is can be seen by trying to re-imagine it written by an English or American poet. Indeed, there is a great William Carlos Williams poem about two workers having lunch called 'Fine Work with Pitch and Copper', but it is nothing at all like Murray's.

It is perhaps another mark of Murray's respect for the Mitchells that he has taken the trouble to write their poem so well. This is not just a passing photograph to illustrate some sociological theory. It is a well-constructed, well-finished artefact, in much the same way as the pole the two men are about to raise will be well cut and solidly placed.

For a start, Murray has written his account of the Mitchells as a sonnet, a form which has an 800-year-old history. It uses the Petrarchan stanza arrangement of two stanzas of four lines followed by two stanzas of three lines – though it doesn't have the rhyme scheme normally associated with the convention. It does, however, have quite a deal of rhyme, if we extend our definition of rhyme to include half-rhyme and assonance. In the first stanza, for instance, where there seems to be no rhyme at all, we have the important internal rhyme of 'pole' and 'hole', plus a whole run of assonances, beginning with 'dinner' in the second line and culminating in the phrase 'shift in unthinning mists'. In the second stanza we have the end half-rhymes 'foam' and 'road' and then the half-rhymes that link the last lines of the second-last and final stanzas 'amusement'/ avenue'. An even more relevant example is the assonance in the two key words 'rich' and 'ritual' that leaps across a distance of two lines. The rhyme is there but it's part of the texture, part of the argument, rather than being something we can count off as *aabb* and so on.

Something similar can be said for the poem's rhythm, too. Murray's sense of rhythm is certainly idiosyncratic but no less real for that. In a sonnet, of course, we expect the iambic pentameter, but Murray rarely, if ever, gives us that satisfaction. The second line, for instance, has 13 rather than ten syllables, but we can still sense the pentameter's five stresses in it: 'they have *dug* a *hole* for and *will*, after *dinn*er, *raise*'. The same use of unstressed syllables can be seen in the line '(and) *look*/(ing) *up*/, (with) *pain*/(and) *subt*/(le) (a)*muse*(ment)' – though one could see the first four feet as being purely iambic, of course. One might also argue that, despite the highly poetic nature of his 'bursaria blossom' image, Murray is producing his own version of the Mitchell's vernacular where an irregular number of unstressed syllables serves to emphasise the stress when it comes, rather in the manner of the irregular four-stress lines in the Anglo-Saxon tradition from which poetry in English derives.

Because it was written only 30 years ago, it may be premature to call 'The Mitchells' a 'classic', but it is surely unlikely that anyone will ever better define and illustrate the essence of at least one important Australian style: the laconic. Paradoxically, one can't imagine the Mitchells making such a large claim for themselves, though. They just go on yarning and slowly eating their lunch (sorry, 'dinner').

J.S. HARRY (1939–)

'Mousepoem'

Her lover departed
to the warm purry
bed of his wife,
with pale blue hands
in the cold dawnlight
she has written a poem so slight
she thinks if a mouse breathed on it,
it would collapse (the
poem, not
    the mouse which is made
of tough, mouse material, whiskers, ears,
small, quick, risk-assessing eyes; the poem
is so light it seems to float, not stand;
the mouse … stands on firm mouse-muscles
& potato-crispy, cat-delighting
bones.) Who would ever think of fucking
a mouse, but its lover? Who would ever
want to be fucked by a mouse but another?
Who would wish for blind, hairless
mouse-children, but a mousy mother?
Does a mouse wish
or are children merely what happens to it
wishless but wanting?
Time: is a moment
a mouse at rest? Pick it up? You cannot.
Relativity (by neither Newton's nor Einstein's
mechanics): when a human moves
a live mouse refuses arrest.

Even a blind mouse
will feel the great weight
of a malnutritioned
skinny human
& dart for the soot-stinky hole
behind a dead fire's
cold grate.

What has her slight poem
to do with a dead fire?
                    Ah ...

First collected in her *Selected Poems* (1995), J.S. Harry's 'Mouse-poem' is a fine, if not definitive example of free verse and free association. It moves from the woman to the mouse and back again as easily as an unmanned vessel drifting with the wind. There is no frame of rhyme, metre or deductive logic to restrain its movement. The poem is entirely a product of the subjectivity of the poet. Or this, at least, is the impression given.

Harry starts with a well-used and perhaps ironic trope. The 'lover' is 'departed', a phrase with echoes going at least as far back as the English love poetry of the fifteenth century. This particular lover, however, has 'departed' 'to the warm purry/bed of his wife' – and the adjective 'purry' is more than a little significant in terms of the mouse soon to be mentioned and speculated about. The woman's response to her lover's departure is to write, with her 'pale blue hands', an extraordinarily slight and frail poem, reflecting, no doubt, her own fragile state while thinking on her lover back in bed with his 'purry' wife.

At this point the mouse, which has previously been just a synonym for smallness and lightness, abruptly takes on a life of its own. Unlike the woman's frail poem, the mouse is made of 'tough, mouse material' and has 'risk-assessing' eyes (in contrast perhaps to the woman herself, caught in her one-sided relationship). The poet (mouselike?) then makes another subjective leap and contemplates the mouse from the cat's point of view, the vulnerability of its 'potato-crispy, cat-delighting/bones'. There is probably another parallel here, too, with the vulnerability of the 'malnutritioned/skinny human' who, unintentionally, will frighten the mouse into its hole later in the poem.

We are now in the mind of the woman thinking of the mouse but also thinking about herself. 'Who would ever think of fucking/a mouse, but its lover?' She seems to imagine herself in the position of a 'mousy mother'. Does a female mouse (like the human female perhaps) 'wish' for children or are they 'merely what happens to it'? The woman has an impulse to pick up the mouse, to look at it more closely, but immediately realises such a thing is impossible – 'a live mouse refuses arrest'. Indeed, at this point she realises that her very presence is a 'weight' which, if she moves, will send the mouse scuttling for its 'soot-stinky hole'.

And now, again, there is a subjective leap. The woman is looking at the mouse's hole in the 'dead fire's/cold grate'. The poem curls back again, almost to its beginning; that is, that 'slight' poem she wrote after the 'dawnlight' departure of her lover. How then did she get from there to this 'dead fire'? We are not told but we may surmise that the relationship with her lover is a 'dead fire' or likely to become one very soon. The lover is back (and breeding?) with his 'purry' wife. There will be no 'blind, hairless/mouse-children' for the woman who has written the slight poem – nor any human ones either, it would seem. It is all these circumstances – and perhaps more – which give such force to the poem's final 'Ah …'.

Some insensitive critics have sometimes accused well-written free verse, such as we see in 'Mousepoem', of being merely 'chopped prose'. While many bad free-verse poets do lack a sense of lineation, J.S. Harry shows herself a master of it. We can see it in the first two lines. She starts with a virtual cliché ('Her lover departed') but in the second line she is already surprising us by ending it at 'purry' – before we go on to find in the third line that the word is describing the 'bed of his wife'. We observe the same process, taken (riskily perhaps) a step further, in line 8 when Harry finishes with '(the'.

This strange truncation sets up the witty contrast about to be made between the frailty of the woman's poem and the relative toughness of the mouse with its 'risk-assessing eyes'. We could even make a similar point about the space left between 'Time' and 'is a moment' further on in the poem. The space here suggests the tentativeness of the woman's mind, as it moves this way and that through the poem. Our minds rarely work by linear and deductive processes. Harry's lineation and spacing reflect this.

Similarly, at a technical level, with its lines of unpredictable length, its occasional naivety of diction ('purry', 'soot-stinky' and so on) and its wayward syntax, 'Mousepoem' may be seen to share the vulnerability of the woman with the 'pale blue hands' – and of the mouse who has to dart for its 'soot-stinky hole' when the need arises. Despite the use of a four-letter word, the poem has something of a children's book feeling to it – the 'blind' mouse children (with their nursery rhyme echoes), the 'slight' poem, the implied cat and so on. Of course, it's a *faux-naiveté* but the feeling of vulnerability is very much there, nevertheless.

'Mousepoem', then, is a fine example of how delicately and obliquely a poem may register human emotions. It's an almost infinitely sensitive seismograph, picking up the most subtle of emotions and presenting them for our sympathy. There will not be many readers who do not at least know something of what that final 'Ah …' means. Conversely, however, there would be very few who could say *exactly* what it does mean. Most of us will be satisfied simply to go back and read the poem again, right through to that culminating 'Ah …'.

CLIVE JAMES (1939–)

'In Town for the March'

Today in Castlereagh Street I
Felt short of breath, and here is why.
From the direction of the Quay
Towards where Mark Foys used to be,
A glass and metal river ran
Made in Germany and Japan.
Past the facade of David Jones
Men walked their mobile telephones,
Making the footpath hideous
With what they needed to discuss.
But why so long, and why so loud?
I can recall a bigger crowd
In which nobody fought for space
Except to call a name. The face
To fit it smiled as it went by
Among the ranks. Women would cry
Who knew that should they call all day
One face would never look their way.
All this was sixty years ago,
Since when I have grown old and slow,
But still I see the marching men,
So many of them still young then,
Even the men from the first war
Straight as a piece of two-by-four.
Men of the Anzac Day parade,
I grew up in the world you made.
To mock it would be my mistake.
I try to love it for your sake.

Through cars and buses, on they come,
Their pace set by a spectral drum.
Their regimental banners, thin
As watercolours fading in
The sun, hint at a panoply
Dissolving into history.
As the rearguard outflanks Hyde Park,
Wheels right, and melts into the dark,
It leaves me, barely fit to stand,
Reaching up for my mother's hand.

Because of his expatriate status – and his extreme versatility in the worlds of literature and show business – the purely poetic talents of London-based Clive James have often been overlooked or underestimated here in Australia. James' predilection for traditional forms and his satirical impulses may have exacerbated the situation. It is not often noticed that exile, of one kind or another, is frequently the condition of Australian poets generally. Several of the best known were born in the country but live (or lived) in our major cities; a few have reversed the process. Some have moved from one capital to another. Others, like Les Murray in Bunyah, have returned to their birthplace only after decades away. There is no reason that being an exile in London should disqualify a poet from being considered Australian or prevent him or her from commenting on what occurs here.

In Clive James' 'In Town for the March' we can sense, in fact, a double exile. The poet returns to Sydney after many years away only to find that the immediate post-World War 2 world he grew up in has 'dissolv(ed) into history' like 'watercolours fading in/ The sun'. He remembers where 'Mark Foys used to be' and notes, with irony, that the shops on the street are now constructed from (and stocked with) items manufactured in the countries we once played a role in defeating. Fortunately, the poet's irritation with this irony is minor compared to the anger he feels against the loud and lengthy discussions on mobile phones all about him.

At this point, James flashes back to the Anzac Day marches he saw as a boy just after the war in which his father had been killed, leaving James' mother a widow. These facts are only implied in the poem but we have them from James' memoirs. While he now describes himself as being 'old and slow', it is only this that permits him to have witnessed the veterans of the 'first war' when they were still 'Straight as a piece of two-by-four'. He then goes on to express an ambivalence felt by many of his generation, the sense that the world those soldiers saved for us was not as uncomplicatedly great as certain patriots would have us believe (James himself, for instance, felt compelled to flee its restrictions). Even so he is proud to say: 'I try to love it for your sake.'

The poet then moves on to superimpose his own memories of those early marches on what is now a 'glass and metal river' with its 'cars and buses' and 'hideous … mobile telephones'. It is this 'spectral' march which embodies the memory of those earlier marches where women such as the poet's mother '… knew that should they call all day/One face would never look their way'. This reference, halfway through the poem, sets up the reader for the intensity of the desolation felt by the mother (and the small boy's less-than-fully comprehending version of it) in the last two lines of the poem. Again there is a double irony here – and a simultaneity. The intervening years have made the poet 'old and slow' – but it is not they that leave him 'barely fit to stand'.

In some ways, the shock of the poem's ending may be even stronger if the reader doesn't know these biographical facts. James has alluded halfway through to those women who should have been able to call out but no longer have anyone to call to. Then, at the end, we understand that the narrator's own mother is in this situation – which, in turn, gives us a deeper insight into why the poet should remember these marches from the Quay to Hyde Park with such intensity. We may also surmise that the little boy is trying to comfort his mother as much as he is seeking to be comforted by her.

Such serious and sincere emotion may seem a long way from the satirical badinage that James is generally better known for. It does, however, have traces of that other tone – and is all the more effective for having them. One can see it right at the beginning with the playful enjambement at the end of the first line and the slight sense of a forced rhyme between 'I' and 'here is why'. This has a childlike naivety that foreshadows the image at the end of the poem. We notice, too, that the whole work is written in iambic tetrameter couplets, a form frequently employed by poets such as Jonathan Swift for satirical or humorous purposes. James likewise uses it for a few wry jokes along the way – for instance in the way the street 'ran' with things made in 'Germany and Japan'. A comparably humorous note is struck when we're forced to pronounce 'hideous' as 'hid-ee-us' to rhyme with 'discuss' in the next line.

Of course, there is much that is serious throughout the poem (most notably the women who do not see a face... to 'look their way'). There are lines, too, which are both humorous and serious simultaneously. When James recalls those soldiers from the 'first war' who were still, in the late 1940s, 'Straight as a piece of two-by-four', he is at once demonstrating an understandable and prevailing national pride and showing off his memory for bits of iconic Australiana. We, the readers, tend to smile slightly – even though most of us share his pride to some degree or other.

It must be remembered, however, that the iambic tetrameter couplet form has not always been used for humorous purposes. Another London expatriate, Peter Porter, used it in a very moving tribute to his first wife (who died by committing suicide). Porter, in turn, took the form from the seventeenth-century poet, Henry King, who used it in 'The Exequy', an elegy for his own wife. James, who has demonstrated the impressive breadth of his reading in various radio programs, could not but be aware of these precedents and the challenges they pose. Like his predecessors, James has also realised the potential for poignancy in this apparently over-simple form. It's as if the convention itself, in all its simplicity, dramatises our human inadequacy when dealing with deeply felt grief. It also, of course, allows the poet to make a few humorous or self-deprecatory asides – which, in turn, only intensify the overall feeling of desolation. Peter Porter for instance, in his poem, recalls: 'I think of us in Italy;/gin-and-chianti- fuelled we …' James gets something of the same effect with his jibes at the mobile telephone users and the slightly humorous self-pity of 'Since when I have grown old and slow'.

Ultimately, however, whatever its form, 'In Town for the March' is a profoundly serious poem – and one very close to something deep in the Australian psyche. We don't like to carry on about such things too much (indeed, we can often make wry jokes about them), but there is still something about those 'regimental banners … fading in/The sun' which we can't easily escape. The image, too, of the post-war widow holding her little son's hand (and being comforted by him in turn) is something we're most unlikely to forget – especially when it is evoked in poetry as clever and as heart-felt as 'In Town for the March'.

GEOFFREY LEHMANN (1940–)

'Parenthood'

I have held what I hoped would become the best
    minds of a generation
Over the gutter outside an Italian coffee shop
    watching the small
Warm urine splatter on the asphalt – impatient to
    rejoin
An almond torta and a cappuccino at a formica
    table.
I have been a single parent with three children at a
    Chinese restaurant
The eldest five years old and each in turn
    demanding
My company as they fussed in toilets and my pork
    saté went cold.
They rarely went all at once; each child required an
    individual
Moment of inspiration – and when their toilet
    pilgrimage was ended
I have tried to eat the remnants of my meal with
    twisting children
Beneath the table, screaming and grabbing in a
    scrimmage.
I have been wiping clean the fold between young
    buttocks as a pizza
I hoped to finish was cleared from a red and white
    checked table cloth.
I have been pouring wine for women I was hoping
    to impress

When a daughter ran for help through guests
    urgently holding out
Her gift, a potty, which I took with the same
    courtesy
As she gave it, grateful to dispose of its contents so
    simply
In a flurry of water released by the pushing of a
    button.
I have been butted by heads which have told me to
    go away and I have done so,
My mouth has been wrenched by small hands
    wanting to reach down to my tonsils
As I lay in bed on Sunday mornings and the sun
    shone through the slats
Of dusty blinds. I have helpfully carried dilly-
    dalliers up steps
Who indignantly ran straight down and walked up
    by themselves.
My arms have become exhausted, bouncing young
    animals until they fell asleep
In my lap listening to Buxtehude. 'Too cold,' I have
    been told,
As I handed a piece of fruit from the refrigerator,
    and for weeks had to warm
Refrigerated apples in the microwave so milk teeth
    cutting green
Carbohydrate did not chill. I have pleasurably
    smacked small bottoms
Which have climbed up and arched themselves on
    my lap wanting the report
And tingle of my palm. I have known large round
    heads that bumped

And rubbed themselves against my forehead, and
    affectionate noses
That loved to displace inconvenient snot from
    themselves onto me.
The demands of their bodies have taken me to
    unfamiliar geographies.
I have explored the white tiles and stainless steel
    benches of restaurant kitchens
And guided short legs across rinsed floors smelling
    of detergent
Past men in white with heads lowered and cleavers
    dissecting and assembling
Mounds of sparkling pink flesh – and located the
    remote dark shrine
Of a toilet behind boxes of coarse green vegetables
    and long white radishes.
I have badgered half-asleep children along
    backstreets at night, carrying
Whom I could to my van. I have stumbled with
    them sleeping in my arms
Up concrete steps on winter nights after eating in
    Greek restaurants,
Counting each body, then slamming the door of my
    van and taking
My own body, the last of my tasks, to a cold bed
    free of arguments.
I have lived in the extreme latitudes of child rearing,
    the blizzard
Of the temper tantrum and my own not always wise
    or honourable response,
The midnight sun of the child calling for attention
    late at night,

And have longed for the white courtyards and
    mediterranean calm of middle age.
Now these small bodies are becoming civilised
    people claiming they are not
Ashamed of a parent's overgrown garden and
    unpainted ceilings
Which a new arrival, with an infant's forthrightness,
    complains are 'old'.
And the father of this tribe sleeps in a bed which is
    warm with arguments.
Their bones elongate and put on weight and they
    draw away into space.
Their faces lengthen with responsibility and their
    own concerns.
I could clutch as they recede and fret for the push
    of miniature persons.
And claim them as children of my flesh – but my
    own body is where I must live.

Geoffrey Lehmann's poem, 'Parenthood', is a good example of how flexible the canon can be. The great poems in English are supposed to be serious, iambic pentameter pieces about Nature or God – or things comparably transcendent. We are not so used to humorous, albeit serious, poems about the sometimes gross details of child rearing. Such things are normally left to newspaper columnists, but poet Geoffrey Lehmann demonstrates just how memorable an account of such activities can be in the hands of a genuine artist.

Another reminder of the canon's flexibility is provided by the poem's opening allusion to Allen Ginsberg's famous poem, 'Howl': 'I have seen the best minds of my generation destroyed by madness, starving hysterical naked …' This cues us in immediately to the fact that 'Parenthood' is not going to be 'that' kind of poem. Rather it's going to be (merely?) about the troubles of enforced single-parent-hood and the 'extreme latitudes of child rearing'. Lehmann hopes his children will 'become the best minds of a generation' but we are not to take this too seriously. Note, too, the contrast between Gins-berg's 'my' generation and Lehmann's much milder 'a' generation. It is as though the latter is warning us to be cautious of histrionics and find instead the poetry of everyday hardship and small rewards.

Significantly, Lehmann (like Ginsberg) uses Walt Whitman's famous long-lined free verse. Ginsberg uses it as a direct *homage* to a mentor, but Lehmann uses the same device no less movingly. He realises that this kind of free verse is the perfect medium for the repetitious, 'rolling with the punches' dimension of child rearing. A neat, Gwen Harwood-like sonnet would not be adequate to his purposes (no matter how well done elsewhere). Lehmann needs a long, rolling, infinitely inclusive line that can accommodate all the telling detail he has in mind to deliver. This doesn't mean that the poem is without form. It does, clearly, have a narrative structure leading to the moment when their 'faces lengthen with respon-sibility and their own concerns' and the poet realises that it is in 'my own body … where I must live'. It also has a considerable formal cleverness on a line-to-line basis. Lehmann does not use the Whitmanesque (or ancient Hebraic) device of parallelism in a simple, repetitive and unvaried way. Not every line begins with 'I have'. Sometimes the 'I have' starts a new sentence in the middle of a line. Other lines start with a different phrase altogether. There is also, too, a sense of the unexpected in the lineation, where the poet cuts suddenly to the beginning of a new line for emphasis, as in the 'small/Warm urine …' of lines 2 and 3 or the 'individual/Moment of inspiration' a little later on.

Similarly, Lehmann's 'free verse' is not necessarily as 'free' as it looks. Take the opening phrase: 'I have *held*/what I *hoped*/would be*come* …' It's not hard to sense the anapaestic rhythm here – even though it quickly changes to something less regular in the rest of the line. In this part we have a kind of roving emphasis with the stress coming down irregularly but hard on the meaning's three key syllables: '*best*', '*minds*' and '*gen*'. 'Parenthood' is also a reminder not only of the effectiveness of metaphor ('the remote dark shrine/Of a toilet'; the 'mediterranean calm of middle age'), but also of well-chosen, closely observed detail ('the small/Warm urine splatter'; 'short legs across rinsed floors smelling of detergent'). Although the poem goes back to Whitman via Ginsberg, it also owes quite a deal to American 'Objectivists' like William Carlos Williams who were probably the first to realise just how effective plain, non-metaphorical details can be.

We are used (generally rightly) to thinking of poetry as something compressed, where the maximum content is to be fitted into the minimum space. As Whitman, Ginsberg and many others realised, this need not always be the case. Over the millennia the writers of epics have always used images and little cameos of remarkable observation, but they were also careful to locate these within an ongoing rhetoric that established the tone of the work as a whole. Many parts of the Old Testament are classic examples of this strategy. Lehmann uses the technique ironically but no less successfully. He often employs circumlocutions rather than naming his object directly. Instead of writing something direct like 'just grateful to flush it away' Lehmann prefers: 'grateful to dispose of its contents so simply/In a flurry of water released by the pushing of a button'. This fits in with the mock-heroic tone of the whole poem (which, though self-effacing, does evoke the unsought heroism in being a single parent – or any sort of parent, for that matter).

A related dimension to this is the poem's undoubted sense of authenticity. We feel these details are extracted from the poet's own life, even if one or two of them could be anecdotes from friends in similar situations. It's not merely a matter of the first person viewpoint; it's a willingness to embrace the experience as a whole and his own role in it. It's also his readiness to admit to his own 'not always wise or honourable response' to his kids' tantrums – and the discretion with which he reveals that he now 'sleeps in a bed which is warm with arguments' as opposed to the minimal comfort of an earlier 'cold bed free of arguments'. The poem thus reminds us how much good poetry comes from life as it is actually lived and not just from speculations about its larger implications. This is 'confessional' poetry at its most convincing, where the particularity of detail takes on almost universal meaning, even for those who have not (or not yet) been parents – or those now reflecting on their own parents' experience.

It's significant, too, that Lehmann chooses to call the poem 'Parenthood' rather than 'Fatherhood', as he might well have done given the circumstances. In our society the situation he describes is more commonly borne by the mother. Seeing it through the eyes of the father seems to lend the experience an extra, less predictable perspective. It is just one more thing that helps to give the poem such wide applicability that it is difficult to imagine any reader remaining unmoved by it.

KATE LLEWELLYN (1940–)

'To a Married Man'

While you look for your underpants
I think about the alternatives
when affairs like ours
are breaking up
you can talk all you like
but it's theory honey theory
it's like listening to the wireless
I long to turn you off and go
and know it's ta–ta time

I'm tired of hearing what a saint
you married
listen pal
if everything's so great in Denmark
what's a tart like me doing there?

don't panic
she won't kick you out
a quick weekend at the Victor pub
two brandies after lunch
and up the stairs
all's forgiven in an hour
you'll drive her home on Monday
talking of retirement trips
and what a naughty boy you've been
and for several months
till you find someone else
you'll be home on time

Kate Llewellyn is best known as a non-fiction writer, but it is as a poet that she first emerged. 'To a Married Man' is from her first book, *Trader Kate and the Elephants* (1982). The poem has worn well over its more than 25 years now and remains a fine example of what can be done with free verse – and with the female colloquial voice in a certain register.

'To a Married Man' appears to tread a fine line between the confessional poem and the dramatic monologue. We surmise that the poem is based on personal experience but we also sense that it is speaking for a category, that it is more universal in its application. The predicament of the unmarried mistress whose lover persists in going home to his wife is not an uncommon one – though on careful scrutiny we see there is no proof in the poem itself that the speaker herself is unmarried. We sense this more in the tone than in any explicit statement. If she had a husband of her own to return to she mightn't be so upset. There's no doubt, however, that the uncertainty about whether the poem is a monologue or a confession helps give the poem an extra edge.

There are many other dimensions of the poem which are no less arresting, however. One, of course, is is the flagrant opening line about the lover haplessly looking for his underpants. This suggests that the sexual encounter has been rapid, even reckless, that they've hurried up the stairs and so on. It also sets the poem's highly critical tone. Is the lover too dumb to find his underpants? We have a nice sense of anger from the very first line.

By the poem's second line the mistress is already thinking of 'alternatives'. She's had enough and realises, incidentally, that she is far from unique in her situation (indeed the penultimate line makes clear she thinks he'll have another woman like her within a few months). The future affair, it seems, will also be 'like ours', a reference that helps give the poem its universality. Her impatience nevertheless continues. Absorbing his fatuous explanations is 'like listening to the wireless', the sort of radio which is left on in the background just below audibility. It's time for practice now, not 'theory'. The woman's impatience is further reinforced by her use of the babyish phrase 'ta-ta time' at the end of the stanza. There will be no long, languorous kisses in this farewell, it seems.

In the second stanza, the speaker objects to her lover's interminable praising of his (absent) wife – the 'saint' he married – and offers instead an allusion to *Hamlet*. The Denmark of her lover's marriage is almost certainly more 'rotten' than 'great', as he insists. We then get the speaker's description of herself as a 'tart'. We see how her self-esteem has been damaged. Instead of being the glamorous mistress she initially considered herself to be, she's now scaled herself back to the dismissive, four-letter monosyllable 'tart' – with all its negative associations of easy virtue, empty-headedness and so on. If we didn't catch the anger in the first stanza we certainly have by the end of the second.

The third stanza fast-forwards the story from the present into the future. The mistress predicts that the lover's wife will not throw him out as he probably deserves. All will be 'forgiven in an hour' if he plays his cards right. The mistress's previous experience has acquainted her with the techniques necessary. It will involve a 'quick weekend' at a seaside resort renowned for the purpose (the 'Victor pub' being in Victor Harbour, not too far from Adelaide), the judicious application of alcohol and a few slick promises on the way home afterwards. It's interesting that the 'sisterhood' is not so very powerful here. The narrator thinks of herself as a 'tart' but the woman she's temporarily supplanted is no brighter if she's to be won over so readily. The reference to 'naughty boy', like the 'ta-ta time' earlier, emphasises a lack of maturity all round, especially on the part of the lover who is serially unreliable.

Despite all this, however, the final stanza is a considerable 'flea in the ear' for the lover to be going away with. He probably hoped, naively, the affair would peter out amicably. Instead he has this contemptuous forecast about how easily his wife will be won back, together with its implication of how stupid she is to be seduced by 'two brandies after lunch' and a quick run 'up the stairs'. The poem doesn't provide the ending he might have wished for, but it's a small punishment nevertheless – though only temporary, it would seem.

Technically, for a conservative reader, 'To a Married Man' might look like the proverbial 'chopped prose' so despised by those who characterise any free verse in this way. They would be even more put off by the poem's lack of punctuation, a device that can be traced back at least to Guillaume Apollinaire's *Alcools* in 1912. Such readers would be wrong on both points.

The rhythm in 'To a Married Man' has the flexibility that one would expect in such a colloquial poem. We can see this in the juxtaposition of the almost straight iambic metre in 'if *everything*'s so *great* in *Den*mark' with the rhythmic violence in 'what's a *tart* like *me do*ing there?'. As with most free verse there are many lines (or parts of lines) which are purely iambic. It's not really as free as it looks – but it is free enough for what it needs to do. Llewellyn, along with Ezra Pound, clearly regards the line as a 'unit of sense' and it is this that justifies such short lines as 'you married' and 'listen pal'. Some inferior users of free verse lineate almost at random; Llewellyn knows what she's doing.

A similar rationale underpins what some would regard as an irritating lack of punctuation. The line endings serve as punctuation in themselves. We don't really need the marks to be spelt out. The reader, admittedly, is forced to do a little more work than usual, but there's no great harm in that. Sometimes there can also be interesting ambiguities, both of whose possible meanings may be true. In the first stanza, for instance, the opening sentence could end after 'up' in 'breaking up' but there could also have been a new sentence starting at 'when' and going through to 'theory'. The speaker is in no mood for fine distinctions of syntax and this shows through in her punctuation (or lack thereof).

A few readers may be reluctant to concede 'classic' status to such a short, seemingly simple poem but, as I hope I've demonstrated, this simplicity is illusory. The emotions in the poem are strong (even if negative); the psychology is as complex as the situation requires; the rhythm is necessarily flexible yet easily within reach of iambic expectations – and the imagery graphic (we don't easily forget the lost underpants, the tart in Denmark and so on). 'To a Married Man' is a poem which has already transcended its time and is likely to continue to do so.

JAN OWEN (1940–)

'Young Woman Gathering Lemons'

The apronful sits on the swell of her belly,
that taut new world she merely borders now.
Above, a hundred pale suns glow;
she reaches for one more and snags her hair.
Citron, amber, white, a touch of lime;
the rind of colour cools her palm.
Extra tubes and brushes she would need –
a three in sable or a two
should catch the gleam around each pore.
Such yellow! If there were only time.
She presses to her face
its fine sharp scent of loss
then sinks her forehead onto her wrist
– the tears drop off her chin –
till the child tugs at her dress.
She kneels to hug him close and breathe him in:
'Who's got a silly old mother, then?'
It dizzies her, the fragrance of his skin.
He nuzzles under the hair come loose.
The fallen lemons, nippled gold,
wait round them in the grass.

Jan Owen's 'Young Woman Gathering Lemons' deals with an issue many poets and many readers will feel close to: how do we divide our lives between our own projects and those other responsibilities that seem to get in their way? For most poets today this will be a conflict between their full- or part-time job and the vocation they are irresistibly drawn to. Even more intense, for many women poets in particular, is the conflict between the loving demands of their young children and the strict demands of their art.

Jan Owen, in this poem, takes one step away from the autobiographical by making her protagonist a painter rather than a poet, but the point is clear nevertheless. What makes the poem especially poignant is the exact balance in which she holds these two contradictory impulses. The woman can see the painting she wants to make almost as if it is finished already, but she is also just as happy, even through tears, to hug her little son 'close and breathe him in'. She can envisage the exact colours she needs, even the brush size, but a mere 'tug ... at her dress' can draw her away from it – even as, ironically, in the last two lines, the painting (which now includes the two of them), is suddenly complete anyway: 'The fallen lemons, nippled gold,/wait round them in the grass.'

Another related irony is that the poem is written in the tradition of ekphrasis, where the poet describes an already-existing work of art and tries to reach, or even re-embody, its 'essence'. The title, 'Young Woman Gathering Lemons', is very much a painter's title and the poem, with its evocative image of the young woman and child under the lemon tree with all its greens and yellows, is, of course, the equivalent of the picture the woman would paint if she were free to do so. The poet, who understands such pressures only too well, has created the work herself and put (perhaps sardonically) the frustrated mother/artist in it.

A closer, line-by-line look at the poem reveals the verbal artistry with which Owen does this. We start right in with an image of plenty: 'The apronful sits on the swell of her belly.' The woman is pregnant with a subsequent child and her ambition to paint will soon be that much further beyond a possibility. Conversely, though, the rhythm of the line, with its roughly anapaestic lilt, indicates that she is not too unhappy about this really. 'The *ap*/ronful *sits*/on the *swell*/of her *belly*.' The gathered lemons comprise a 'taut new world' that she is now only dreamily on the edge of. In the tree there are 'a hundred pale suns'; she sees them with an artist's eye and is immediately calculating the relevant tubes of paint – the brushes, too. And she is doing this, even while she is disconcerted by her hair being caught in the branches (symbolic, perhaps, of how she is irretrievably entangled in her situation). Later her son ('sun'?) will be nuzzling in under that same hair.

Soon the 'sharp scent of loss', however, has her in tears – which, of course, the child can sense and so 'tugs at her dress' for reassurance. She kneels down to him and gives him, without resentment – in fact, with joy – all the attention he is demanding. 'Who's got a silly old mother, then?' And we remember, ironically again, the 'Young Woman' in the title.

The poem ends in an epiphany. The mother is dizzied by 'the fragrance of his skin' and the son also has a moment of pure pleasure 'nuzzl(ing) under the hair come loose'. The fallen lemons, 'nippled' like the breasts she has earlier fed him with (and with which she'll soon be feeding the new child), are symbolically lying all 'round them in the grass' (in a painterly *nature morte* perhaps). We notice, too, that they 'wait' rather than just lie there – in parallel, it would seem, to the waiting our artist/mother will have to endure before, some time in the future, she can do justice to this scene (or its memory).

So far we've seen the artistry with which Owen arranges the details of the poem, moving from one part of her picture to another like a painter – but also like a storyteller. The painter's initial assessment, her plans, her tears, the son's tugging, her kneeling to him, his nuzzling her and the final cinematic 'pull back' to show the scattered lemons all comprise a mini-narrative building to the epiphany already mentioned. In addition to this, though, Owen shows herself a master (or mistress?) of that flexible mixture of iambics and free verse that is used by many of the best poets in English these days.

As suggested above, she starts with a rather anapaestic line, but by the second the poem is already turning iambic: 'that *taut* new *world* she *merely border*s *now*'. Most of the other lines are iambic too, but Owen can also run two or three important words together so that they seem equally stressed ('*pale suns*'; '*fine sharp scent*' and so on).

Comparably subtle is Owen's use of rhyme. At first glance the poem seems unrhymed, but we soon notice that half-rhymes abound and several full rhymes occur throughout the poem, often widely separated: the half-rhyme 'now' with 'glow', for instance, or the 'lime'/'time' rhyme separated by five lines. Similarly, we can't miss the almost insistent 'chin', 'in', 'skin' rhyme and the half-rhyme 'loose' and 'grass' that so nicely rounds off the poem. One can't help observing, too, how the poem is clinched by that old device of having a four-stress line followed by a three-stress line (in the manner of ballads and many old hymns).

To some (male?) readers 'Young Woman Gathering Lemons' might seem an overly 'domestic' or 'female' poem, concerned to paint a simple Madonna-and-child from an idyllic childhood. It's hardly Tennyson's 'The Charge of the Light Brigade' – or Wilfred Owen's 'Anthem for Doomed Youth', for that matter – but it does address something almost all of us are concerned with and it does so with impeccable poise. The poem is understated in its techniques but, at the same time, is psychologically acute and profoundly moving. It's the sort of small-scale, delicately observed poem that seemed to come into its own in the twentieth century, even if (as in Coleridge's rather longer 'This Lime-tree Bower my Prison') there were a few forerunners.

GEOFF PAGE (1940–)

'The Publisher's Apprentice'

Selected and discussed by Peter Pierce

Sometimes she hears their
central stillness:
these paragraphs, the silent house,

the way a spouse has gone to bed.
She sees the writer at his screen
among his myriad corrections,

musing on the lives he's typed,
transparent but with colour.
She sees the diagram on his wall;

the line is like a small yacht tacking.
Somewhere, too, there is a childhood's
damaged photographs.

She smiles at Faulkner's definition:
a novel is a narrative
with something wrong with it.

This well-worked opening page or two
will need to be re-written;
some other pieces don't quite fit;

the characters too well recall
the models they derive from.
The floor-plan of a crucial scene

doesn't quite make sense —
where was that couch again?
But, even so, the world exists —

for all its imperfections.
The cast converge, conspire, make love,
enact their small betrayals.

Borne by its momentum now,
she needs to reach the end.
These people are, she knows, still vivid

inside their maker's brain —
and in a spouse's too, perhaps,
and one or two good friends,

just as they are in hers.
She finds she's come to care.
Sitting in her late-night chair,

she has another five beside her,
weighted with their limitations.
Those suits who mind the bottom line,

though rarely eloquent,
must have the final word.
The minds where all these true creations

might once have bloomed and waved a while
are flipping through their eighty channels,
a scotch perhaps to sink the day,

some salted nuts beside them.
She sees the coloured shadows shimmer.
But in this room with lamp and chair

she's reached the final page.
The characters encounter fates
both plausible and not unkind –

although a few – like life, she knows –
must run on unresolved.
She gives a sigh to see them leave –

then wanders stiffly to the kitchen,
the outline of a soft rejection
forming in her mind.

Published in Geoff Page's late career, *Seriatim* (2007) is his eight-eenth collection of poetry; he has also written many novels in both prose and verse. Some themes emerge strongly, treated with the seriousness of mind combined with suppleness of poetic tech-nique that we expect from, and take delight in, Page's work. Among them, miscellaneously, are mothers, music, Muslims (and minarets) and the very different but alike, exacting claims that they can make on us. But the poem from *Seriatim* that I want to address at length is not topical, nor necessarily autobiographical, but possesses an elusiveness and plangency that quietly compel our attention. This is 'The Publisher's Apprentice' (which was selected for the anthology of *The Best Australian Poems 2007*).

Now Page is old enough, as other poems in this collection ruefully inform us, to know about Mickey Mouse's famous mischief-making as 'the sorcerer's apprentice' in Walt Disney's film *Fantasia* (1940). However the apprentice in this poem is not intent on play-ing tricks, or doing harm, although she will cause pain to another person whom she has never directly met. Still, and sympathetically, she imagines his presence, and recognises the solitude that she has in common with him due to the nature of their work. He is a novelist. She has his manuscript in her hands, reading it on behalf of the publishing house that employs her: 'Those suits who mind the bottom line'. This is how she introduces the invisible connections between them: 'Sometimes she hears their/central stillness:/these paragraphs, the silent house'.

Then she elaborates on the scene that she is creating in her mind, 'sees the writer at his screen/among his myriad corrections'. He, too, is engaged in an exercise of imagination, 'musing on the lives he's typed,/transparent but with colour'. It is his solitude that registers most strongly with her: the writer in his silent house, the spouse gone to bed, the creative task his alone to complete. Next she thinks of one of the prescriptions about literary form from the American author, William Faulkner, who declared that '*a novel is a narrative/with something wrong with it*'. That reflection focuses her mind on her own undertaking; she turns to the manuscript before her: 'This well-worked opening page or two/will need to be re-written'. Under her eyes, in her hands, his whole arduous enterprise could fall apart.

By now we are beginning to gain a quiet sense of how Page has structured 'The Publisher's Apprentice'. In essence, this is through the use of parallels. The poem's design is scenic, theatrical. We move between separate rooms, and vocations, between two silent, engrossed, nocturnal workers – the novelist and his unknown reader. He sits before his screen, she in her 'late-night chair', where in the lamp light 'she sees the coloured shadows shimmer'. The other parallel involves the twin and entwined stories of the two characters. Through her thoughts, the process of his writing the novel she holds is reconstructed. Now we follow, as steadily she reads through the text, with increasing interest and admiration, but with not quite enough of either.

Mediating between the publisher's reader and the author are the characters and incidents that he has created. She has reservations – 'the characters too well recall/the models they derive from', but 'even so, the world exists –//for all its imperfections'. This is a novel of domestic life whose 'cast' (she is still thinking dramatically) 'converge, conspire, make love,/enact their small betrayals'. 'These people', so 'vivid//inside their maker's brain' have begun to be so for her as well. She has 'come to care', as has his spouse perhaps, 'and one or two good friends' (in the poem's most desolate line). But the 'suits', her employers, 'must have the final word' on this, and the other five manuscripts that also await her. Their minds (like so many others who once were readers) are indifferent to 'all these true creations'; their night-time recreation involves flipping through television channels with 'a scotch perhaps to sink the day'.

The 'apprentice' reaches the final page (as Page, the author, allows himself a heartfelt pun) wherein 'the characters encounter fates/both plausible and not unkind'. Engaged now, she 'gives a sigh to see them leave', but nonetheless she turns down the bid, the gift, the supplication which are embodied in the author's manuscript: 'the outline of a soft rejection/(forms) in her mind'. And that is the 'plot' of 'The Publisher's Apprentice', although plot is rather what we look for in a novel (even a rejected one) than in poems. In this case, however, we begin to feel that there is another story, a further parallel. At its core, if by analogy, this is a poem of disappointed love.

For here are a number of the situations and circumstances of a love story: passion, reflection, entreaty, obsession, empathy, hope, separation, rejection – abstract nouns that correspond to stages in a relationship that ends 'unresolved', in one of the last words of the poem. The tentative approaches, the emotional expense, the desire for union – these aspects of what might have been a love relationship are shadowed forth in Page's tale of the writer and his reader. So much might have been, for two who never met. The tone of 'The Publisher's Apprentice' is tender, but sorrowing. Of what may follow, the readers of the poem are not encouraged to guess.

The pace of 'The Publisher's Apprentice' is slow and ruminative. The diction is simple – words for everyday things that summon up their emotional correlatives, such as the two chairs where the main characters spend so much of their working time. Here Page's fond deftness in the use of rhyme is also employed: 'care' is rhymed with 'chair'. In these two rhyme words, as elsewhere ('kitchen'/ 'rejection'), lies a narrative in miniature. In its scenic way, the poem is also a miniature, a diptych which features at once connection and apartness and which – for all the modesty of its scale and manner – makes a brilliant reckoning of that 'world' that exists 'for all its imperfections'.

JOHN TRANTER (1943–)

'North Light'

He looks around his son's room: the bed
unmade, the globe of the world with an
imaginary voyage plotted in blue ink,
the clutter of books and plastic toys,
a life gathering its tackle together and
pushing forward. He stares at the backyard
and the thick bushes growing upwards.
The only movement is the glitter of leaves,
and the washing his wife hung out,
before she went to work, flapping
in its circus. Something you can't see
holds it all together. What is it? Last
spring they painted the house: amateurs,
but doing the job as best they could, then
they laid bricks in a pattern in the yard –
what is it, that makes the pattern hold?
That party where they squabbled, the dinner
where old friends got drunk and happy ...

He sits at the kitchen table, half dressed,
drinking a glass of orange juice,
and wonders about the delicate adhesive
that holds it all together. Once, long ago,
he'd been divorced: a sad, frightened drunk
living in a rented room.
　　　　　When the washing's dry
he'll gather it up, in armfuls, and bring it in.
He turns on some music. The house has a
northerly aspect; it is full of light.

The classics of the past can tell us much, but, in some ways, the classics of the present can tell us more. John Tranter's 'North Light' has had less than two decades to establish itself as a 'classic', but it's likely to be around as long as anyone is interested in how we city-dwelling Australians have lived our lives over the past 40 years or so.

Paradoxically, it's a poem of both puzzlement and assertion. Three times the protagonist wonders what 'holds it all together' and each time we are not really given an answer. On the other hand, there is no mistaking the positivity of the poem's last sentence: 'The house has a/northerly aspect; it is full of light'.

Years ago, the poem's 'hero' was 'a sad, frightened drunk', but in the opening lines he is looking around his son's room, noting its chaos but also how the boy's life is 'gathering its tackle together and/pushing forward'. His own situation is more static but not dissatisfyingly so. Somehow, his wife and he, with some difficulty, have more or less 'got it together'. Of course, we can easily imagine a few arguments over why she's out at work and he's at home – bringing the washing in, admittedly, but not hanging it out. The ironing, perhaps, is another issue again.

The 'house-husband' is enjoying the stillness, broken only by the 'glitter' of the bushes growing outside and the 'circus' of washing on the line. He thinks back to their 'home improvements', the painting, the paving. They have 'renovated' their marriage as much as their house by sharing the enterprise, despite their lack of expertise. Their 'squabbles' at a party don't destroy it; the happiness of friends at a dinner party consolidates it.

In the second stanza we cut to the kitchen. The protagonist, significantly, is drinking orange juice. There was a time when it would have been something stronger – and he's still wondering what 'delicate adhesive … holds it all together'. Perhaps one of them is his being 'on the wagon' these days. He doesn't want to go back to that 'rented room'. He's happy with the house (and its mortgage, no doubt). The house, as the real estate agent would say, 'has a northerly aspect' – and, as the poet would say, 'it is full of light', both literally and metaphorically.

There are not many contemporary poems about happiness but Tranter's 'North Light' is one of them. It's not a glorious, Hollywood happiness; it's not an easily attained happiness – but it's a real one. A state of mind achieved by a certain good sense, by trust, by shared enterprise and (dare one say it?) by love.

Of course, the poem is contemporary not only in its portrayal of the limited but actual happiness most of us aspire to, but in its technique. Traditionalists will look in vain for rhyme or a regular metre. The poem seems to be written in free verse, the rhythm changing all the time beneath our eye. 'He *looks around* his *son's room*: the *bed*' seems irregular enough, but if we swap one word we suddenly have a pure iambic pentameter: 'He *looks around* his *daughter's room*: the *bed*'. In fact, 'North Light' has a good deal of the flexible iambics seen in Matthew Arnold's 'Dover Beach' – and something of its mood, too: a less grandiloquent version, perhaps, of 'Ah, love, let us be true/To one another!'

Like most current poets who've done their homework, Tranter likes to refer back obliquely to the old, even while creating something that is new. In many ways 'North Light' is a single blank verse paragraph going back to the blank verse of Milton and Wordsworth. He even emphasises this continuity by breaking the line fourth from the end and indenting its conclusion ('When the washing's dry...').

It's interesting, also, to count the number of syllables in a few random lines and see how often they come to nine, ten or eleven, the normal range we expect in pentameters where one syllable too few or too many is nothing to fuss about. Tranter likes to raise traditional expectations and then crack them slightly. Some poets would have written, 'he'd *been divorced*: a *sad* (and) *fright*ened *drunk*', which would have been a neat pentameter, but Tranter uses a comma instead of the 'and'. He brings the two crucial stresses together: '*sad, fright*'.

It's instructive to consider, too, what makes the poem's ending work so well. Of course, there's the sense of plenitude in 'armfuls' and the reassurance of the washing being 'dry' as it's meant to be. There are also all the symbolic associations of 'light' – from divine

revelation through to the 'enlightenment' of the French philoso-
phers. The man has emerged from the long-ago darkness of his
'rented room' into the 'light' of an inexplicable but real happiness
with his wife and son. The 'music', too, is significant. We're not told
which idiom it is; the reader has to provide his or her own. In some
cases, modern jazz – in others, high baroque or Dolly Parton. The
factor that gives the absolute touch of finality, however, is the half-
rhyme of 'light' with 'dry' just four lines earlier. There's a suspension
we've been unaware of until its resolution is achieved with the half-
rhyme in the last line.

How long John Tranter's 'North Light' will be around we cannot
know, but, given its level of human insight and its technical subtlety,
one can expect it has quite a few years ahead of it yet.

ROBERT ADAMSON (1943–)

'Canticle for the Bicentennial Dead'

They are talking, in their cedar benched rooms
on French-polished chairs, and they talk

in reasonable tones, in the great stone buildings
they are talking firmly, in the half-light

and they mention at times the drinking of alcohol,
the sweet blood-coloured wine the young drink,

the beer they share in the riverless river-beds
and the backstreets, and in the main street –

in government coloured parks, drinking
the sweet blood in recreation patches, campsites.

They talk, the clean handed ones, as they gather
strange facts; and as they talk

collecting words, they sweat under nylon-wigs.
Men in blue uniforms are finding the bodies,

the Uniforms are finding the dead: young hunters
who have lost their hunting, singers who

would sing of fish, are now found hung –
crumpled in night-rags in the public's corners;

discovered there broken, illuminated by stripes
of regulated sunlight beneath the whispering

rolling cell window bars. Their bodies

found in postures of human-shaped effigies,

hunched in the dank sour urinated atmosphere
near the bed-board, beside cracked lavatory bowls

slumped on the thousand grooved, fingernailed walls
of your local Police Station's cell –

Bodies of the street's larrikin Koories
suspended above concrete in the phenyle thick air.

Meanwhile outside the count continues, on radio
the TV news; like Vietnam again, the faces

of mothers torn across the screens –
And the poets write no elegies, our artists

cannot describe the shape of their grief, though
the clean handed ones paginate dossiers

and court reporter's hands move over the papers.

The majority of Robert Adamson's best poems are set on his native Hawkesbury River, NSW, but there are some notable exceptions. 'Canticle for the Bicentennial Dead' is one of them. Here, we have a political poem which memorably defines the confused and uncomfortable feelings experienced by many Australians as the bicentenary of the settlement at Port Jackson loomed and was celebrated – feelings which were intensified by the Royal Commission on Aboriginal Deaths in Custody held between 1987 and 1990. The sesquicentenary in 1938 had been a relatively uncomplicated event (with only a few Aboriginal protesters, well ahead of their time). The 1988 affair proved much more problematic.

Adamson's treatment of these paradoxes begins with his title. A canticle is defined as a 'little hymn' – a hymn presumably in honour of those Aborigines who have been killed (or, more recently perhaps, have killed themselves) under the impact of white 'settlement'. Thus, in a sense, the poem is more an elegy than a 'little hymn' even though Adamson says towards the end of the poem that 'the poets write no elegies' about these unfortunate Australians.

The poem is also a kind of canticle in that it is written more or less in the form of an Aboriginal song cycle. It employs the present tense throughout and uses lots of repetition and parallelism. Many different things are happening at the same time and their meaning somehow resides in their simultaneity. In a whole poem made of couplets, we see the 'clean handed ones' with their 'nylon-wigs' gathering 'strange facts' while those who live in the 'riverless riverbeds' and 'government coloured parks' are drinking themselves into oblivion – or ending up in cells with 'stripes/of regulated sunlight' where, increasingly, they are found 'suspended above concrete in the phenyle thick air'.

Adamson is concerned with more than a static situation, however. He has constructed the poem with a particular narrative, which adds to its political impact. Initially we have the judges in their 'cedar benched rooms' and their 'French-polished chairs' who 'talk//in reasonable tones'. Then we cut to the alcohol-consuming Aborigines whom the judges are writing about so detachedly. These two worlds are in abrupt contrast. They are linked only by the 'Men in blue uniforms' who are 'finding the bodies', the bodies of the 'young hunters' and 'singers' who sing and hunt no more but are found 'crumpled in night-rags in the public's corners'; that is, where they have been totally marginalised and/or imprisoned.

The focus is then held for several stanzas on these particular cells, on the 'dank sour urinated atmosphere(s)', the 'phenyle thick air' and the 'cracked lavatory bowls'. These are hardly circumstances which might discourage people 'at risk' from killing themselves. The poem doesn't exclude the possibility that these 'larrikin Koories' have been murdered, but it's clear that an act of murder would hardly be necessary. The circumstances are sufficient in themselves to bring about that result.

Adamson then cuts away to a more public, less claustrophobic atmosphere, where the body 'count continues' on the media. It's like the war in Vietnam all over again, with the casualty reports and 'the faces//of mothers torn across the screens'. Unlike the Vietnam war, however, where many protest poems and art works were created (not many of them memorable), the Aboriginal deaths in custody bring forth no elegies or paintings which might 'describe the shape of their grief'. Ironically, of course, the poem we are reading is an exception to its own rule.

Eventually, we are back where we began with the 'court reporters' hands mov(ing) over the papers'. The 'clean handed ones paginate dossiers' but nothing has changed. The 'blood-coloured wine', the 'government coloured parks', the 'regulated sunlight' and the 'phenyle thick air' continue unalloyed. As do the 'cedar benched rooms', the 'French-polished chairs' and the 'nylon-wigs'. Everything is the same – despite our vivid excursion into Aboriginal realities and those 'strange facts' which the judges write about so uncomprehendingly.

It's interesting to note, too, how Adamson intensifies the tragedies of these deaths in custody. The victims are not mere statistics. They are 'hunters/who have lost their hunting', 'singers who// would sing of fish' and 'larrikin Koories' who all might have done much more with life than it offered them. The 'larrikin' term is particularly effective here since mainstream Australians have for so long admired the so-called 'larrikin' in themselves but fail to see its merits in others where it's regarded as merely 'offensive behaviour'. Adamson, admittedly, risks sentimentalising the Aborigines here but he does make the essential point that these wasted lives did not have to be so. In an earlier time, their culture would have sustained them physically and spiritually. Even for the post-settlement 'larrikin Koories' things could have been different.

Other less obvious ingredients also contribute to the poem's success as both art and politics. The song cycle influence has been mentioned, but so too should the poem's syntax and its rhythm. At first glance the metre may seem like a series of iambic pentameter couplets, but on closer inspection one sees a rhythmic irregularity more typical of the 1611 Bible or Walt Whitman. The syntax, too, with its long sentences and frequent parentheses, helps develop this almost biblical feeling. We sense the importance, too, of the many unstressed syllables seen in lines such as: '*Bodies of the street's larrikin Koories*/sus*pen*ded above *concrete* in the *phenyle* thick *air*.' Some lines in the poem appear to have six main stresses; others five – but in these we also hear the force of the old Anglo-Saxon four-stress line with its irregular number of unstressed syllables.

Of course, a major difficulty with all political poems is that not everyone will agree with them. Even those tempted to assert that Aborigines have not been particularly ill-treated since 1788 will be disarmed, I suspect, by the poem's evocative presentation of detail, both of the 'clean handed ones' and of those who drink the 'sweet blood-coloured wine'. Such readers would be drawn in, too, by the poem's narrative structure and by the way it circles back to the beginning, illustrating that nothing very much has changed.

As art, 'Canticle for the Bicentennial Dead' works equally well. Whatever our politics or our position in the 'history wars', we are struck by the poem's graphic images, its clever comparisons, its echoes of other forms (the song cycle, the Hebrew psalms and so on), its appropriately complex syntax and, finally, by its rhythmic variety and subtlety.

Auden may well have been wrong when he said: 'Poetry makes nothing happen.'

'In Departing Light'

My mother all of ninety has to be tied up
to her wheelchair, but still she leans far out of it
      sideways;
she juts there brokenly,
able to cut
with the sight of her someone who is close. She is
      hung
like her hanging mouth
in the dignity
of her bleariness, and says that she is
perfectly all right. It's impossible to get her to
      complain
or to register anything
for longer than a moment. She has made Stephen
      Hawking look healthy.
It's as though
she is being sucked out of existence sideways
      through a porthole
and we've got hold of her feet.
She's very calm.
If you live long enough it isn't death you fear
but what life can still do. And she appears to know
      this
somewhere,
even if there's no hope she could speak of it.
Yet she is so remote you think of an immortal – a
      Tithonus withering
forever on the edge
of life,

although with never a moment's grievance. Taken
    out to air
my mother seems in a motorcycle race, she
the sidecar passenger
who keeps the machine on the road, trying to lie far
    over
beyond the wheel.
Seriously, concentrated, she gazes ahead
towards the line,
as we go creeping around and around, through the
    thick syrups
of a garden, behind the nursing home.

Her mouth is full of chaos.
My mother revolves her loose dentures like marbles
    ground upon each other,
or idly clatters them,
broken and chipped. Since they won't stay on her
    gums
she spits them free
with a sudden blurting cough, that seems to have
    stamped out of her
an ultimate breath.
Her teeth fly into her lap or onto the grass,
breaking the hawsers of spittle.
What we see in such age is for us the premature
    dissolution of a body
that slips off the bones
and back to protoplasm
before it can be decently hidden away.
And it's as though the synapses were almost all of
    them broken
between her brain cells

and now they waver about feebly on the draught of
    my voice
and connect
at random and wrongly
and she has become a surrealist poet.
'How is the sun
on your back?' I ask. 'The sun
is mechanical,' she tells me, matter of fact. Wait
a moment, I think, is she
becoming profound? From nowhere she says, 'The
    lake gets dusty.' There is no lake
here, or in her past. 'You'll have to dust the lake.'
It could be
that she is, but then she says, 'The little boy in the
    star is food,'
or perhaps 'The little boy is the star in food,'
and you think, More likely
this appeals to my kind of superstition – the
    sleepless, inspiring homunculus.
It is all a tangle and interpretation,
a hearing amiss,
all just the slipperiness
of her descent.

We sit and listen to the bird-song, which is like
    wandering lines
of wet paint –
it is like an abstract expressionist at work, his
    flourishes and
then
the touches
barely there,
and is going on all over the stretched sky.

If I read aloud skimmingly from the newspaper, she
    immediately falls asleep.
I stroke her face and she wakes
and looking at me intently she says something like,
    'That was
a nice package.' In our sitting about
she has also said, relevant of nothing, 'The desert is a
    tongue.'
'A red tongue?'
'That's right, it's a
it's a sort of
you know – it's a – it's a long
motor car.'
When I told her I might be in Cambridge for a
    time, she told me, 'Cambridge
is a very old seat of learning. Be sure –'
but it became too much –
'be sure
of the short Christmas flowers.' I get dizzy,
nauseous,
when I try to think about what is happening inside
    her head. I keep her
out there for hours, propping her
straight, as
she dozes, and drifts into waking; away from the
    stench and
the screams of the ward. The worst
of all this, to me, is that despite such talk, now is the
    most peace
I've known her to have. She reminisces,
momentarily, thinking I am one of her long-dead
brothers. 'Didn't we have some fun
on those horses, when we were kids?' she'll say,

giving
her thigh a little slap. Alzheimer's
is nirvana, in her case. She never mentions
anything of what troubled her adult years – God,
    the evil passages
of the Bible, her own mother's
long, hard dying, my father. Nothing
at all of my father,
and nothing
of her obsession with religion, that he drove her to.
    She says the magpie's song,
that goes on and on, like an Irishman
wheedling to himself,
which I have turned her chair towards,
reminds her of
a cup. A broken cup. I think that the chaos in her
    mind
is bearable to her because it is revolving
so slowly – slowly
as dust motes in an empty room.
The soul? The soul has long been defeated, and is all
    but gone. She's only productive now
of bristles on the chin, of an odour
like old newspapers on a damp concrete floor, of
    garbled mutterings, of
some crackling memories, and of a warmth
(it was always there,
the marsupial devotion), of a warmth that is just in
    the eyes, these days, particularly
when I hold her and rock her for a while, as I lift
    her
back to bed – a folded
package, such as,

I have seen from photographs, was made of the Ice
    Man. She says,
'I like it
when you – when
when
you …'
I say to her, 'My brown-eyed girl.' Although she
    doesn't remember
the record, or me come home
that time, I sing it
to her: 'Da
da-dum, de-dum, da-dum … And
it's you, it's you,' – she smiles up, into my face – 'it's
    you, my brown-eyed girl.'

My mother will get lost on the roads after death.
Too lonely a figure
to bear thinking of. As she did once,
one time at least, in the new department store
in our town; discovered
hesistant among the aisles; turning around and
    around, becoming
a still place.
Looking too kind
to reject even a wrong direction,
outrightly. And she caught my eye, watching her,
and knew I'd laugh
and grinned. Or else, since many another spirit will
    be arriving over there, whatever
those are – and all of them clamorous
as seabirds, along the walls of death – she will be
    pushed aside
easily, again. There are hierarchies in Heaven, we

remember; and we know
of its bungled schemes.
Even if 'the last shall be first,' as we have been told,
	she
could not be first. It would not be her.
But why become so fearful?
This is all
of your mother, in your arms. She who now, a
	moment after your game, has gone;
who is confused
and would like to ask
why she is hanging here. No – she will be safe. She
	will be safe
in the dry mouth
of this red earth, in the place
she has always been. She
who hasn't survived living, how can we dream that
	she will survive her death?

Of course, compression is the essence of poetry – or one of them anyway. This does not mean that every poem has to be short, however. Sometimes a poem's subject, like a novel's subject, requires elaboration. Sometimes we need more, not less. Robert Gray, who began with the influence of haiku and the short, almost photographic poems of William Carlos Williams, understands this well and with 'In Departing Light' he gives us one of his most moving and indelible poems.

For reasons too complex to address here, mothers often seem to be of extraordinary importance to poets, both male and female – but this is perhaps just an intensification of an experience enjoyed by most people. In Gray's case we have a good understanding, but not a lot of detail, of how the poet/mother relationship worked in earlier days. We are told of her 'obsession with religion' – and the relationship with the poet's father which 'drove her to (it)'. We are given a little of her childhood – and a reference to her own mother's 'long, hard dying'. It's not a complete picture, but it's enough to see why he's there wheeling her around the lawns of the nursing home.

'In Departing Light' is broken into four long stanzas, each one showing a different aspect of the mother's condition. The first focuses on the mother's physical situation – 'a sidecar passenger' in her wheelchair as she is pushed through the 'thick syrups/of a garden, behind the nursing home'. The second stanza, starting with 'Her mouth is full of chaos', concentrates on what she says, her (uneven) tendency towards surrealist poetry which shows merely that her brain is failing to work properly any more: her chaotic speech merely indicates the 'slipperiness/of her descent'.

The third stanza of 'In Departing Light' casts the situation in a more biographical context. We see scraps of coherence, such as her response to news of her son's intention to go to Cambridge for a time, but we also get her almost meaningless metaphors, such as 'The desert is a tongue'. The poet muses on how much of her past has been swept away by the disease and on how she is calm 'as dust motes in an empty room'. Her husband, who seems to have been problematic while he lived, has gone from her memory entirely – as have 'the evil passages/of the Bible' and other things that used to trouble her. She has become no more than 'a folded/package'. Only her physical attributes, such as her 'odour/like old newspapers on a damp concrete floor', have any real presence now.

It is in the last stanza, however, (beginning with 'My mother will get lost on the roads after death') that the real force of the poem comes home to us – and we see how the first three stanzas have all been an essential build-up to the last one. The poet gives us just one more episode, the time his mother got lost in a department store and 'grinned' when she saw that her son had been watching her 'turning around and around'. The main point here is that, as with life, 'she will be pushed aside'. Gray has no faith in Christ's assurance that 'the last shall be first'. That, for him, is just another of Heaven's 'bungled schemes'. She 'could not be first. It would not be her.' Unlike the death notices which so often assure us that mothers are safe in Heaven, the narrator here believes instead that 'She will be safe/in the dry mouth/of this red earth, in the place/she has always been'. No longer will she have to 'fear … what life can still do'.

It's at this point that Robert Gray delivers his hammer blow to the traditional religious viewpoint on death. 'She/who hasn't survived living, how can we dream that she will survive her death?' If there is an afterlife he is sure his mother will be pushed aside by all those other souls, 'clamorous/as seabirds, along the walls of death'. If there isn't such an afterlife then she will be 'safe/in the dry mouth/of this red earth', a fate her son clearly prefers — and believes will be the case.

The impact of these last lines is very much a result of all that has preceded them — the images of her in the wheelchair, the images of her lost in the department store, the humiliating episodes with the false teeth, the chaos of her conversation. All these, and more, illustrate only too convincingly how she 'hasn't survived living'. Why, then, should we think she would survive her death?

Some readers may puzzle over the extreme variations of line length in this poem. It seems likely that it reflects the changing emotions of the narrator, all the way from humour to sadness. Sometimes, new sentences begin at the end of an already long line; sometimes a line may comprise only one or two words for emphasis (take, for instance, the vague 'somewhere' on a line by itself in the first stanza). The line, as Ezra Pound once recommended, can be a 'unit of sense' but in this context, because of the confusion in the mind of the poet's subject, that 'sense' is frequently and deliberately undercut by successive extensions and truncations of the line.

Some readers may also consider Gray's free-verse rhythms to be too close to prose rhythms but, if they pause to consider the contrast between the rhythm of most lines in the poem and the prose being written here, they will see a significant difference between the two. '*She*/who *hasn't* sur*vived liv*ing, *how* can we *dream* that *she* will sur*vive* her *death*?' We not only have the clever syntactical balancing between each part of this sentence but also their quasi-iambic feeling, broken only by the adjacency of a couple of stressed syllables ('sur*vived liv*ing') and an extra unstressed syllable in the phrase '*she* will sur*vive*'.

In summary then, we may see Robert Gray's 'In Departing Light' as a triumph of the longer poem. It's extensive but there's nothing in it which is inessential to its final effect – as summarised and delivered by the poem's unforgettable last sentence: 'She/who hasn't survived living, how can we dream that she will survive her death?' You may find you've remembered it already.

'Portrait of the Artist as an Old Man'

In my father's house are many cobwebs.
I prefer not to live there – the ghosts
disturb me. I sleep in a loft
over the coach-house, and each morning cross
through a rearguard of hedges to wander in the
    house.
It looks as though it grew out of the ground
among its oaks and pines, under the great
ark of Moreton Bay figs.
My study is the largest room upstairs;
there, on wet days, I write
archaic poems at a cedar table.
Only portraits and spiders inhabit the hall
of Courland Penders … however,
I check the place each day for new arrivals.
Once, in the summerhouse, I found a pair
of diamond sparrows nesting on a sofa
among warped racquets and abandoned things.
Nobody visits Courland Penders; the town
is miles downriver, and few know me there.
Once there were houses nearby. They are gone
wherever houses go when they
fall down or burn down or are taken away on
    lorries.
It is peaceful enough. Birdsong flutes from the trees
seeking me among memories and clocks.
When night or winter comes, I light a fire
and watch the flames
rise and fall like waves. I regret nothing.

M ichael Dransfield was, and remains, a controversial figure in Australian poetry. Opinions about the worth of his work still vary widely – though his early death, his drug-affected lifestyle and the late-Romantic elements in his poetry have always found him an audience with the young. Psychologically, Dransfield was a complex figure and there were many contradictory elements in his poetry, too.

One of these was his feeling for the aristocratic. Opposed to the Vietnam war and in many ways considering himself a political radical, Dransfield also had a weakness for the trappings of nobility, whether back in England or here in their watered-down Australian version. A number of his poems (not necessarily the best ones) create the personal mythology of Courland Penders, an extensive rural family property, long since in romantic decline and where the poems' narrator is the last of his line. While this myth was clearly important to Dransfield personally, it may also have a more universal resonance.

We need perhaps to remember that the poem was written by a very young man. Dransfield was 22 when *Streets of the Long Voyage*, the collection which included 'Portrait of the Artist as an Old Man', was first published and the poem may well have been written a year or two earlier. The narrator, by contrast, is in his declining years – as is the property on which he's living in contented isolation. Though most of the poem's details are nostalgic and affectionate the poem actually starts with an irony, a distortion of Christ's assurance that 'In my father's house are many mansions'. The narrator's lineage and country seat has only 'many cobwebs'. He does not complain, however, nor lay any blame. Indeed, he never really explains how Courland Penders came on such hard times. Was it a succession of impractical owners like the narrator himself or were there more objective factors? The 'houses', workman's huts presumably, have fallen down or been burnt or 'taken away on lorries', but we're not told why. It all seems to have happened in an earlier generation.

The big house itself, however, remains an interesting mixture of English aristocratic expectations and Australian realities. It's surrounded by 'oaks and pines' but also lives 'under the great/ark of Moreton Bay figs'. It looks as if, almost organically, it 'grew out of the ground', but it also has the 'coach-house' and 'summerhouse' that any self-respecting English country mansion would feature. The 'warped racquets' on the sofa poignantly remind us of the 'Anyone for tennis?' cliché.

We should note, too, what this old man is doing (and not doing). His life has a certain discipline; he is not in a self-indulgent alcoholic stupor. He writes 'archaic poems on a cedar table' – but only on 'wet days'. Clearly he composes only when he's in the mood – and, since the poems are 'archaic', they're not likely to have much commercial value. Clearly, however, they're important to him – even if no one else will ever read them. He writes in the 'largest room upstairs' purely for the pleasure of it. Dransfield may be suggesting that such dreaming impracticality should always be a part of writing of poetry, but it's hard to be sure of this. It may just be the preference of the poem's narrator.

It's important, too, that writing poetry is not all the old man is doing. He 'check(s) … for new arrivals'; he watches the diamond sparrows with indulgence; he hears the 'birdsong' fluting from the trees and is pleasurably absorbed with his 'memories and clocks'. All these are pretty much aristocratic concerns. We're not told where the money comes from for him to afford them. Presumably, he's running down the last of the family's assets – and clearly has no descendants of his own to worry about.

The narrator's noble unconcern is further emphasised in the phrase 'When night or winter comes'. He doesn't much seem to care whether night or winter is the relevant factor in lighting a fire. We don't know if he himself has gathered the wood (and/or chopped it) or whether, at some stage, someone else has done it for him. He's reached a fine objectivity here. He watches 'the flames/rise and fall like waves', just as his own family has done. The poem's last sentence is movingly defiant. 'I regret nothing' – nothing of what it took to build up the property (and take it from the Aborigines perhaps) and nothing in what has led to its decline. Like Nietzsche, it seems, he has moved 'Beyond Good and Evil' into the inevitable pattern of human events.

It is hard to be clear about exactly what this poem offers the reader – as opposed to the self-mythologising satisfactions it clearly offered its author. One thing perhaps is its angle on poetry – that poetry is something to be written from desire rather than from social obligation or any other lesser motive. Another, perhaps, is the undeniable attractions of the aristocratic lifestyle, despite its obviously shaky moral foundations. We could learn a lot, the poem implies, if we were free to ignore the pressure and moralising of others and live alone in a big house, checking the diamond sparrows and enjoying our memories and clocks. Perhaps the aristocratic is what everyone should aspire to.

It's possible that Dransfield, in the poem, is aware of the relative decadence of this position. The narrator is, after all, the last to enjoy the pleasures of the house. Although he 'regret(s) nothing', he may also realise that an inheritance built on some, possibly remote, injustice is not something that can endure forever. Its end was somehow built into its beginning.

On a technical level, it's tempting to wonder whether 'Portrait of the Artist as an Old Man' is an example of the 'archaic' poems the narrator is writing on those wet days. In some ways the poem feels like Tennysonian blank verse. There are certainly quite a few regular iambic pentameters scattered through it. ('I *check* the *place* each *day* for *new arrivals*' and so on). Several of the poem's images, too, are explicitly late Romantic, for example 'Birdsong flutes' – and 'memories and clocks'. Dransfield, unlike almost every other Australian poet of his generation, loved the poetry of Victorians such as Tennyson and Swinburne. Its presence in 'Portrait of the Artist as an Old Man', though cleverly diluted and altered, is manifestly one of the poem's charms.

ALEX SKOVRON (1948–)

'Eclipse'

for Gwen Harwood

Our memories stretch to fit us,
    extend our days
between one dream of darkness
    and the next.
Landscapes unsettle, we awake
    mysterious to seek
the compass of each myth until
    the shutters fall
and we climb back to the skin,
    elastic, and we ban
the riddles of the dark, murky
    terrain, the library
we can never quite locate, cave
    never quite leave.
We peer into the ever-fading map,
    the colours jump
into and out of focus; we devise
    colourful glories
and elaborate ghosts, or flecks
    of paradox
over the perfect irony of mind
    which is our bond
and hostage. Meanwhile, indistinct
    avenues connect
and disconnect, eerie vehicles ply

their dim territory,
figures, voices foreshorten, bend
        beneath the wand
of contrapuntal sleep: we reach
        into dark, the latch
lifts or dissolves, the gate swings
        open, awkward songs
and longings visit us – we sleep,
        forget the drop
of knowledge trembling on one half
        of the fragile leaf,
the other perpetually dark, forever
        strange, forever
locked eclipse, just its silhouette
        serrated with light.

Not all poems are designed to amuse us – or to move us to wonder or compassion. Some, such as Alex Skovron's 'Eclipse', can be brief but searching essays in philosophy or psychology, intellectual speculations about how the mind operates – the mind examining itself, if you will. In 'Eclipse' Skovron is concerned chiefly with 'the riddles of the dark … the library/we can never quite locate'. How does this dream world relate to the waking world where we 'climb back to the skin' and watch our tiny 'drop/of knowledge trembling on one half/of the fragile leaf'? What we know in the conscious world, Skovron suggests, is significantly outweighed by its more mysterious counterpart.

The poem is dedicated to Gwen Harwood, an Australian poet who also had a considerable interest in philosophy, particularly that of Ludwig Wittgenstein. Skovron starts by noting the elasticity of memory but also how we move in and out of each 'dream of darkness'. In the subconscious, in the dream world, we 'seek/the compass of each myth' but it is an unavailing search. We have to 'climb back to the skin' and 'ban/the riddles of the dark'. Paradoxically these dream regions are both a 'library/we can never quite locate' and a 'cave' we can 'never quite leave'.

On waking, Skovron suggests, we 'peer into the ever-fading map' of what we have just seen. We use the dream material there to create 'colourful glories' or 'elaborate ghosts' for ourselves. We might even use our mind to play with 'flecks/of paradox' that originate in those regions. The mind, we're reminded, is both a 'bond/and hostage', our only connection with the dream dimension – but also in danger from it.

Skovron then resumes his on-going description of the subconscious, its 'indistinct/avenues', its 'eerie vehicles'. It's a terrain where both figures and voices are distorted by foreshortening, a world to which we are taken involuntarily by 'the wand/of contrapuntal sleep'. It is in this world of 'awkward songs/and longings' that we are able to (or prone to?) forget 'the drop/of knowledge trembling on one half/of the fragile leaf'; that is, that hard-won, scientific knowledge of the daylight world built up by generations of scientists and thinkers. Clearly, the two worlds coexist; the fragile world of our day-to-day knowledge backed by the 'strange' and 'perpetually dark' one behind it. Around this conscious world the unconscious world forms some sort of corona. We see its 'silhouette' around the edges of our waking world. There's a paradox here, too. The world of darkness is creating a 'serrat(ion)' of light, implying perhaps that the strangely dark, subsconscious dimension may be more 'enlightening' than the rational one we live in, unproblematically, each day.

When we look back at the intellectual progress of the poem we can see it's been quite a journey. Skovron, like Freud, has sought to emphasise the importance of the subconscious, to suggest its indispensability. He has done this not through research or case studies but through what we might call 'poetic' thinking. By using a series of images such as 'the library/we can never quite locate' and the 'cave/(we) can never quite leave', by talking of its 'indistinct avenues' and its 'eerie vehicles', the poet seeks to convince us not only of the existence of such a world (not really a difficult task) but, more importantly, of its relevance to, and interaction with, our conscious world.

It's interesting, too, that the poet has sought to do this in what amounts to a series of couplets with the second line indented below the first. It's as if the unpredictable and quirky twists of his argument (and imagery) need to be reflected in the form used. It's not a smooth presentation in blank verse but rather an 'awkward' line-by-line presentation reflecting the difficulties and elusiveness of what the poet is talking about. We sense this technique of tension and resolution particularly in the last two lines where the poet talks of the subconscious being merely a 'silhouette' before he points out in the last line that it is 'serrated with light'.

Intellectually ambitious poems like 'Eclipse' are rarely understood at a single reading, but neither is the philosophy and psychology with which they compete. To be persuaded of something by means of a sequence of images, however, may well be more enjoyable and more permanent than labouring through pages of densely argued prose towards a position which is not necessarily any more convincing, particularly at that deeper level where it counts.

ALAN WEARNE (1948–)

'A World of Our Own'

Will Claire attend the Boat Race dance?
Have I a pre-selection chance?

In my study Nigel twitched:
'It's Lucy, Dad, we must get hitched.'

And I, to ease us from this jolt,
poured both a treble single malt.

Name the ratio, what's the blend
of house guests for a Lorne weekend?

But Fleur's a gem since up she musters
professors, senators, messrs justice.

Whilst life improves up 'all right'
if I can make an Old Boys night.

Angus and Polly were around
that Sunday when the PM drowned.

Alan Wearne is best known for his verse novels, particularly *The Nightmarkets* and *The Lovemakers*, but his peculiar talent for social observation and dry humour also shines through in his less-frequent short poems, too. One of the most perfect of these is his relatively recent, 'A World of Our Own'. Here, in a mere 14 lines (the poem is a sonnet by some definitions), Wearne gives us a light-hearted but deadly portrait of what, in a note to the poem, he describes as '1967; the upper middle class of eastern suburban Melbourne'.

Australia, especially to visiting Britons over the past century or two, has often been described as 'class-free', but it only takes a few social encounters outside one's own group to realise this is hardly the case. We may not do it as well as the British, but we do it even so. It's interesting, too, to see how often class is observed from the 'outside', as it were.

In 'A World of Our Own' the characters are allowed to speak for themselves, but it's fairly obvious that the poet himself doesn't consider himself one of 'Our Own'. He's met them, presumably, and may have been invited 'around' a few times, but it's not his world – for all of its fascination. Such distance, of course, is essential to satire. If he were in the group he would scarcely notice its oddities.

The poem begins its theme of self-absorption with a couple of questions that could only be of interest to the speaker and his group. We don't know who 'Claire' is but she's clearly someone of social importance to the group (and possibly of personal interest to the speaker). The second question beautifully sums up the some-times cavalier approach to politics among conservatives. It's not as though he's been to scores of boring party branch meetings and expects that his turn has come around at last. He just needs to have a sense of his own popularity among the few people who will make the decision. Presumably, it will be a 'blue-ribbon' seat, which will guarantee election. We notice, too, perhaps that the pronunciation of the word 'dance' is a class-signifier in Australia. 'Dahnce' suggests class; 'Dants' implies the lack of it.

In the next two couplets we are given a little family scenario. The narrator is confronted by his somewhat embarrassed son, Nigel, who (back in 1967) has lined himself up for a 'shotgun' marriage to Lucy. One can sense how resonant those two names, Lucy and Nigel, will sound on the wedding invitations. The speaker, however, is just a little disconcerted (it's a matter of class never to be *too* disconcerted). Not unexpectedly, he feels the need for a triple strength high-quality Scotch whisky. Who wouldn't? His son, Nigel, will apparently need one even more.

After this little bit of consternation, the poem then cuts away to the equally pressing problem of what's the right 'ratio' for a 'Lorne weekend'. Non-Victorians may need reminding that the seaside resort of Lorne was highly fashionable in 1967 – and remains so. We're not told what 'blend' or 'ratio' is being referred to, but its clearly got something to do with male to female and/or a blend of the truly genteel with those who might serve to entertain them or give them a clearer sense of themselves, people such as professors, senator and judges who may or may not have come from their own class but have done things in the world which merit attention and confer prestige on those who may ask them 'around'. We don't need to be told much about 'Fleur' to get a sense of her personality.

At this point the narrator seems to diverge a little, musing on the limited but real pleasure of getting together with his mates on an 'Old Boys night'. A similarly mild detachment marks the last couplet, too. Our monologist recalls that it was 'Angus and Polly' he (and his wife, presumably) had 'around' on that particular Sunday when Harold Holt, prime minister, drowned off Portsea beach (another fashionable location).

This last couplet is certainly a rather devastating satire if one thinks about it a little. To the question of 'what were you doing when Harold Holt was lost off Portsea?' they can cheerily answer we were having 'Angus and Polly ... around'. Naturally, everyone in the charmed circle knows who 'Angus and Polly' are. And, naturally, 'Polly' sports a name like 'Polly' as an in-group (boarding school?) nickname to be used by friends while 'Angus' has rather Scottish (if not Calvinist) echoes of a serious fellow who has brought credit to his family and not let down the (Anglo-Celtic) 'side', as it were. 'Angus and Polly' are plainly of more significance than Harold Holt, even if Holt himself shared much the same background. At least the narrator (and his wife?) do recall that it was a 'Sunday' when the PM disappeared. He did not slip away entirely without notice.

In this connection we might remind ourselves, too, of how effective the old *aabb* rhyme scheme can be when used in conjunction with the iambic tetrameter – as opposed to the pentameter preferred by Alexander Pope and many others. With the tetrameter it's as if the jokes are pouring down on us in quick succession. We smile at the apparent forcedness of 'musters' and 'messrs justice', the cleverness of 'jolt' with 'single malt', the unbelievable offhandedness of 'around' and 'drowned' in the last stanza – and so on. There's not a rhyme in the whole seven couplets that doesn't bring a smile, one way or another.

And so it is just one of the many charms of 'A World of Our Own' that Wearne manages to capture the exact intonation and preoccupations of those satirised while doing it effortlesly in a form used so well by Jonathan Swift in the early eighteenth century. 'Verses on the Death of Dr Swift', for instance, uses the iambic tetrameter couplet mercilessly to satirise those 'friends' who distractedly note the death of their friend, the dean, while busy at their card games ('The Dean is dead: (Pray what is trumps?').

Wearne does much the same thing (though less personally) to send up a rather later self-absorption. 'Will Claire attend the Boat Race dance?/Have I a pre-selection chance?' Who cares? Of course we don't give a fig about Claire – or our hero's pre-selection chances – but we do care deeply about cleverly written satire and its capacity to show us the foibles of others, to offer us a smile along the way and, perhaps less certainly, assist us in avoiding the same shortfalls in our own lives.

ALAN GOULD (1949–)

'A U-Boat Morning, 1914'

will come as we perform the mundane toil,
say, tossing the breakfast scraps astern,
or washing down the maindeck among the oblongs
of sail-shadow. The morning sun
will mint its coins across a lazy sea,
the weather tacks and sheets will rise and fall
in languid intersectings of the sea-rim.

And there, so sudden, ordinary, too close
to dodge, or do anything about but wait for
with quiet interest, will be the thing of hearsay,
cigar profile, stub tower, little gun, so credible,
for all that it will be the first such vessel
we will have seen outside some journal's
crude picture.

      Through his loudhailer,
the officer will be polite, but firm,
reading the English translation from a card.
Fifteen minutes. We'll stow such extra food,
water, charts, as time will allow,
also oilskins, a mouth organ, a piece
of unfinished scrimshaw perhaps, nothing bulky,
then lower the boats, and stand off from the barque
at the distance we will have been directed to.
Oddest for our sense of what is proper
will be the sight of the helm unmanned out there
in open sea.

And this will be the manner
a moment in time will surface to say, *Of course*
your lives are free. Of course they are compelled,
as we watch, quiescent, attentive, the lifeboats
gentle as hammock sway in the swell beneath us,
the little gun puffing its little smoke,
and thin smoke oozing from somewhere on board.
Gradually our home will lean into
its odd stricken angle, and spill wheatgrain
from the holes in her side, slipping under,
natural as a sleeper turning under blankets.
When it is done, the captain will salute us
just once, the submarine chug away, routine
as a mailboat.

And without undue hardship
we will survive, but no-one there will serve
in sailing ships again. This is how
an ancient confidence will vanish
casually like a fashion in jokes. Instead
we'll live into a time strange to us,
we'll live aware of how the unborn have
their faces turned away from all we took
for granted, as stubborn or quizzical, we will
submit to someone else's scheme of what
is pressing, waste on the floor of life's renewal.
And if this quiet impending morning leaves
one thought in mind, it might be wheatgrain
fanning from a ship across the ocean's dark
like brassy beads, like fabulous golden blood.

Alan Gould's poem, 'A U-Boat Morning, 1914', is one of his most typical but also one of his best. Characteristically, Gould views the grain ship's sinking from at least two removes in time. The poet is writing a dramatic monologue in the mid-1990s from the viewpoint of someone who is anticipating by some years an event that will happen in 1914.

There is much more to this poem, however, than any mere cleverness with viewpoint. Gould wants to emphasise both the extraordinary and the ordinary aspects of the sinking. It all happens while the sailors are at 'mundane toil'. The boat slips under the water 'natural as a sleeper turning under blankets'. And, afterwards, the submarine will 'chug away, routine/as a mailboat.'

Conversely, however, for the narrator, it is an event without precedent and one that will change his life forever. For him and his fellows 'it will be the first such vessel/we will have seen outside some journal's/crude picture'. Afterwards, he understands he will be merely 'waste on the floor of life's renewal'. The event may *seem* ordinary but the wheatgrain (and all that it symbolises) fans out from the ship 'like fabulous golden blood'. This is hardly a mundane image. To hold such contradictory elements in balance is a key element in the poem's charm. No less important, however, is the way the poem offers a last glimpse into a time when war was still a little chivalrous and played by the rules. Within two years of this relatively merciful sinking, there would come the massive destruction suffered by both sides in the battle of the Somme. Back in 1914, however, the German U-Boat commander, 'polite, but firm,/read(s) the English translation from a card'. The sailors are given time to escape; even to survive the rest of the war. It will not be this way again, we may be sure of that.

What lends this situation even greater poignancy is Gould's use of the future tense. Such small decencies are anticipated by the sailor, but we know from our perspective how short-lived they would be. It is another thing that the poet holds in a delicate balance – a future event predicted from the past, which, in turn, is seen again from the future as a past event. It's a clever but meaningful conundrum. It's not hard to see why Gould called his selected poems *The Past Completes Me*.

Some critics and readers have, over time, misread Gould's career-long preoccupation with sail. Though a kind of nostalgia for this graceful and highly skilled mode of transport is certainly part of the interest in 'A U-Boat Morning, 1914', Gould is much more concerned here, as in many of his other poems, with sailing as a vehicle for moral and metaphysical speculation. His spokesmen rarely recall or predict events simply for their own sake or for their visual beauty. So what, then, are the moral speculations to be found in 'A U-Boat Morning, 1914'?

One obvious one is the relative reluctance with which human decency gives way to internecine slaughter on an industrial scale. Gould is reminding us that there were once (relative) decencies in humanity's seemingly unavoidable war business and that they might be retrieved if only we had perhaps the courage to imagine such a development. That is, if we do not fall into despair, cynicism and apathy.

Another, more benign concern is the disappearance of successive technologies and the artisanship that goes with them. Gould's narrator does not wax excessively about this. He accepts that his 'ancient confidence will vanish/casually like a fashion in jokes'. He is left, not so much with bitterness at the destruction of his way of life and the relevance of his skills, but with a single image: 'wheatgrain/fanning from a ship across the ocean's dark/like brassy beads, like fabulous golden blood'. The narrator laments but he also accepts. This, Gould is implying, is as it should be.

Technically, the poem supports the continuing relevance of blank verse as a vehicle for narrative poetry. It's a device that goes back to Milton's *Paradise Lost* and to the plays of Shakespeare. Gould establishes the metre in the opening line ('will *come* as *we* per*form* the *mun*dane *toil*'), but it is not until the fifth line that we see it again without modification: 'will *mint* its *coins* a*cross* a *la*zy *sea*'. The poet allows the metre to bend as the demands of the narrative and the narrator's speech patterns require. There is a prosaic ordinariness to the line '*read*ing the *Eng*lish trans*la*tion *from* a *card*', created by the poet's insertion of a couple of extra unstressed syllables. It is the sort of variation that makes the narrator's voice convincingly colloquial (despite his often sophisticated imagery). It is a very different effect, for instance, from that achieved by Tennyson in 'Ulysses' – another great maritime poem with which Gould's poem forms a notable contrast in manner, but not in quality.

Les Murray has called Alan Gould Australia's 'best history poet'. 'A U-Boat Morning, 1914' is very much the sort of poem he must have had in mind. The past, for Gould – and for the rest of us – is accessed not only by 'facts', but by the force of our imagination, as seen clearly in this poem.

JENNIFER MAIDEN (1949–)

'Costume Jewellery'

('Let's get one thing straight. You're behind the
    counter because you have to work for $6.00 an
    hour. I'm on this side asking to see the good
    jewellery because I make considerably more'
    – reported remark by U.S. National Security
    Advisor Condaleezza Rice to shop assistant
    who had pulled out some costume jewellery on
    seeing her.)

You wear on TV gold earrings, necklace
heavier than Mrs. Albright's to hold your
head steady. Your small brows tighten
together to balance the weight. Your half smile
wills the viewer to think you astute, not
lively since neatness takes all your
energy, and neatness is the best thing
against evil. You knew some girls growing
up in Birmingham and they were bombed
to bits in church one Sunday. Untidy agony
is dirty, terror hungers loudly, but you learned
music. Your mother named you after
con dolcezza and you always were that.
Provost of Stanford U., partly because, its President
    said,
you were a young black woman, you
don't like Positive Discrimination. You sacked
a Chicana dean and her students went on hunger
strike, but you shrugged, 'I'm not hungry.
I'm not the one who's not eating.' Descended

from slaves in a white house, you're proud
how 'Granddaddy Rice' changed religion
to get on. 'Praise Be,' you said, smiling.
Evil is never Birmingham. Evil must
be Iraq and you must have power, proper
jewellery, to fight, protect kids like church,
be well-presented, plausible and neat. Always
the White House was bright as a cake
with candles, fiery nothings. The lights
of the White House are blazing
cubic zircona, con dolcezza, but
you're not hungry with terror, you're not starving.

To write a protest poem at a distance from the relevant events is always risky, but there is no reason, in principle, why it should not be done. Indeed, there are quite a few reasons why it should be. W.H. Auden's 'Musée des Beaux Arts' is not based on any particular suffering experienced by its author. Ezra Pound, a non-combatant, wrote, in 'Hugh Selwyn Mauberly – Parts IV and V', one of the great denunciations of World War 1. Each day in Australia, via television, press and internet, we are (rather softly) bombarded with images, visual and verbal, from wars around the world, particularly those in which the Americans (and we Australians) are involved. It would be less than human, even in our armchairs, not to respond to them in some way.

The best of these poems, as is the case with Jennifer Maiden's 'Costume Jewellery', pick up on some contradiction, some detail that evades or complicates the simplicities of the propaganda machines of either side. Such poems see through into the complexities that make the relevant protagonists human – though they're not necessarily any more admirable for that. In 'Costume Jewellery' Maiden begins with an epigraph where the then U.S. National Security Adviser, Condoleezza Rice, reportedly behaved snobbishly towards a shop assistant who subjected her to racist assumptions. It is this small but significant incident which, clearly, has generated Maiden's poem.

As suggested earlier, protest poems are dangerous to write. In some countries, indeed in many countries, you can be arrested or killed for your efforts. In Australia we have the luxury of publishing them with impunity – which is not, in itself, a reason not to write them but it should give us pause. Not everyone is as lucky as we are. Maiden's poem is addressed to Condoleezza Rice directly though there is no assumption that she will ever read it, let alone allow it to change her behaviour. It is a useful rhetorical strategy even so.

Maiden thus begins by admitting that her image of Rice is derived from television where she (Rice) is seen wearing earrings and a necklace that are even heavier than her predecessor as Secretary of State, the Democrat Madeleine Albright. Almost as an ekphrastic exercise, Maiden describes Rice's 'portrait' from the screen. She has 'small brows' and a 'half smile'. She looks 'neat' because, as Maiden says ironically, 'neatness is the best thing/against evil'.

We then get the first thing in Rice's back story which helps explain the woman and the politician she was at the time of writing – namely, the racist murder of several of her classmates in a Birmingham, Alabama, church in 1963. This is where Maiden takes the first of her risks. How can she criticise, as a white Australian, an African-American who has had to live with such a traumatic childhood experience? How can Maiden, as a woman, complain of the way in which Rice has raised herself from such unpropitious beginnings to break through the patriarchs' 'glass ceiling'?

The poet's answers to these potential attacks are seen both in the poem's epigraph itself where Rice shows a comparable incomprehension to that which Maiden might be accused of – and in Maiden's arguments about how Rice reacted in her (Rice's) life subsequent to the Birmingham bombing. According to Maiden, Rice sees neatness as a way of fighting evil – and refuses to believe that 'Evil is … Birmingham' (or the rest of the U.S., for that matter). Music training, academia and a little bit of Positive Discrimination lifted her out of the chaos of Birmingham and into positions of power such as Provost at Stanford University, U.S. National Security

Adviser and, ultimately, Secretary of State. The ascent, says Maiden, has toughened her so that she has no trouble withstanding a student hunger strike or venting her anger on a shopgirl who makes the racist assumption that because a customer is black she will be able to afford only costume jewellery, not the real thing.

Throughout all this is the constant theme of Rice's childhood, of the need to be 'well-presented, plausible and neat'. Rice is shown as feeling a continuity (if a little cynically) with the apparent spiritual opportunism of her 'Granddaddy Rice' – and, as a descendant of slaves, she is proud to be working in the White House, even if, as Maiden suggests, the building is only 'a cake/with candles, fiery nothings'. The problem with Iraq and the American intervention there, Maiden suggests, is that it is not 'neat'. Rice's neatness has isolated her from Iraqi hunger, terror and starvation. Genuine jewellery, not 'costume jewellery', is a defence against such things, a way of keeping chaos (such as the events in 1963 Birmingham) at a distance. Parodoxically, Condoleezza is *con dolcezza* ('with sweetness'), a musical marking she'd be more than familiar with from her years of studying piano to professional level.

Of course, an outline of a poem's argument does not make it a great poem – though with political poetry, in particular, such a backbone is an essential part of any possible greatness. The attack on Condoleezza Rice is savage, but it is well argued and well illustrated. What is it, however, that takes this poem beyond being merely a superior op-ed piece through to a powerful piece of political poetry? In addition to the risks taken, the particularities and the weight of Maiden's argument, we also feel the force of her imagery. We recognise the 'tight smile', the 'neatness'. We flinch at the phrase 'bombed/to bits' even though it's not an original one. We pick up on the anecdote about the 'Chicana dean' and the hunger strike, just as we do on the epigraph. We circle back to the Birmingham church but not to see it the way Rice does. Rice, as U.S. National Security Adviser, is concerned to protect the 'kids' of America. Maiden, in her turn, wonders about the kids in Iraq. We note too, at the end, the '*dolcezza*' of the White House, its almost celebratory lights which are so much in contrast to the hunger, terror and starvation above which Rice has raised herself – and which she now, according to Maiden, is happy to see imposed on others in a distant country.

No one said political poetry needs to be fair. This poem would hardly find sympathetic readers in the U.S. Republican party, but it does have subtlety. Maiden is careful to see her political enemy in three dimensions, to see 'where she is coming from', as it were. It doesn't incline the poet to forgiveness, far from it, but it does make for a complex and forceful poem. Some might still ask what right does a relatively safe white woman in Australia have to such opinions? What could she learn just from television and newsprint alone? The poem, however, persists in standing firmly by itself. It makes its point, quite a complicated one, and it really doesn't matter who wrote it – or what her circumstances were.

JOHN FORBES (1950–98)

'Europe: A Guide for Ken Searle'

Greece is like a glittering city
though only in a political speech

but Italians believe in *bella figura*
& mis-use the beach. In Germany there's

Kraftwerk & acres of expressionist kitsch.
Oil-rich Norwegians don't need to ski

they just like it & Iceland is famous
for its past. Doing their physical jerks,

a quiet pride permeates the Swedes.
Denmark is neither vivid nor abrupt

& Belgians have a ringside seat
to observe the behaviour of the Dutch.

The French invented finesse but it's
their self-regard that intrigues us.

We pity the English, though they get on
our wick, pretending to understand us

& Scotland is old-fashioned like a dowry
but unusual, like nice police. Mention

Ireland & you've already said enough.
The Spaniards are not relaxed about sex

& tourists are attracted to this. Some
Portuguese exist entirely on a diet of fish

but rich cakes, finance & guest workers
sustain the Swiss. Consult my *By Trailbike*

& Hot-Air Balloon Through Middle Europe
for details of the Austrians & Czechs

but don't forget Bavaria's Octoberfest
or that Rococo architecture was designed

to be passed out under, pissed, & it's
aesthetically edifying to do this.

For the rest: give Russia a miss,
the Poles will appreciate hard currency

but only as a gift & the fleshpots of
Split will leave you a physical wreck.

This guide stops short at the Balkans,
as it omits the Finns. I won't apologise

– many guides to Australia include
New Zealand or leave out Tasmania.

No doubt some thorough American manual
can give you the lowdown on Europe's margins

but mine, designed for only one traveller,
is better written & much shorter.

Besides, if you remove the art, Europe's
like the US, more or less a dead loss

& while convenient for walking
& picturesque, like the top of a *Caran*

D'Ache pencil case or a chocolate box,
what do you make of a landscape

that reminds you of itself? Is this why
the people are sure they're typical

not standard? I can't advise you on this
but I know how I enjoyed myself: though

knocked out by what convinced me
'Great Art' without inverted commas is

(but not because of this) I hung around
with other Australians & hit the piss.

W ritten more than 20 years ago, and with all the changes which
have occurred both here and in Europe, one might think
John Forbes' classic, 'Europe: A Guide for Ken Searle', would by
now be seriously out-of-date. A careful reading, however, suggests it
is no less relevant than it ever was. While at one level purporting to
summarise (light-heartedly) the supposed national characteristics of
Europeans (from the Irish through to the Russians), it may in fact
be about something else entirely.

In the background somewhere, as a given, is our knowledge of
the inevitable superficiality, even fatuity, of any guide to a pheno-
mon as complex as Europe. Forbes speaks disdainfully of 'some
thorough American manual' and asserts that his is 'better written &
much shorter'. He knows, too, that there is a deep human tendency
to oversimplify others. In 'Europe: A Guide for Ken Searle' Forbes
has taken this to a self-satirising extreme. Rather like an 'ocker'
version of a Henry James heroine, the poem's narrator has inno-
cently come to 'old' Europe and is trying to make sense of it. After,

we assume, just one or two short trips, the poet is presuming to pass on his knowledge to a similarly naive fellow countryman intending to make the same trip. It's not accidental that, as an Australian, the narrator recommends passing out under Rococo architecture 'pissed' and that, intimidated by 'Great Art', he spends much of his time getting drunk with other Australians.

The crucial joke in this series of generally dismissive 'one-liners' is that Forbes has actually located (almost as if by accident) something which is not entirely wrong. There *is* a significant variety among the countries of Europe, despite the best efforts of the European Union and its parliament in recent decades. These differences run far beyond the obvious one of language. No less crucial, however, is the attitude of the Australian narrator who is trying to encapsulate them.

Given space restraints, it's worth examining at least a few of these and trying to categorise them. While many if not most of the observations are dismissive, some are insultingly so. Among these would be: Iceland ('famous/for its past'); Ireland ('... & you've already said enough'); Russia ('give Russia a miss'); Finland ('it omits the Finns'). Only slightly more generously treated are: Denmark ('neither vivid nor abrupt'); the Poles ('appreciate hard currency//but only as a gift'); Croatia ('the fleshpots of/Split will leave you a physical wreck').

Forbes keeps his most interesting jibes for what might be called the 'major' countries of Europe: Germany, France, Britain and perhaps, at a stretch, Greece and Italy. Germany not only has the avant-garde rock band, Kraftwerk, but 'acres of expressionist kitsch' – and 'Bavaria's Octoberfest' is an ideal destination for beer-drinking Australians, it would seem. France has its immutable 'self-regard' and, admittedly, its 'finesse'. England is more problematic for Australians since the English 'get on/our wick, pretending to understand us'. Greece and Italy, those fabled tourist destinations, are dismissed in turn for being merely a 'glittering city' and, in Italy's case, for its belief in the '*bella figura*' and for its inhabitants 'mis-us(ing) the beach'.

These are all sly, if somewhat unfair, digs. Comparable 'arguments' are employed to dismiss the Norwegians, Swedes, Belgians, Dutch, Scots, Spanish, Portuguese, Swiss, Austrians and Czechs. It's quite a list to add to those already dealt with. Although Forbes (or his narrator) claims his guide is 'much shorter' than its not-so-well-written competitors, it's surprisingly comprehensive even so.

At last, towards the end of the poem, our guide begins to generalise about the continent as a whole. 'Europe's/like the US, more or less a dead loss'. He asks the very telling question for a non-European, particularly one from a country settled (or invaded) by Europeans: 'what do you make of a landscape//that reminds you of itself?'. He does concede, however, that 'I know how much I enjoyed myself', even if, impressed by 'Great Art' without the inverted commas, much of the trip involved hanging 'around/with other Australians & hit(ting) the piss'.

What, finally, are we to make of all this? The poem is no doubt a satire on Europeans, their pretensions and peculiar habits, but even more it is a satire on the Barry McKenzie type of Australian who goes to Europe but is too ignorant to understand what he (or she) encounters. Since Forbes has addressed the poem to his friend, the painter Ken Searle, it's reasonable to assume the poem's narrator is Forbes himself. On the other hand, the range of reference in the poem tells us that the poet is not merely an ignorant and heavy drinker at the Bavarian Octoberfest or an Aussie who passes out, 'pissed', under Rococo architecture. For all his potpourri of prejudices, the narrator is quite well-informed, tossing terms like 'bella figura', 'expressionist' and 'Rococo' about with offhanded élan. This mixing of 'high' and 'low' was a particular skill of Forbes and this poem, among quite a few others, demonstrates the length to which the technique may be taken by those with the necessary expertise. It's not often that the words 'pissed' and 'bella figura' appear in the same poem.

The poem's attractions, however, go well beyond the mere content discussed so far. They also include Forbes' playful technical assurance – and his knowledge of the English poetic tradition. The poem is arranged in couplets which remind us (distantly, at least) of the heroic couplets used by Augustan satirists such as Alexander

Pope and Jonathan Swift. Forbes doesn't rhyme *aa, bb, cc* and so on as they did, but there is plenty of rhyme right through the poem – usually to humorous effect. We have, for instance, the 'speech'/ 'beach' rhyme in the first four lines, but note how Forbes avoids putting 'beach' at the end of the line where we might expect it. Then we have the half-rhyme 'kitsch' (echoing 'speech' and 'beach') before, in turn, we hear a series of short '*u*' rhymes: 'abr*u*pt', 'D*u*tch, '*u*s' and so on. This again is soon followed by a run of short '*i*' rhymes (or half-rhymes), as in 'th*i*s', 'f*i*sh', 'r*i*ch' and 'Sw*i*ss'. They're echoed by the 'p*i*ssed', 'th*i*s' and 'm*i*ss' rhymes a few lines later. All this not only keeps us guessing in a way that an *aa, bb, cc* series wouldn't, it also sews the whole poem together, disguising thereby that it is essentially a mere listing or sequence of one-liners. The rhyming teasingly suggests that there might be a coherent argument even if there isn't one.

Forbes has similar fun with his syntax and lineation, often refusing to finish his sentences at the end of a line. Some sentences run on for stanzas with lots of parentheses; others are just a line or two (often running across a stanza gap). This is another device for keeping the reader on his or her toes. A few lines, for example '& *Bel*gians *have* a *ring*side *seat*' are the exact iambic tetrameter which is implied throughout (even in irregular lines such as 'but un*u*sual, like *nice po*lice. *Men*tion'). Forbes was often thought of as being extremely avant-garde and under the impress of the 'New York School' of John Ashbery, Frank O'Hara and others, but there is no doubt that he had a clear knowledge of the tradition he was taken to be working against. It is this depth which has already kept a supposedly superficial poem like 'Europe: A Guide for Ken Searle' alive and well many years beyond the point where some of its details may have become inaccurate. There is no reason to think it will not continue to do so.

'Another Country'

She said she loved being a woman.
Her skin pressed mine, my face her hair.
And I a man? Just being human
Can sometimes seem too much to bear:

The hands remember what they held,
The tongue recalls the salt-sweet skin.
Who was it said that 'her hair smelled
Like a country I could be happy in'?

It's not in human form that I
Have leave to stray in that domain
But only now as the swept sky
Or a thin fall of cold sweet rain.

Stephen Edgar's 'Another Country' is the second poem in a ten-poem sequence called 'Consume My Heart Away'. Very little biographical information is given in the whole group, let alone in this poem, so it is probably best to read it not as 'confessional' poetry but a contribution, and very memorable one, to the long history of love poetry in English. Like many famous love poems, it is quite short and not without its ambiguities.

To go through the poem looking for its so-called 'prose meaning' is a first, though minimal, step. We note that the poem is in the past tense and that the love affair is almost certainly over – though we are not told how it ended. At the outset, the protagonists seem to be thinking of the relevance of their gender in all this. The female declares that she 'love(s) being a woman'. The male may or may not have been asked directly what he thought about being a man. His answer is to duck – or perhaps expand – the question. 'Just being human/Can sometimes seem too much to bear.'

In the second stanza the poet goes on to give some sense of what he means by this; how his hands hold the memory of her body and his tongue itself 'recalls (her) salt-sweet skin'. We may surmise from that 'salt-sweet' that the affair had its sweeter and its saltier moments, though salt in the language of eroticism is, of course, not necessarily negative. The narrator then goes on to 'borrow' someone else's line (or more properly, as T.S. Eliot recommended, to steal it): 'her hair smelled/Like a country I could be happy in'. Notice how we're not given the irrelevant colour or texture of her hair; it's just a place he felt he 'could be happy in'. If we assumed the relationship was already over in the first stanza it becomes even more clear in the second. There's an unstated 'could have been' buried in there somewhere. Her hair is not a country he's still happily living in – though he clearly remembers its potential as such a place.

In the third stanza the narrator takes this image further. The 'domain' mentioned is primarily that country of potential happiness though, by extension perhaps, it could be the woman herself in her totality – that body, that 'salt-sweet skin'. Now, however, since the affair is over, he has no way of getting back to her in any human or physical form. It is only in certain sorts of weather that she returns to him, taking the form of 'the swept sky/Or a thin fall of cold sweet rain'.

It's worth thinking for a moment what these two images say about the woman in question. She has become insubstantial as the sky, but it is a 'swept' sky which implies the finality of her having been 'swept' away. She is also a sensuous memory. The eroticism mentioned in the first stanza (and the second, for that matter) returns here as the sensuousness of a 'fall of cold sweet rain'. The memory is 'cold' because she is gone – but also, perhaps, because coldness itself can be bracing. The rain is 'thin', reflecting her distance from him. It is still a 'sweet' rain, however, which implies that the impulse that drew him to her in the first place may not have yet abated. She is still very much a memory even though she is also 'Another Country', as the title suggests.

Stephen Edgar is known these days as being the only Australian poet who almost invariably uses regular metre and rhyme. His employment of it in 'Another Country' is essential to its success. It's impossible to re-imagine the poem into free verse. Edgar's steady, though occasionally varied, iambic tetrameters give a dignity and a sort of hard-won formality to the poem. Love has been called a 'disorder of the senses' but here, after the event, the feelings are 'straightened' into metre and into a tight *abab* rhyme scheme. The original experience may have been chaotic perhaps (almost 'too much to bear'?), but that confusion has been caught and somehow made permanent by these technical regularities.

The slightly elevated, incantatory feeling created by the steady tetrameters also has the effect of lifting the affair to another level. This has not been some seedy one-night stand to be remembered with smiling bemusement or vague regret. This has been an experience worthy of the form it has now been given. Indeed, with these regularities, it becomes an experience worthy of being memorised. It will thus stay in the reader's mind just as the affair itself has persisted in the mind of the poet who remembers it with such pleasure – and, in a sense, pain. As readers, the form has brought us closer to the experience itself, albeit vicariously.

Of course, these tetrameters and *abab* rhyme schemes have been responsible for much forgettable poetry over the centuries. It's interesting to see how Edgar avoids the fate that has overtaken so many of his predecessors. One small way is, perhaps, the half-rhyme he uses between 'woman' and 'human' (though it is, admittedly, the only half-rhyme in the poem). More important, however, is the slight rhythmic irregularity to be found in many of the lines. We note the adjacency of the stressed syllables of *'loved'* and *'be'* in the first line where the normal pattern would be 'She *said* she *loved* be*ing* a *woman'*. This idiomatic variation gives the line (and the poem that follows it) a conversational straightforwardness it wouldn't have if all the lines were as regular as, say, 'It's *not* in *human form* that *I'* or 'The *hands* re*member what* they *held'*.

In some cases, these variations are minimal, but that only intensifies their effect. Take the line 'The *tongue* re*calls* the *salt*-sweet *skin'*, for instance. We know that the scansion should be as indicated but we can't help giving those three important monosyllables equal force, as if to savour each one in turn – '*Salt-sweet skin'*. Something similar happens with the irregularities in the last two lines of the poem with the adjacencies of *'swept sky'* and *'thin fall'*. We are forced to slow down and give each word its unique value. And yet, at the same time, we have the satisfaction of having all these things in a formal context which provides the enhancements already mentioned.

If one goes looking for minor criticisms with which to 'balance the budget', as it were, one discovers that some of these conceivable defects are, in fact, advantages. Take, for instance, the omission of the second verb in the poem's second line 'my face her hair'. This may seem confusing at first but it actually brings out the closeness of the narrator's face and the hair he was pressing it into, so much so that they appear to risk becoming the same thing. A similar rebuttal can be made of the poet's apparent laziness in not saying who wrote the convenient line 'her hair smelled/Like a country I could be happy in'. When one is in love, or perhaps is remembering being in love, one is not inclined to footnoting. One remembers the appositeness of the phrase, not where it came from. Admittedly, Edgar does mention the source in the acknowledgements in the book in which 'Another Country' was first collected (Chapter 27 of Russell Hoban's *Fremder*, in fact), but such scrupulosity is not for the poem itself – nor for the mood from which it emerged.

The American-derived free-verse orthodoxy of the past half-century or so would have us believe that poems such as 'Another Country' must inevitably sound 'dated' and sentimental because they use forms which have been around for hundreds of years. Stephen Edgar in this poem – and in many others – has shown this to be a truly mistaken notion. The resources of traditional metres and rhyme schemes are just as available, just as powerful, as they ever were. It's just a matter of knowing how to use them.

KEVIN HART (1954–)

'The Last Day'

When the last day comes
A ploughman in Europe will look over his shoulder
And see the hard furrows of earth
Finally behind him, he will watch his shadow
Run back into his spine.

It will be morning
For the first time, and the long night
Will be seen for what it is,
A black flag trembling in the sunlight.
On the last day

Our stories will be rewritten
Each from the end,
And each will end the same;
You will hear the fields and rivers clap
And under the trees

Old bones
will cover themselves with flesh;
Spears, bullets, will pluck themselves
From wounds already healed,
Women will clasp their sons as men

And men will look
Into their palms and find them empty;
There will be time
For us to say the right things at last,
To look into our enemy's face

And see ourselves,
Forgiven now, before the books flower in flames,
The mirrors return our faces,
And everything is stripped from us,
Even our names.

M ost of us do not have to hand the fine detail of Christian
resurrection theology, but there is no doubting the force
of Kevin Hart's account of it, whether you're a Christian or not.
The prophecies vary a little from one denomination to another, but
most of them involve a 'last day' and some sort of physical resur-
rection. Hart's account of these things may or may not be exactly
in line with the official Catholic doctrine (it certainly wouldn't be
expressed in such a poetic way); as poetry, however, Hart's account
is more than compelling.

Before working through the poem's images in detail it's worth
noting how much Hart's 'last day' is a matter of reversals. The
ploughman's shadow will 'Run back into his spine'; our stories will
be rewritten backwards and end at our birth (or, more likely perhaps,
with a new birth). There will be time, he suggests, to look back and
'say the right things at last'. On the other hand, the extent of the last
day's transformations are, according to Hart, total. The 'long night'
leading up to it will be obliterated by a new 'sunlight'; 'Old bones'
will be re-covered with flesh; the books of our long human herit-
age will 'flower in flames' and 'everything (will be) stripped from
us/Even our names'.

We should remember, too, that this poem was written and
published in the early 1980s when the threat of nuclear annihila-
tion was at its most likely since the Cuban missile crisis of 1962.
The probable flashpoint was in Europe and it is no accident that
Hart begins his poem there. The 'shadow' running back into the
ploughman's spine has something of a nuclear flash about it. The
'books ... in flames' also suggest it – as does the 'black flag', with its
implications about the patriotisms and ideological conflicts prevail-

ing at the time. We should note, too, in passing, Hart's fleeting allu-
sion to W.H. Auden's poem, 'Musée des Beaux Arts' – and, in turn,
to Breughel's painting, 'The Fall of Icarus', which inspired it.

Ultimately, however, it is not the nuclear holocaust that Hart is
concerned with. For him, as a Catholic, the last day will be the so-
called 'Day of Judgement', the idea which preoccupied Renaissance
painters who so delighted in depicting sinners on their way to Hell
– or already enduring its tortures. Hart, to the almost certain relief
of agnostics and atheists, puts a more generous spin on this. He sees
the last day as more of a moment of reconciliation, of forgiveness
and self-knowledge. Admittedly, 'everything (will be) stripped from
us' (even our beloved egos, it seems) but that, according to Hart, will
simply be a necessary part of a transformation where the 'black flag'
of human sin will no longer be relevant. Though the term 'born
again' has been much abused, this is more or less what Hart means
here. If we're born again our previous names will be irrelevant.

This analysis is, however, a little too simple. It's worth look-
ing more closely at some key images in the poem and considering
the theology behind them. We notice that the whole of human
history up to the last day – including, presumably, all our intellec-
tual and scientific achievements – has been a 'long night' and can be
symbolised as a 'black flag trembling in the sunlight'. The sunlight,
of course, being the new dispensation.

The poem's third stanza suggests our stories 'will be rewritten/
Each from the end,/And each will end the same'. It's as if the sin in
all our lives will be removed as we are sent back to the innocence
of our birth (though Hart seems to have forgotten the doctrine of
Original Sin for the moment here). There is a suggestion, too, that
the non-sentient parts of God's creation (the 'fields and rivers') will
reveal themselves as having been conscious all along and 'clap' with
approval at God's transformations.

In the fourth stanza the reconciliation motif dominates. 'Spears'
and 'bullets' from our endless wars will 'pluck themselves/From
wounds already healed' – implying that those wounds hadn't healed
as well as we thought they had (or that mere human healing isn't
enough). The image of women 'clasp(ing) their sons as men' is a little

more difficult, recalling perhaps the medieval dispute about exactly what age the saved would be in heaven (33, some suggested). It may refer to mothers who lost their young sons before they saw their full potential as men. The men, in turn, in stanza 5, merely 'look/Into their palms and find them empty'. Men, unlike women perhaps, are more materialistic and acquisitive, but any such gains on that final day will be irrelevant. Hart then returns to his reconciliation theme, noting our inability to say what should be said when needed and our tendency to transfer our own inner conflicts to our enemy. Finally, on the last day, when we 'look into our enemy's face//… (we) see ourselves,/Forgiven now …'.

The last stanza's reference to mirrors implies that on that last day we will see ourselves as we 'really' are and not merely the confected personality we created for ourselves. That face, along with the name of that same pseudo-being, will be 'stripped from us'. It sounds harsh but it's a necessary step, Hart implies, on the way to something profoundly better than the 'long night' (of human history?) we've been living in so far.

Not surprisingly, the poem has a somewhat Old Testament-like rhythm, being written in a free verse that goes back to the 1611 Bible. There may be a shadow of a nuclear holocaust behind the poem, but almost all of its details and vocabulary could be found in the Bible without much trouble. We can hear the biblical heavy stresses, too — and the wide separations between them — quite clearly in the opening lines of stanza 2. 'It will be *morning*/For the *first time*, and the *long night*/Will be *seen* for *what* it *is*.' Notice, too, the way the rhythm in the third line resolves towards the iambic just as the sentence approaches its final meaning.

Unlike Walt Whitman (or, more recently, Allen Ginsberg), Kevin Hart has arranged his free verse in lines of various lengths and has cut the poem up, almost arbitrarily, into five-line stanzas. This enables certain effects, such as the suspension between the end of stanza 2 and the beginning of stanza 3. After the phrase 'On the last day' at the end of stanza 2 we naturally ask 'What?' — then we have the answer, after an appropriate pause, in the first line of the next stanza: 'Our stories will be rewritten'. Such variations of line length also make it possible for the poet to emphasise key phrases with single lines such 'Old bones' or 'And see ourselves' (the latter also after a stanza break).

Though Hart, as free verse requires, doesn't use rhyme here he does allow himself a nice finalising rhyme by matching 'flames' with 'names' in the closing stanza. The two ideas are related anyway (the 'flames' will burn away our 'names') but, more importantly, the rhyme gives a necessary finality to a poem which is, after all, called 'The Last Day'.

It was T.S. Eliot who suggested that a successful religious poem ought to make one feel what it's like to have convictions other than one's own. By this criterion alone, Kevin Hart's 'The Last Day' is a memorable poem whether you're an atheist, agnostic or orthodox Catholic. Hart's poem is a highly personal version of an eschatology that we're all at least partly familiar with. One doubts whether the official doctrine from Rome has 'fields and rivers clap(ping)' on the last day, but in Hart's expert hands we have no trouble suspending disbelief (or extending our belief a little).

Kevin Hart, in this poem, has managed to say some very profound things very simply – and in a language far more persuasive than the nit-pickings of official theology. He insists on full value from his 'poetic licence' and takes us to places that only poetry can reach.

DOROTHY PORTER (1954–2008)

'Exuberance with Bloody Hands'

What do the Minoans teach us –
exuberance with bloody hands?

The wind the Goddess brings
is both wonderful and vicious

she flies into your soul
she flies into your face

and what will you do to see her?

Become the stone altar
become the moist fetish
become the bird screaming down on you

it's just a trance
you tell yourself
you'll wake up tomorrow
your lover sleeping on your shoulder

it was just the wine
it was just the drugs

it's all over
I can't remember
nothing happened

no-one got hurt

but there was something
a wind, a bird, a sense
of being taken up and over

dancing and dying
dancing and not dying
dancing and living forever

but your mortal lover snores
and snuffles into your mortal skin

the rattle, the trees, that perfume,
that fantastic presence

what are you fit for now?

whose throat would you cut
to have it happen again?

D orothy Porter is best remembered as a verse novelist but in the years between *Little Hoodlum* in 1975 and her death in 2008 she also published at least six collections of individual poems. Among these is *Crete* (1996) from which 'Exuberance with Bloody Hands' is taken. In the first 50 pages of this book, Porter examines some of what we know (or think we know) about the civilisation and religion of Minoan Crete and energetically turns it to her own purposes.

In 'Exuberance with Bloody Hands' she is concerned with the overpowering force of what we might genteelly call lust or eroticism, the impulse that throws people off their moral bearings and has them waking up next morning wondering what happened and who got hurt. This is a knowledge even older than the Minoans, but they will more than do for what Porter has in mind.

She starts by restating the title and the central image of the poem – 'exuberance with bloody hands'. Dictionaries rather mildly define 'exuberance' as 'the state of being exuberant'; that is, 'being lavish, effusive and full of vigour'. Clearly, Porter refers to something larger than this – and her whole poem is a perfect definition of what she means. The 'bloody hands' are an inextricable part of it. Someone is going to get hurt, whether in the roughness of the sexual encounter, or that person offstage who has been sexually betrayed. The ruthlessness of the whole business is brought home to us in the final stanza: 'whose throat would you cut/to have it happen again?'

Although the poem has a very contemporary feeling in parts ('it was just the wine/it was just the drugs'), it is also very much derived from the pre-Christian, pre-Enlightenment world when goddesses were taken seriously. The 'Goddess' (we're not told of what but it's pretty clear) brings a 'wind' that is 'both wonderful and vicious'. What, says Porter, will you be prepared to do to offer yourself to her completely? Reduce yourself to an inanimate 'stone altar' or a 'moist fetish'? Metamorphose into 'the bird screaming down on you'? All of these things and more, it would seem.

Almost at once, however, the rational side of the mind starts making excuses. It was just 'a trance'. Everything will be okay tomorrow with 'your lover sleeping on your shoulder'. Perhaps the whole experience was not transcendent or metaphysical but merely a side-effect of 'the wine' or 'the drugs'? In any case – and rather conveniently – you 'can't remember'. You tell yourself 'nothing happened' and that 'no-one got hurt'.

All these excuses and denials are not enough, however. Something did happen and you know it. There was 'a wind, a bird, a sense/of being taken up and over'. Over what? The limits of your rational being, presumably. Then Porter gets to the paradoxical essence of the experience. There is an awareness of intense mortality but, at the same time, a transcendence of it (however brief). You are 'dancing and dying' but you are also 'dancing and not dying'. You are even 'dancing and living forever', but this is quickly shown to be an illusion in the next stanza where your 'mortal lover snores/ and snuffles into your mortal skin'. The repetition of 'mortal' here is crucial. We are taken up by the Goddess, given a whiff of immortality, and then dumped back again with only the memories, 'the rattle, the trees, that perfume,/that fantastic presence'.

'What are you fit for now?' Porter asks eventually. Not much, it would seem, but the memory does not disappear. 'Whose throat would you cut,' Porter asks, 'to have it happen again?'

To moral conservatives 'Exuberance with Bloody Hands' might seem a profoundly immoral poem, but if they read it more carefully they may find it more like Shakespeare's famous sonnet 129 which begins 'Th' expense of spirit in a waste of shame/Is lust in action' and concludes by recommending that we 'shun the heaven that leads men to this hell'. Like Shakespeare, Dorothy Porter knows that what she writes about is very real – and intensely pleasurable – but the cost is 'bloody hands', even a preparedness to cut throats. She makes it clear that it's pointless to pretend that 'no-one got hurt'. Porter balances the pleasure and the cost exactly and, to those of a more rational turn of mind, the poem is more likely to deter people from encountering the Goddess than encourage them to do so. The vividness and sexual energy is there – but wouldn't we be just as happy simply waking up with our everyday 'lover sleeping on (our) shoulder' and having that person 'snuffle into (our) mortal skin'?

This is a poem from which it takes a while to recover. When we do, we might also consider why it works so well and why it has proven so memorable. One obvious reason, of course, is the graphic imagery: the 'bloody hands', the 'moist fetish', the 'dancing and dying', the throat cutting and so on. Another is the way the argument of the poem is structured. We start with a question; we get a rush of an answer; then we try to talk our way out of the situation; then we remember (cannot avoid remembering) the intensity of the experience, despite the reassuring presence of our rational 'mortal lover'. Finally, we are left with two questions, the answers to which we may not like. It's been a roller coaster of a narrative and there's been no chance to get off.

A less obvious factor in making the poem work so well is how Porter handles her free verse, including the business of lineation, stanza formation and rhythmic variation. She uses lineation and stanza length as a form of punctuation, a way of making the essential ideas of the poem stand out (the self-deceiving single stanza 'no-one got hurt', for example). She's also happy to employ that old free-verse technique of parallelism to build up her ideas, as in the stanza where every word starts with 'dancing'. She likes to move the rhythm around, too, taking advantage of the freedoms offered by the medium. While there are quite a few straight iambic lines such as 'The *wind* the *Goddess brings*' and 'she *flies* into your *soul*', there are also many places where she bangs stressed syllables down beside each other with memorable force – as in, for instance, the '*stone altar*', 'the *moist fetish*' and the '*bird screaming*'.

'Exuberance with Bloody Hands' is an extreme poem. There's no denying that. It's not one we bounce back from quickly. Its morality is not simple, however. For all of her verbal energy, Dorothy Porter ultimately establishes a thoughtful balance between the rational and the irrational, between the 'lover sleeping on your shoulder' and the Goddess who will have you cut throats just to make you feel (however briefly) that you're 'dancing and not dying/dancing and living forever'.

'Glass Harmonica'

In her busking cloche
velvet dress and army boots
her Salem air of ashes …
she clears a space in Harvard Square
to play the musical glasses.

Tucked along a spindle,
each rim larger than the last,
beneath her wetted fingers
the bowls begin to sing
of Faneuil Hall and Kirchgässner,

of feathered snow and wolverines,
of broken fans and wreathless things –
The Woman without a Shadow
echoes through tabernacles
with eyes of broken tin.

Iced air is rising from the river –
call me Ishmael call me Ishmael –
a wave to drown the soul of bowls
and now the sea has taken on
the burden of the song.

September shakes down leaves
to make the branches simple …
one high note might light a pyre
of bundled birch –
                    but today she has no bowls for death.

She plays a wintry madrigal.
In the city of white swans
she reaches for the smallest bowl,
and then the smaller one.

Jennifer Harrison's 'Glass Harmonica' is one of those poems that somehow demand you do your research. In a public read ing such background information can be provided readily by the poet but as readers we must, as we do with T.S. Eliot's 'The Waste Land', track down at least some key references for ourselves. Not all poems deserve this, of course, but the mysteriousness of poems like 'Glass Harmonica' will send many of us off at least to Wikipedia or Google.

There you will find that the glass harmonica was invented by Benjamin Franklin in 1761 and that Mozart composed a Quintet for Glass Harmonica in 1791 for the virtuoso on the instrument, Marianne Kirchgässner. You might also discover that Faneuil Hall has been a popular marketplace in Boston, Massachussets, since 1742 – and that Harvard Square is a comparable landmark in nearby Cambridge.

The important thing about the poem, however, is the sound – and the implications of that sound – which the female busker is creating on her instrument. The poet watches the lady with bell-shaped hat (a 'cloche'), 'velvet dress and army boots' and an air of having come from Salem, still best known for its persecution of witches in the late seventeenth century.

The poet/observer is already impressed by the woman's appear-ance, let alone by the sounds she begins to make on her 'musical glasses' with those 'wetted fingers'. As she listens, the poet begins to have a slow rush of associations; she thinks of the old marketplace at Faneuil Hall; she remembers the eighteenth-century virtuoso on the instrument, Marianne Kirchgässner. We soon learn that it is winter and the listener is thus reminded of wolverines in the 'feathered snow', an image which might well apply to both New England and 'Old Europe'. The reference to 'broken fans and wreathless things' remains obscure but, nevertheless, intensifies these highly subjective associations set off by the strange, glassy music being listened to.

In the next stanza, the poet feels the 'iced air' from the river. It makes her think of Ishmael, the narrator of Melville's novel, *Moby Dick*. It's as if the sea itself has somehow taken up the mysterious music, akin perhaps to its own restlessness and unpredictability. The poet notes, too, that autumn is shaking down the birch leaves and fantasises that just one of these sustained notes might start a fire in the way a soprano's voice can break a wine glass if it stays on the right pitch for long enough.

Although, on this occasion, the musician 'has no bowls for death', the poem ends bleakly enough with a 'wintry madrigal' in this 'city of white swans' where the woman plays the highest note on her instrument and then appears to go on to an even higher note – on an invisible glass which is even smaller than the smallest one on the instrument. It's as if the listener has been lifted towards heaven by these strange, glassy tones that seem to go up indefinitely beyond human hearing – clearly a transcendent note in more ways than one.

'Glass Harmonica' is very much one of those poems which tries to capture, or at least evoke, something on the edge of human experience, something not fully understood but which we nevertheless feel to be significant. The glass harmonica, compared to most other instruments, is intrinsically strange. Its music is even stranger. Harrison underscores this strangeness by making all sorts of risky allusions in an attempt somehow to convey it. It's a highly subjective poem with all sorts of private references, the full range of which very few readers would know without some research. Harrison, however, is not deterred. She takes the risk and at the end takes the reader out, or up, into that ethereal realm beyond the already high pitch emanating from the 'smallest bowl'.

This aesthetic process is intensified by the rather formal quality of the poem, the way it's arranged into a series of five-line stanzas with considerable use of rhyme or half-rhyme. It is only in the last stanza that Harrison cuts back to four lines, as if she's deliberately omitting the sound of the smaller than smallest bowl whose note we can only imagine. The rhythm keeps a regular iambic pattern ('a *wave* to *drown* the *soul* of *bowls*') with just a few variations such as the reversed foot in '*ech*oes through *tabernacles*' where the pattern would normally be 'ech*oes* through *tabernacles*'. This overall consistency reinforces the sense we have that the musician knows exactly what she's doing – even if we don't. There is certainly, for instance, a ballad-like inevitability about the four stress/three stress pattern in the last two lines: 'she *reaches for* the s*mallest bowl*,/and *then* the s*maller one*'.

It is probably this sort of technical accomplishment which, on a first reading, takes us breezily past obscurities about the little-known Marianne Kirchgässner and the rather better-known opera by Richard Strauss, *The Woman without a Shadow*. It makes us feel that some research on the poem's allusions would be well justified. We feel we need to work our way into the subjectivity of Harrison's poem and find out more for ourselves. We want to know how she got to that 'feathered snow' and those 'wolverines' – and think a little more on what she might mean by those 'broken fans and wreathless things' even if we never do quite understand their significance fully. Eventually, we too will have heard what the poet heard, or something very like it, and will sense the sound of that 'smaller' bowl beyond the 'smallest bowl'. The strange woman and her glass harmonica sing on in the memory.

'Bahadour'

The sun stamps his shadow on the wall
and he's left one wheel of his bicycle
spinning. It is dusk, there are a few minutes

before he must pedal his wares through
the streets again. But now, nothing
is more important than his kite working

its way into the wobbly winter sky.
For the time he can live at the summit
of his head without a ticket, he is following

the kite through pastures of snow where
his father calls into the mountains for him,
where his mother weeps his farewell into

the carriages of a five-day train. You can
see so many boys out on the rooftops this
time of day, surrendering diamonds to

the thin blue air, putting their arms up, neither
in answer nor apprehension, but because
the day tenders them a coupon of release.

He does not think about the failing light,
nor of how his legs must mint so many steel
suns from a bicycle's wheels each day,

nor of how his life must drop like a token
into its appropriate slot; not even

of constructing whatever angles would break

the deal that transacted away his childhood –
nor of taking some fairness back to Nepal,
but only of how he can find purchase

with whatever minutes of dusk are left
to raise a diamond, to claim some share
of hope, some acre of sky within a hard-fisted

budget; and of how happy he is, yielding,
his arms up, equivalent now only to himself,
a last spoke in the denominations of light.

With only three collections so far, Judith Beveridge has made her name as one of Australia's most sophisticated contemporary poets. Though written in free verse, her poems are invariably polished to an almost translucent shine. For all her craftsmanship, however, Beveridge is no mere aesthete. Her poems are dense, not only with imagery but with moral imagination. She is able to feel her way into the situation (or plight) of other humans (or animals) and convince us, at once, of their integrity and complexity.

At one level, 'Bahadour' is a triumph of the much-maligned 'tourist' poem, that genre where someone from the first world visits the third and jots down, in postcard manner, their passing observations and, perhaps, their moral queasiness. Beveridge, in 'Bahadour', shows what can be achieved in this mode, if the poet takes the time to think, to empathise thoroughly and to craft his or her insights. It is rare to see poems that are simultaneously so moral and so complex as this one.

The morality begins in the opening line when the poet notes that the sun has already 'stamp(ed)' the boy's shadow on the wall. There seems to be no undoing this. Later she will refer to how the boy's life is merely a 'token' to be dropped into the 'appropriate slot' of India's 'hard-fisted' economic system. The boy has been sold into childhood servitude, presumably by parents who felt they had no other option. He is a 'five-day train' away from the mountains and snow of his native Nepal and must mint 'so many steel/suns from a bicycle's wheels each day'.

If this insight constituted the whole poem we would simply have orthodox Marxism. Where Beveridge goes well beyond this, however, is in her determination to peer deeply into the boy's human situation and discover what he is – despite his (undeniable) exploitation. Flying his kite in the few minutes he has off at dusk 'he can live at the summit/of his head without a ticket'. He can join the other boys 'surrendering diamonds to//the thin blue air'. He has been given his small 'coupon of release'. These images are not a mere 'poetification' of the situation. They reflect the intensity of the boy's aesthetic and, in a way, physical experience.

Like the rest of us (but more desperately) he can be taken out of himself into something more substantial, more transcendent. It is his equivalent, perhaps, to experiencing a symphony concert, a great painting (or even the final moments of an AFL grand final). He has come here 'to claim some share/of hope, some acre of sky …'. He doesn't (as a proto-Marxist would) concern himself with how he might undo 'the deal that transacted away his childhood'. He doesn't dream of 'taking some fairness back to Nepal'.

While not overlooking these omissions, Beveridge is much more interested in the way the boy celebrates how, at such a moment, he is 'equivalent … only to himself'. He doesn't have to be merely an insignificant part of someone else's narrative (his employer's, most obviously). He possesses, despite what he suffers, his own integrity and his own humanity. In all the huge unfairness of India the young peddler is 'a last spoke in the denominations of light'.

Perhaps the most convincing dimension of 'Bahadour' is how Beveridge has worked her way through technically to the insights noted above. This has clearly been no easy or formulaic journey. Each visual element in the situation has been seen and transformed so that it has, in itself, something of the same transcendence that the young kite flier experiences. The sky is not merely the sky; it is a 'wobbly winter sky' of 'thin blue air' with its own particularity.

The kites are 'diamonds' rather than mere constructions of paper, wood or wire. The coins he must earn each day are 'steel/suns', not just rupees. The whole situation is fully imagined, not simply jotted down in a journal or scribbled on a postcard.

Imagery of this quality contributes much to the poem's delicate tone, but so, too, do Beveridge's syntax and rhythms. The sentences run freely across lines and stanza breaks, but tend, generally, to be about a breath in length. A few may be longer when extra details seem to force their way in – as in the sentence beginning 'For the time …' in the third stanza. The poem moves at its own reflective and observant pace; there is no sense of hurry despite the 'failing light'.

Some may see the way the poem is divided into tercets as arbitrary, since the syntax so often runs across stanzas. This technique, which goes back to the American poet, William Carlos Williams, can give the illusion of form where, some would say, none exists. Actually, Beveridge's dignified, free-verse rhythms are already present and would still be felt even if the poem were printed as a continuous stanza. The tercet arrangement, however, tends to slow the reader down, to make him or her think more deeply about what is being presented. It can also provide, as a kind of bonus, some interesting, even arresting disjunctions, such as we feel when a stanza gap intervenes in the middle of the phrase 'would break//the deal'.

Another feature of Beveridge's free verse that may be of interest here is the shadow of the iambic pentameter that seems to lie underneath it. On a random count the lines seem to average about ten syllables, though few are actually a regular pentameter. 'He *does* not *think* about the *failing light*' is one of the few. Note, though, as an index of the poet's flexibility, the sense of release in the anapaests 'For the *time* he can *live* at the *summit*' – and the jarring proximity of the two stresses in the poem's opening phrase 'The *sun stamps* …', the way it reinforces the boy's predicament.

Of course, such sophistications are nothing in themselves. They are relevant only if they contribute to the poem's total effect. There is no doubt, however, that in 'Bahadour', as in many of her other poems, Judith Beveridge has shown that her complex free-verse rhythms and carefully honed images are at the core of the deep moral and psychological insights her poems develop. These are no mere flourishes. It is unlikely, having read 'Bahadour', that one will ever again see Indian child labourers in quite the same simplistic light. Human beings are much more than economics, even though injustices will remain injustices.

ANTHONY LAWRENCE (1957–)

'The Drive'

My father could not look at me
as we sat in the back of a white sedan
on our way to the police station.
But I looked at him. He was staring
straight ahead through all the years
his son had disappointed him.

News had come through of the boy
who'd fire-bombed the car outside
the Methodist Church. When the detectives
arrived, I was having a family
portrait taken. I saw the suits and ties
in the window, then the doorbell rang.

I smiled into the flash, ran to the bathroom
and vomited my head off. I wanted to make
the Australian team as a fast bowler.
I wanted Frances Clarke to love me.
But instead I'd struck a match and immolated
the minister's new Valiant, my breath

punched out of my lungs by the boom.
I ran behind the Sunday-school buildings
and confessed to the lawn-raking currawongs.
I watched black smoke like useless prayer
gutter into the Sydney sky.
The sirens were a long time coming.

As we pulled into the station carpark,

dead leaves and the two-way static
sounded like years of thrashings: blue
welts across the backs of my legs like
indelible neon, and my mother's weeping
for the times I'd nailed her with insults

to the wall. But now, after breakdowns,
divorce and a distance of eighteen years,
we can talk about the sound a belt makes
as it flies in the bathroom; about
the violent spirit of a teenage son.
My mother kisses my eyes to stop

the sadness we've known from breaking
through. My father tells me about his life
instead of brief reports from the office.
I love them, these parents and strangers,
these friends who appear from time to time,
sharing their names, their blood.

Many good poems are autobiographical, but it is rare in Australian poetry to see it done as directly as it is in Anthony Lawrence's 'The Drive'. Most poets prefer to use distancing devices such as mythical personae or rewriting the experiences as monologues for someone else. It was American poets such as Robert Lowell, Sylvia Plath and Anne Sexton in the late 1950s who first began to show the potential – and the dangers – of what became known as 'confessional' poetry. They demonstrated the explosive force that is available when a skilled poet drops the disguises and writes directly out of his or her own, often traumatic, experience using the real names and places and so on.

Naturally, we can't be sure that some small details haven't been modified for aesthetic purposes, but the reader has no difficulty smelling the authenticity and the risk-taking in 'The Drive'. It's as plain as the 'black smoke' that 'gutter(s) into the Sydney sky' after the 'minister's new Valiant' is set alight. Many of the most successful confessional poems have a well-shaped story to tell and 'The Drive' is no exception.

Lawrence begins *in medias res* (in the middle of things) and then goes back to explain just how he comes to be in the police car with his father. Even the lineation in these first three lines is clever narration. The first line mysteriously tells us 'My father could not look at me'; the second delays the explanation while the third at least tells us where the events are occurring – 'on our way to the police station'. The rest of the stanza provides us with more generalised but essential background – 'all the years/his son had disappointed him'.

In the second stanza we have more revelations though we don't yet know for sure that the narrator is the same 'boy/who'd fire-bombed the car outside/the Methodist Church.' We also have the ironic arrival of the 'suits and ties' of the police just as a 'family/portrait' is being taken. The third stanza, which the reader would expect to provide some sort of motivation for the crime, seems instead to emphasise the lack of it. The narrator is merely musing on how what he's done will get in the way of his sporting and romantic ambitions. The dramatic force with which his breath was 'punched out of (his) lungs by the boom' gives some sort of clue however. He remembers, again ironically, confessing to the church currawongs – and attempting a 'useless prayer' analogous to the 'black smoke' from the destroyed car. The explanation for all this is, like the sirens of the fire engine, 'a long time coming'.

At this point, however, Lawrence cuts back to the police car and, more importantly, to the revelatory brutality of his teenage relationship to his parents, the thrashings he got from his father and the insults he offered his mother. If the poem ended here it would make a certain sense – brutalised boy acts out repressed violence and so on – but it is in the last two stanzas of the poem that its real force is revealed. There, we skip ahead 'eighteen years' and see that after the 'breakdowns (and) divorce', the narrator is at last able to speak to his parents, albeit separately, about those chaotic years, 'about/the violent spirit of a teenage son' and 'the sound a belt makes/as it flies in the bathroom.' His mother 'kisses (his) eyes to stop//the sadness'. His father gives him more than just 'brief reports from the office'. There is a sense of recognition, of reconciliation, even redemption. But it is not a relatively straightforward thing like the parable of the prodigal son. The parents are still (or have become?) 'strangers'. They are now 'friends' more than parents, but the last line is surely also the poem's bottom line. The narrator recognises that despite everything that has occurred, and irrespective of whose fault it was, he still '(shares) their names, their blood'.

As suggested already, 'The Drive' is as much a triumph of narration as it is of poetic description. It's like a short redemption movie, but the compression of poetry enables it to swell with implications. On 'unpacking' the brief references to how the three characters have damaged or disappointed each other, we see the full extent of what has happened. We also sense its full humanity, however. We see that it's not a simple matter of right and wrong, of who is to blame for what (although the Methodist minister with his wrecked Valiant may have had more simple ideas). We see all three characters, 18 years later, now beginning to understand the maelstrom they were caught up in. We think about the crucifixion implications in 'I nailed her with insults//to the wall'. We wonder at the objectivity of two grown people talking about 'the sound a belt makes/as it flies in the bathroom'. All of these densely compressed images open out with implication when one really begins to think about them.

A further dimension to Lawrence's skill with narration is the way the poem appears to be almost arbitrarily broken up into five-line stanzas and yet each stanza is a self-contained 'chapter' in the story. We get acute enjambements across stanzas such as 'breath// punched' and 'stop//the sadness', but these seem only to intensify the points being made rather than acting as distractions. It is a similar case with the poem's rhythm. Although there are a few lines of completely regular iambic ('The *sirens were* a *long* time *coming*'), most lines seem to have the colloquial quality of well-written narrative prose while, paradoxically perhaps, retaining through their rhythmic force and imagery, their quality as poetry. We have, for instance, a sense of the anapaestic in lines like 'and con*fess*ed to the *lawn*-raking *curra*wongs'. Such lines are certainly not iambic but they're not arrhythmic either.

Ultimately, however, beyond all this is the force of the story – the graphic suburban violence and the reconciliation (albeit with 'strangers' and 'friends') 18 years later. 'The Drive' is a poem with no punches pulled and there must be very few readers left unmoved by its final lines. This sort of completion and incompletion is the world as we know it – and Lawrence's poem serves very well to remind us of this fact.

'Shooting the Dogs'

There wasn't much else we could do
that final day on the farm.
We couldn't take them with us into town,
no-one round the district needed them
and the new people had their own.
It was one of those things.

You sometimes hear of dogs
who know they're about to be put down
and who look up along the barrel of the rifle
into responsible eyes that never forget
that look and so on,
but our dogs didn't seem to have a clue.

They only stopped for a short while
to look at the Bedford stacked with furniture
not hay
and then cleared off towards the swamp,
plunging through the thick paspalum
noses up, like speedboats.

They weren't without their faults.
The young one liked to terrorise the chooks
and eat the eggs.
Whenever he started doing this
we'd let him have an egg full of chilli paste
and then the chooks would get some peace.

The old one's weakness was rolling in dead sheep.

Sometimes after this he'd sit outside
the kitchen window at dinner time.
The stink would hit us all at once
and we'd grimace like the young dog
discovering what was in the egg.

But basically they were pretty good.
They worked well and added life to the place.
I called them back enthusiastically
and got the old one as he bounded up
and then the young one as he shot off
for his life.

I buried them behind the tool shed.
It was one of the last things I did before
we left.
Each time the gravel slid off the shovel
it sounded like something
trying to hang on by its nails.

'Shooting the Dogs', by Philip Hodgins, is one of the most laconic poems ever written in this country – which is supposedly full of them. Some of its lines are as 'unpoetic' as it's possible to be. Take, for instance, the opening line: 'There wasn't much else we could do'. Another example is '… but our dogs didn't seem to have a clue'. The double negative in 'They weren't without their faults' is a slightly wordier equivalent to the answer Australians normally give the question 'How are you going?' 'Not bad', we say, not wanting to overstate the point. Again the sense of a yarning narrative (to be told perhaps while leaning on some stockyard rails) is felt in the simple sentence 'But basically they were pretty good'. It's not a line one can imagine being penned by any of the great figures of the English canon even though all its words have been around for a millennium or more.

The remarkable thing about 'Shooting the Dogs', however, is not that it's a nice a piece of local colour or wry 'outback' humour but that it's ultimately so moving. Obviously, the poem's last line is the crucial one but the build-up towards it starts from the beginning. Right from the opening, the poem starts with loss, even dispossession (the title of Hodgins' verse novel on a comparable theme). It's the 'final day on the farm' and 'There wasn't much else we could do'. We're not told much about the 'new people' except they've already got dogs of their own. Presumably, they've been luckier than the narrator and his family.

In the second stanza, the narrator emphasises how unaware the dogs were and contrasts them almost humorously with those archetypal dogs who 'look up along the barrel of the rifle', knowing what's going to happen to them. In the third stanza, Hodgins mentions their brief bemusement with 'the Bedford', stacked with furniture not hay. Then the dogs finally realise. And here the poet allows himself his first artistic flourish, the memorable simile 'like speedboats' to describe the dogs' heads above the grass.

In the fourth and fifth stanzas, just like an old bush storyteller, the narrator goes off on a tangent with information that is, we realise later, crucial to the punchline later on. The dogs, like us, are unique animals. One is fond of chasing chooks; the other delights in rolling about in the carcasses of dead sheep. The humour with which we're told this makes it all the sadder when we hear of their death and burial just a couple of stanzas on. The poet admits that 'They worked well and added life to the place' – namely the place that he's now leaving with some reluctance. Given their imminent demise, the word 'life' here has an extra resonance, too.

The poignancy of all this is intensified by the trust and enthusiasm with which the dogs come running to the narrator's call – and by the broken trust which makes the young dog '(shoot) off/for his life'. We already know at this point, however, that he's been 'got'. The poignancy goes up another notch with the fact that they are buried 'behind the tool shed', no more or less functional than the tools which were stored there. Then, at last, we have the final image for which the poem is so well known: 'Each time the gravel slid off the shovel/it sounded like something/trying to hang on by its nails'.

There are several implications here, of which the most obvious is the dogs' (already posthumous) reluctance to give up their lives. They 'added life to the place' while they lived and now, like almost all of us, they're unwilling to let go. The gravel on the shovel symbolises what it is burying. The second level here, of course, is the narrator's sadness at having had to give up the farm. 'Shooting the Dogs' is the last thing he has to do before he leaves. A third, extra-literary, level here is the fact known to many but not all of Hodgins' readers when the poem was published that he was dying from leukaemia and had been for quite a few years.

Many of Hodgins' later poems used strict metres and regular rhyme schemes (as if he wished to avoid making things too easy for himself), but in 'Shooting the Dogs' he has wisely let his extraordinarily low-key free verse do the job. One of Hodgins' few concessions to formality is to divide the poem into seven stanzas of six lines each, even though those lines are sometimes of radically uneven length. The short lines, in particular, are used to striking effect – as, for instance, in 'not hay' and 'for his life'.

The free-verse rhythms (which are sometimes almost prose-like) are employed not just to convey the flatness of the narrator's tone but also to drive home key points in the story. This can be sensed most strongly in the poem's closing lines, though it occurs quite often elsewhere, too: '… it *sounded* like *something*/*trying* to *hang on* by its *nails*'. There is a suggestion of an anapaestic (almost happy) regularity in the penultimate line. This, however, is then brutally broken by the stress on the two adjacent syllables '*hang on*' in the middle of the last line. It can also be felt in the two unstressed syllables which make us land so heavily on the crucial monosyllable '*nails*'. Such irregularities are certainly a part of the poem's overall laconic tone, but they also come down heavily on the words which carry the poem's emotional force.

There are, admittedly, quite a few regular iambic lines – which serve only to illustrate the irregularities elsewhere. 'We *couldn't take* them *with* us *into town*' and 'The *stink* would *hit* us *all* at *once*' are just two examples of this classic iambic. It's the way Hodgins goes against these expectations that creates the memorably flat tone of the whole poem – and the prevailing understatement which leaves the reader so devastated by the simile in its last three lines.

During his short life, Philip Hodgins built up a reputation as one of the most convincing of contemporary poets writing about Australian farm life. He knew it well from personal experience, remembered it without exaggeration or sentimentality – and, in poems such as 'Shooting the Dogs' (and quite a few others), found a tone that has remained true to its essence.

JOHN KINSELLA (1963–)

'Drowning in Wheat'

They'd been warned
on every farm
that playing
in the silos
would lead to death.
You sink in wheat.
Slowly. And the more
you struggle the worse it gets.
'You'll see a rat sail past
your face, nimble on its turf,
and then you'll disappear.'
In there, hard work
has no reward.
So it became a kind of test
to see how far they could sink
without needing a rope
to help them out.
But in the midst of play
rituals miss a beat – like both
leaping in to resolve
an argument
as to who'd go first
and forgetting
to attach the rope.
Up to the waist
and afraid to move.
That even a call for help
would see the wheat

trickle down.
The painful consolidation
of time. The grains
in the hourglass
grotesquely swollen.
And that acrid
chemical smell
of treated wheat
coaxing them into
a near-dead sleep.

John Kinsella, like the Portuguese poet Fernando Pessoa (1888–1935), writes in several very different styles. It is in his 'wheatbelt pastoral' mode, however, that he is most sure-footed. 'Drowning in Wheat' is one of his best-known and memorable poems in this genre.

Deaths of the kind Kinsella presents here do happen in wheatbelt towns from time to time. Children (universally) like to play and, often, they like to play dangerously. The admonitions of grown-ups are cast aside, especially when the spirits of adventure, competitiveness and recklessness overwhelm them.

Kinsella begins by emphasising how 'They'd been warned' and told that 'You sink in wheat./Slowly.' There is even an unattributed bit of folklore about 'a rat sail(ing) past/your face' as you start to sink. The rat, paradoxically, is 'nimble on its turf' but you are stuck and slowly going down. The ironies and contradictions continue. 'Hard work', unlike at other times, 'has no reward' when you're floundering in a silo of wheat.

Predictably, the children (we're not told exactly how old they are but 'old enough to know better' presumably) establish a competition: 'how far (they) could sink/without needing a rope'. The game goes well for a while but, as is the way of these things, 'rituals miss a beat', a safety routine is forgotten and suddenly they find themselves 'Up to the waist/and afraid to move.' At least they remember that much of what they've been told. At this point, Kinsella starts employing incomplete sentences to suggest their panic. He talks, without finite verbs, about 'The painful consolidation/of time' and 'The grains/in the hourglass/grotesquely swolien'. Even the final sentence is incomplete, based as it is on the present participle, 'coaxing'. We, as readers, are left suspended grammatically as we watch and meditate on what has happened.

It is interesting to speculate what wider reference Kinsella intended this poem to suggest. What of the irony in the title itself, for instance? 'Drowning in Wheat' could mean that, luckily, the farmers have got more wheat this season than they can expect to sell. But, again paradoxically, it is in this surplus that two of their children will drown. Another implication may be that, in any comparably desperate situation, it is always best not to panic – though in this case, that argument is undermined a little by the fact that not panicking will only delay the inevitable, not avoid it. More probably then, the poet is concerned with the poignancy of the situation itself – the fact that children have ignored the advice and they're going to die suffering the consequences of their actions. Some might be tempted to see the poem as a 'cautionary tale', but it seems more likely that the poet is more interested in evoking what has happened rather than imagining his poem will somehow in the future prevent its happening again.

'Drowning in Wheat' is in some ways analogous to Robert Frost's famous poem, 'Out, Out', the one about the young boy who dies after his hand is cut off by a buzz-saw – though Kinsella doesn't in any way display the relative callousness that marks the end of Frost's poem. In 'Drowning in Wheat' we last see the victims in the middle of their death, sinking down in the wheat and slowly being overcome by fumes. Kinsella thus leaves them 'on view' in their 'hourglass' rather than showing them inert and asphyxiated a few metres below the wheat's surface.

Technically, some readers might question the short lines in which Kinsella has written his poem. Under the not-always-beneficial influence of the American poet, William Carlos Williams, a lot of failed poems have been attempted in this form. Beginner poets often imagine that cutting up a prose statement into lines of three or four words will somehow transmute mundane prose alchemically into powerful poetry.

Kinsella, however, has a much better reason for employing the short line. The children are playing in a silo – and the poet has more or less enclosed them in a long, thin silo-like structure. We read down through the poem in a way analogous to how the children sink down through the wheat. At last, we get to the bottom – neatly tied-off with the half-rhyme 'wheat' and 'sleep'. This 'thin' form also forces us to take the poem slowly, one line at a time – a process which will allow its meaning to be absorbed and its implications meditated upon. Williams was the first to realise the potential of writing poetry like this – but the so-called 'toothpaste' technique has always depended on the quality of what's in the tube.

As with most free verse, 'Drowning in Wheat' is not quite as 'free' as it appears. There are quite a few iambic lines, for instance – and, strangely enough, the admonitory bit of folklore we're given is almost entirely in iambics: 'You'll *see* a *rat* sail *past*/your *face*, *nimble on* its *turf*,/and *then* you'll *disappear*'. The regularity here mnemonically enhances the sentence's memorability.

Ultimately then, Kinsella has left us with a graphic and poignant description of two young accidental deaths. He doesn't appear to want to go much beyond this. He'd rather let the poem sit there and resonate while readers draw their own conclusions. As quite a few of Kinsella's other poems demonstrate, there are many toughnesses in Western Australia's increasingly marginal wheat-belt. We have been shown just one of them.

BRONWYN LEA (1969–)

'Girls' Night on Long Island'

We drink vodka martinis
with tiny onions and green olives,
eat popcorn and salty pork and talk
about circumcision. That's their problem,
we decide, their insecurity, the root
of their castration anxiety. Teresa laughs,
she's not complaining,
she thinks it's worth the sacrifice.
I shrug, fixing another drink, either way.
'What does she care?' Ruth asks,
'She's Australian!' and everybody laughs.
But Meg is happy at least one
woman's not fussy
because when her premature son
was born they stuck dozen of tubes
into his little red body,
and when he came out of ICU,
she just decided forget it. Ruth says
it was the same with her son,
though longer ago,
his lung burst in the delivery room
from a resuscitator set at adult pressure –
and they took him to another hospital
to have the lung re-inflated.
For a week she cried,
without her child or any visitors,
and when she finally got him back,
she wouldn't let another doctor

touch him. And besides,
she laughs chewing on an olive,
all of her grandparents
and all of her uncles and all of her aunts
died at Auschwitz,
and she thought about this,
as she suckled her newborn son,
that if another Hitler came to power
at least he wouldn't get
this little Jew. And her words fall heavy
on the living room, just like the rain
falling outside. Meg is asleep.
Her second martini too much
after half a Xanex. Some of us turn
to the fire. Some of us turn
to the rain.

'Girls' Night on Long Island' is a timely reminder that not all Australian poetry has to be set in its own landscape. Australians are great travellers and livers-abroad. Bronwyn Lea spent several important years of her life living and studying in the U.S. – and the tentativeness of her connection with the Long Island women in the poem shows. As a female she is one of them, but as an Australian she is something of an outsider, a butt for wisecracks. The poem itself, however, shows significant American influences, reminding us that quite a deal of recent Australian poetry has a 'mid-Pacific' aura to it.

The conversations in 'Girls' Night on Long Island' might well have been turned into a short story but, by using the flexible and conversational free verse she does here, Lea compresses the material and makes it resonate, leaving more room for the reader to interpret and to ponder connections. Such interpretations begin, necessarily, at the beginning. Who exactly are these women? What are their affiliations? The name Teresa sounds Catholic rather than Jewish and she jokes about preferring circumsized men. Ruth, on the other hand, has had almost all her relatives murdered in Auschwitz. The group is eating 'salty pork' so we can assume they're not orthodox Jews. Meg, who may or may not be Jewish, is 'happy at least one/ woman's not fussy' about the issue; she doesn't want her uncircumsized son to be disadvantaged, as it were. It's a multicultural gathering with a Jewish tinge perhaps.

The evening itself in real life may well have lasted several hours but the narrator cleverly focuses on a few key episodes, each one of them having a particular poignancy and revealing some of the difficulties involved with being female, in Long Island or elsewhere. Men may have their problems too, it seems ('castration anxiety', for one), but they're offstage – though never entirely out of the picture. The fact that two of the women talk about the misadventures of their male babies seems to ensure this – as does the initial joking about the sexual pros and cons of circumcision.

It's interesting to trace the attitudes of the women through the poem. Teresa, almost certainly non-Jewish, jokes about circumcision's being 'worth the sacrifice'. She prefers men that way. The narrator, through either shyness or genuine uninterest, shrugs and turns to fix another drink. Meg, who at the end of the poem has passed out from a 'second martini' added to prescription drugs, is glad that at least one woman is 'not fussy' about all this since she (Meg) just didn't feel like inflicting any more pain on the 'little red body' of her newborn son after he came out of ICU. We're not told what the father of her son thought of all this but, plainly, he didn't successfully disagree with her.

At this stage, Ruth (who is certainly Jewish) takes things one step further by narrating her tale of medical ineptitude and telling them of her fierce determination not to 'let another doctor/touch (her son)'. At this point we reach the climax of the poem with Ruth's revelations about her relatives being killed in Auschwitz. She tells this while 'chewing an olive' and laughingly remembers that, as she suckled her uncircumsized Jewish son, this would be at least one 'little Jew' that a re-born Hitler wouldn't 'get'. The narrator then tells us how Ruth's 'words fall heavy/on the living room, just like the rain/falling outside'. The banter is over. Decades after the events in Europe – and an ocean away – the aftermath is still being felt. And not just by the relatives but by everyone in the room. The Xanex that Meg has taken is one way of 'dealing' with it. Alcohol and female companionship (with attendant jokes) are others. At this stage the party starts to break up. Some women look into the fire and wait for the conversation to resume. Others decide they'd better go, that it's time to face the rain that has been falling outside throughout the evening.

Inevitably, both the fire and the rain bear a symbolic load. The fire paradoxically so, since it's at once a comfort to the women who are staying on and a reminder of the crematoria that incinerated Jews in Europe under Hitler. The rain, on the other hand, suggests the rest of the women's lives, the part they have to go back to when the 'Girls' Night' is over. There may be an echo here, too, of Ernest Hemingway's famous conclusion to *A Farewell to Arms* where the narrator, after the death in childbirth of his girlfriend, says: 'After a while I went out and left the hospital and walked back to the hotel in the rain'. These women, too, are going out into the rain. It is this mixture of complex symbolism and literary echoing that lends the poem's ending its particular force – and so, retrospectively, the poem as a whole. After the joking earlier on we readers, whether male or female, are left stunned by the intensity of the stories we've heard, particularly the last one. Like the women, we see for the moment there is nowhere else to go. We stare silently into the fire – or we call it a night and step out into the rain.

A slightly less obvious component in this overall effect is Lea's mastery of enjambement and lineation. Most of the lines are 'units of sense' but every now and again Lea varies this to powerful effect. At the end of the long sentence about Ruth's son's misadventures, for instance, Lea starts a new line for the key words 'touch him' – and then begins a tough new sentence right on that same line: 'And besides …' An equally moving example is the enjambement between 'he wouldn't get' and 'this little Jew'. It's almost as if the baby is being hidden away protectively in the next line. Lea also finishes the poem with that classic free-verse device parallelism ('Some of us turn/to the fire. Some of us turn/to the rain.') but, characteristically, she puts her own stamp on it by not starting each line with the same word as is done traditionally.

Of course, it's premature to be hailing a poem published less than ten years ago as a classic. What makes one confident about this poem, however, is that it embodies so much of what the best poetry has so often done (though every rule has its exceptions, of course). It builds something universal from the specific. It entertains and moves us by turn. It leaves us with that sense of having been (if only a little) permanently transformed. We are never going to be able to think of a girls' night in Long Island (or anything loosely comparable) without thinking of Lea's poem: its raw humour, its pain-filled anecdotes, its fierce revelations − and those last two sentences. I don't think one needs to repeat them.

COPYRIGHT

Kevin Hart: the author

William Hart-Smith: The William Hart-Smith Estate (Brian Dibble)

Gwen Harwood: Penguin Group (Australia)

Dorothy Hewett: Fremantle Press

Philip Hodgins: Janet Shaw

A.D. Hope: Geoffrey Hope

Clive James: the author

John Kinsella: the author

Anthony Lawrence: the author

Bronwyn Lea: the author

Geoffrey Lehmann: the author

Kate Llewellyn: the author

James McAuley: HarperCollins Publishers (Australia)

Ronald McCuaig: HarperCollins Publishers (Australia)

Jennifer Maiden: the author

David Malouf: the author

John Manifold: University of Queensland Press

Les Murray: the author

Oodgeroo of the tribe Noonuccal: from My People, 4e, © 2007. Reproduced by permission of John Wiley & Sons, Australia

Jan Owen: the author

Geoff Page: the author and Salt Publishing

Dorothy Porter: from *Crete* courtesy the author and Jenny Darling and Associates

Peter Porter: the author

GLOSSARY

Alexandrine A line of six feet (also called hexameter), usually iambic.

Alliteration The repetition of consonants at the beginning of words; for example, 'dived down deep'.

Alliterative verse Anglo-Saxon verse where there are four stressed syllables in the line, of which the first three are normally alliterative; for example (in translation), 'There was Shield Sheafson, scourge of many tribes' (*Beowulf*).

Anapaestic A metre made up of two weak syllables followed by a strong one; for example, 'There's the *hap*/less young *po*/et I *told*/ you a*bout*'.

Apostrophe When a person not present, or an abstraction, is addressed; for example, 'Hence, loathed Melancholy!' or 'Milton! thou shouldst be living at this hour'.

Ars poetica A poem expressing the poet's ideas about the art of poetry.

Assonance The repetition of vowel sounds; for example, 'large charge'.

Ballad stanza A four-line stanza arranged with lines of four stresses, three stresses, four stresses, three stresses, using an *abcb* rhyme scheme; employed for centuries in narrative poetry but also in hymns, folk songs and so on.

Blank verse Unrhymed iambic pentameter, as used in Shakespeare's plays, Milton's *Paradise Lost* and many other poems in English.

Caesura A pause in the middle of a line of verse; for example, 'A little learning//is a dangerous thing' (Pope).

Conceit An extreme or fanciful comparison; for example, when Donne says of a flea that has just bitten him and his mistress: 'This flea is you and I, and this/Our marriage bed, and marriage temple is'.

Consonance The repetition of consonants, usually elsewhere than at the beginning of words (in which case it is called 'alliteration'); for example, 'big dog'.

Couplet Two successive lines of verse, often rhyming, in which case they are called 'heroic couplets'.

Dactyllic A metre made up of one strong syllable followed by two weak syllables; for example, '*Warily/Wil*fred was/*walk*ing a/*long* with her'.

Diction The vocabulary used in a poem. In some periods poetic diction became very old-fashioned and had to be updated and made more colloquial; for example, by the Romantics and the Modernists.

Dimeter A line of two feet (or two stressed syllables).

Dramatic monologue When the poet puts himself or herself in the mind of another person and writes from that point of view; for example, Browning's 'My Last Duchess'.

Elegy A poem mourning someone's death; for example, Auden's 'In Memory of W.B. Yeats'; originally the term 'elegiac' referred to a particular metre in Greek and Latin, and was used for many different sorts of poem; for example, by Catullus.

Enjambement Where a sentence in a poem runs on from one line to the next without a significant pause – as opposed to 'end-stopped' where there is a punctuation mark or a definite pause.

Epic A long poem, often telling an heroic story but sometimes, as in Byron's *Don Juan*, an unheroic or humorous one. The best-known examples are Homer's *Iliad* and *Odyssey*, Virgil's *Aeneid*, Dante's *Divine Comedy* and Milton's *Paradise Lost*.

Epigram A short, witty poem, the ancestry of which goes back at least to the Latin poet, Martial (40–104 CE).

Feminine rhyme Where the rhyme is polysyllabic and the stress is not on the last syllable; for example, '*cler*ical/*spher*ical'.

Foot The basic unit of metre, comparable to a bar in music. Usually marked by a slash; for example, 'So *all*/day *long*/the *noise*/of *batt*/le *rolled*/' has five feet. It is best to think of each foot in English verse having just one stressed syllable and a number of unstressed syllables.

Free verse (*vers libre* in French) Poetry that doesn't have a regular metre or a rhyme scheme. Sometimes called 'mixed verse' because it mixes several kinds of feet together in one line; for example, 'A *wet/leaf* that/*clings* to the/*threshold*' (Ezra Pound).

Haiku A three-line, unrhymed Japanese verse form with lines of five, seven and five syllables respectively.

Half-rhyme A rhyme where either the final vowel or the final consonant is not the same as the one in the word rhymed with; for example, 'dig/dug' or 'large/bath'.

Heptameter A line of seven feet (or seven stressed syllables).

Hexameter A line of six feet (or six stressed syllables) (also known as an Alexandrine).

Iambic A metre made up of an unstressed syllable followed by a stressed syllable; for example, 'So *all/*day *long/*the *noise/*of *batt/*le *rolled/*'.

Iambic pentameter An iambic line of five feet, as above; by far the most common line in English.

Iambic tetrameter An iambic line of four feet, quite often used in humorous or satirical poetry; for example, by Swift.

Imagery The making of something more graphic by using some sort of comparison; for example, a simile, metaphor or simply a well-chosen adjective and noun. See example below under *Imagists*.

Imagists A group of poets in England and America around 1912 who believed that compression and the image were the essence of poetry. Pound's 'In a Station at the Metro' is often considered the classic Imagist poem: 'The apparition of these faces in the crowd;/ Petals on a wet, black bough'.

Inverted foot Where the normal arrangement of syllables in a foot is reversed, usually at the beginning of a line for dramatic purposes; for example, Frost's '*Some*thing/there *is/*that *does/*n't *love/*a *wall*' (in 'Mending Wall').

Laconic Saying a lot in a little; sometimes used in the sense of 'laidback'; from the Spartans in Laconia who were known for their brief, pithy speech.

Lineation The issue of when a poet goes on to the next line and why he or she does so at that point; most important in free verse. Various tension and release effects are gained by this device; for example, 'I saw a girl with one leg/over the edge of a balcony' *from* William Carlos Williams, 'The Right of Way'.

Line length The number of feet (or stressed syllables) in a line of verse; for example, monometer, dimeter, trimeter, tetrameter, pentameter, hexameter, heptameter and so on.

Long vowels Long vowels, as in 'w*a*vers and f*a*des', can have a different effect on one's mood to that created by short vowels such as 't*i*p t*o*p'.

Lyric A poem written to be sung to the accompaniment of a lyre; originally, in ancient Greece; now refers more generally to a short poem of a celebratory, rather than of a dramatic or satirical, nature.

Masculine rhyme Where the rhyme is monosyllabic or where the rhyme is on the last syllable of a polysyllabic word; for example, '*prize*/monopol*ise*'.

Metaphor A comparison made by saying one thing is something else; for example, 'The moon was a ghostly galleon …'.

Metonym Literally 'name change'; for example, in Milton's line 'When I consider how my light is spent' where 'light' refers to his vision.

Metre The underlying pattern of stressed and unstressed syllables in a line – in contrast to 'rhythm', which is what actually happens in a particular line; for example, the inverted foot in Donne's '*Death*, be/not *proud*', as opposed to the metre underlying it: 'Death, *be*/not *proud*'.

Negative capability Keats felt that the best poetry is written 'when man is capable of being in uncertainties, mysteries, doubts, without any irritable reaching after fact & reason'; in other words, the poet should have the ability to follow the poem where it leads rather than to determine it excessively from outside.

Objective correlative A term coined by T.S. Eliot in his essay on *Hamlet* where he wrote: 'The only way of expressing emotion in art is by finding an "objective correlative"; in other words, a set of objects; a situation, a chain of events which shall be the formula for that *particular*, such that when the general facts which must terminate in sensory experience, are given, the emotion is immediately evoked'. According to Eliot, the poet should find an equivalent ('an objective correlative') for his or her emotion and not try to describe it directly.

Octave The opening eight-line section of a sonnet.

Ode Originally a poem to be sung and danced on a public occasion; for example, a victory at the Olympic games; now simply a poem of some length, normally on a serious subject.

Onomatopoeia Where the actual sounds of words seem to reinforce their literal meaning; for example, 'Over the cobbles he clattered and clashed ...'.

Ottava rima An eight-line iambic pentameter stanza rhyming *ababab cc*; originally used for serious epics in Renaissance Italian; used by Byron in his mock epic *Don Juan*.

Oxymoron A contradiction in terms. Some have unkindly suggested 'military intelligence' or 'nice police'.

Paradox An apparent contradiction that suggests a deeper truth.

Parallelism The repetition of the same grammatical structure, particularly at the beginning of lines; often used in free verse (and in the Bible).

Parody An imitation of a poem or a kind of poem designed to make it seem ridiculous.

Pastoral Originally a love poem about idealised nymphs and shepherds in ancient Greece; now sometimes used more generally about poems located in an idealised rural setting.

Pathetic fallacy A form of personification, where something inanimate is described as though it were animate.

Pentameter A line of five feet (or five stressed syllables).

Persona The narrator or central figure of a poem who can be distinguished from the poet himself or herself.

Personification A kind of metaphor where something inanimate (or abstract) is given living characteristics; for example, 'The sun beats lightning on the waves' (Hart Crane, 'Voyages I').

Petrarchan sonnet A sonnet with an octave and a sestet, normally rhyming *abbaabba cdecde* (as used by the Italian poet Petrarch (1304–74) and many after him. It also normally has a *volta*, or turn of thought, at the end of line 8.

Prosody Theory of versification, concerned with metre, rhyme schemes, stanza forms and so on.

Quantitative verse In Greek and Latin, verse metre was based on long and short syllables rather than on stressed and unstressed syllables. Terms like iambic and dactyllic originally referred to quantitative metres.

Quatrain A stanza of four lines, normally rhyming.

Refrain A reiterated line, like the chorus of a song.

Rhyme scheme The pattern of rhyme throughout a poem; described by calling the first rhyme *a* and any following rhyme *a* also; the next end-word is called *b* and so on. See rhyme scheme of *Petrarchan sonnet* above.

Rhythm See *Metre* above.

Scansion The marking of stressed and unstressed syllables in a particular line or throughout a poem. A poem with a regular metre is said to 'scan'.

Sestet The last six lines of a sonnet.

Sestina A form from Medieval Provence in which the final words of six unrhymed stanzas are repeated in a certain fixed order. It finishes with a tercet, which incorporates three or six of the terminal words.

Short vowels See *Long vowels*.

Simile A comparison explicitly using the words 'like' or 'as'; for example, 'He ate like a horse'.

Sonnet A poem of 14 lines. Two earlier forms of sonnets are the Petrarchan and the Elizabethan (as used by Shakespeare and Donne). Contemporary sonnet writers often use blank verse and some have even used free verse. Many sonnets have a *volta* (or turn of thought) at the end of line 8. Some, for example the Elizabethans, have a rhyming couplet at the end.

Sprung rhythm A rhythm used mainly by Gerard Manley Hopkins in which the first syllable of a foot is always stressed but can be followed by any number of unstressed syllables. '*High* there, how he/*rung* upon the/*rein* of a/*wimpling/wing* …'.

Stanza A group of lines within a poem; often regular in traditional verse (for example, the quatrain), but frequently irregular in length in free verse. Sometimes, less satisfactorily, called a 'verse'.

Stanza gap The break between stanzas, often used in free verse to gain certain effects; for example, a longer pause.

Strong lines Irregular lines used by the Metaphysical poets where several stressed syllables are placed next to each other, thus seeming to interrupt the otherwise smooth flow of the underlying metre. For example, in Donne's line, 'Nor hours, days, *months*, which are the *rags* of *time*', where the underlying metre is, 'Nor *hours*, days, *months*, which *are* the *rags* of *time*'.

Syllabic verse Where the number of syllables in a line (rather than the position of stressed and unstressed syllables) is the basis of composition; for example, the five-, seven- and five-syllable structure of the Japanese haiku.

Symbol A word, sign or image that stands for something other than itself; for example, the cross in Christianity or the albatross hung around the neck of the mariner in Coleridge's 'Rime of the Ancient Mariner'. There is often a productive disagreement about the meaning (or even the presence of) symbols in a particular poem.

Synaesthesia When one sensory impulse is experienced in terms of another e.g. the 'honey-voice' of the sirens in Homer's *Odyssey* or Blake's image where a 'hapless Soldier's sigh/Runs in blood down Palace walls' ('London').

Synecdoche A figure of speech where a part of something is used to stand for the whole: 'He owned many horses and was addicted to the turf'.

Tanka A Japanese syllabic form arranged 5/7/5/7/7.

Tautology Pointless repetition; for example, 'In my opinion, I think …'

Tercets Three-line stanzas.

Terza rima An Italian linked rhyme scheme, used by Dante in his *Divine Comedy*, which is arranged *aba bcb cdc* and so on.

Tetrameter A line of four feet (or four stressed syllables).

Trimeter A line of three feet (or three stressed syllables).

Trochaic A metre made up of one stressed syllable followed by one unstressed syllable; for example, Blake's '*How* the/*Chimney/sweepers/cry*' ('London'). Note: the unstressed syllable in the final foot is often left out.

Trope From the Greek 'a turn'; means 'figure of speech'; for example, metaphor, simile, personification and so on.

Villanelle A French form of five tercets and a quatrain all based on just two rhymes with some repetition of lines.

Volta The turn of thought at the end of line 8 of a Petrarchan sonnet.

APPENDIX

Some additional modern or contemporary Australian classics

Adam Aitken 'At the Registry'

Jordie Albiston 'The Fall'

Chris Andrews 'Pittosporum'

Peter Bakowski 'Portrait of Erik Satie, Composer'

Judith Bishop 'Doña Marina'

Ken Bolton 'Tiepolo'

Peter Boyle 'Paralysis'

R.F. Brissenden 'Samuel Johnson Talking'

David Brooks 'Bush-Mouse'

Kevin Brophy 'What I Believe'

Pam Brown 'Paris, France'

Andrew Burke 'Mother Waits for Father Late'

Joanne Burns 'Carnal Knowledge'

Adrian Caesar 'Mid-Term Report'

Michelle Cahill 'Narcolepsy'

Heather Cam 'Majestic Rollerink'

Gary Catalano 'The Empire of Grass'

Lee Cataldi 'kuukuu kardiya *and the women who live on the ground*'

Nancy Cato 'The Dead Swagman'

James Charlton 'Koonya'

Christine Churches 'My Mother and the Trees'

Julian Croft 'Labour and Capital'

Alison Croggon 'The Elwood Organic Fruit and Vegetable Shop'

M.T.C. Cronin 'Dawnflower'

Luke Davies 'Totem Poem'

Jack Davis 'Warru'

Sarah Day 'Chaos'

Laurie Duggan 'Adventures in Paradise'

Geoffrey Dutton 'Our Leisured Ladies'

Adrienne Eberhard 'George Augustus Robinson III'

Anne Elder 'School Cadets'

Brook Emery 'My Father's Eyes'

Russell Erwin 'Troopship'

Steve Evans 'Old Codgers'

Diane Fahey 'Danaë'

Lionel Fogarty 'Drunk Cricket Field No. 1'

John Foulcher 'Reading Josephus'

Jane Gibian 'Ardent'

Kevin Gilbert 'Consultation'

Barbara Giles 'Fireworks and Champagne'

Peter Goldsworthy 'The Nice'

Lisa Gorton 'Press Release'

Jamie Grant 'Mon père est mort'

Jeff Guess 'The Priest and the Cockroach'

Emma Lew 'Riot Eve'

Tony Lintermans 'Stone Wall about to Fall'

Kathryn Lomer 'Vortex'

Ian McBryde 'Stalingrad Briefing, 1943'

Shane McCauley 'Advice on How to Become a Bohemian Poet'

Hugh McCrae 'Song of the Rain'

Roger McDonald 'Bachelor Farmer'

Kenneth Mackenzie 'An Old Inmate'

Rhyll McMaster 'Residues' *from* 'My Mother and I Become Victims of
    a Stroke'

'Ern Malley' 'Petit Testament'

Chris Mansell 'Definition Poem: Pissed as a Parrot'

Billy Marshall-Stoneking 'Wash Day'

Philip Martin 'A Sacred Way'

Philip Mead 'The Man and the Tree'

John Millett 'Meat'

Peter Minter 'Knitcap Sutras'

Mal Morgan 'Watsons'

Vera Newsom 'The Red Silk Dress'

πO 'Politz'

Mark O'Connor 'The Beginnng'

Esther Ottaway 'Headless Portrait of a Pregnant Woman'

K.F. Pearson 'And Abroad'

Craig Powell 'Madonna and Child'

John Quinn 'Argument'

Jennifer Rankin 'Cicada Singing'

Vicki Raymond 'Chat Show'

Nigel Roberts 'The Quote from Auden'

Peter Rose 'Renascence'

Jacob G. Rosenberg 'Mother'

David Rowbotham 'Three Horses'

J.R. Rowland 'Cairo Hotel'

Robyn Rowland 'Ausculta'

Graham Rowlands 'Uncle'

Brendan Ryan 'Maternity Paddock'

Gig Ryan 'Interest Rates'

Tracy Ryan 'First Burn'

Philip Salom 'Elegy for My Father'

Kirsty Sangster 'Erasmus in the High Country'

Andrew Sant 'The Mineral Boom'

Jaya Savige 'Exchange at Skirmish Point'

John A. Scott 'Changing Room'

Margaret Scott 'Elegies'

Michael Sharkey 'History'

Craig Sherborne 'Journo'

R.A. Simpson 'Judge and Prisoner'

Peter Skrzynecki 'Seeing My Parents'

Vivian Smith 'Family Album'

Edith Speers 'Love Sonnet (9)'

Nicolette Stasko 'Dwelling in the Shape of Things'

Peter Steele 'The Academy of Contempt'

Harold Stewart 'The Leaf Maker'

Jennifer Strauss 'Loving Parents'

Andrew Taylor 'Developing a Wife'

Tim Thorne 'A Letter to Egon Kisch IV'

Richard Tipping 'Against or For Beauty'

Dimitris Tsaloumas 'The Return'

Samuel Wagan Watson 'White Stucco Dreaming'

Ania Walwicz 'fairytale'

Petra White 'Ricketts Point'

Jane Williams 'Emissary'

Lauren Williams 'Unannounced'

Amanda Wilson 'Vigil'

Fay Zwicky 'Akibat'

Also published by UNSW Press

Big Elephants are Useful
A Compendium of Mnemonics & Idioms

SJ Hartland

Do you know why Big Elephants Are Useful To Indians For Unloading Logs? Because it's a BEAUTIFUL way to get a tricky spelling right.

Have you ever lost an arguement? Or was it an argument? If you can just remember 'I lost an "e" in an argument', then you'll never get it wrong again.

This fascinating collection provides hundreds of simple mnemonics to help you remember awkward spellings, grammatical rules and useful facts and figures.

It also wanders through the weird and wonderful byways of English idioms, where nothing means what it says.

If someone said you were 'a sandwich short of a picnic', would you be upset? Or could you be described as someone who 'fell asleep in a greenhouse'?

If you want a little traditional wisdom or some cracking new insults, this book offers a treasure trove of curious, witty and downright obscure English idioms.

Sally Hartland was born in 1959 in Knutsford, Cheshire, where she lived until 1981 when she married and moved to London. Sally began writing when her fascination with mnemonics prompted her to begin researching the weird and wonderful memory aids that form a delightful and witty part of our language. Sally now lives in Bath with her husband, two daughters and elderly Labrador.

ISBN 978 1 74223 027 6

Also published by UNSW Press

The Little Red Writing Book

Mark Tredinnick

'This is a book for every writer's backpack.'
– Nicholas Jose

'Good writing says something very honest, very clearly.
It's partly a matter of technique, but mostly a matter of
courage. Mark Tredinnick's book is great on sentences,
paragraphs, and practice – but its brilliance is in its ability
to inspire, and its exhortation to be brave.'
– Anna Funder

The Little Red Writing Book is a workbook on technique, style, craft and manners for everyone who writes and wants to do it better. It is a manual of good diction, composition, sentence craft, paragraph design, structure and planning. It is a guide to the poetic disciplines of creative writing and the functional disciplines of a professional prose. It is a reflection on the moral obligations and creative agonies of the writing life. And it is an argument for, and a short course in, grace on the page.

Enriched by examples of fine prose from great writers; flush with exercises; informed by the author's expertise in both creative writing and functional prose; and written with flair, *The Little Red Writing Book* is a lively and readable guide to lively and readable writing.

It's a writing book for people who write because they love to and for people who write because they have to.

MARK TREDINNICK is a poet, essayist and writing teacher. He is a former book editor, publisher and lawyer.

ISBN 0 86840 867 0

Also published by UNSW Press

The Little Green Grammar Book

Mark Tredinnick

This is a grammar book for the writer in everyone. No matter what you write – novels, poems, papers, reports, emails, blogs, letters to the council, instructions, wine labels or Christmas cards – this fuss-free book will help you say what you mean to say as neatly and unmistakably as you can.

Mark Tredinnick's companion to *The Little Red Writing Book* dispenses with the smug attitude of 'how not to' guides. It is a 'how to' guide, intent on showing the difference between what works, what doesn't, and why the difference matters.

MARK TREDINNICK is a poet, essayist, critic and writing teacher. His books, all published in Australia and the USA, include *The Little Red Writing Book, The Land's Wild Music* and *A Place on Earth*, an anthology of Australian and US nature writing.

ISBN 978 0 86840 919 1